Breaking the Siegfried Line

Breaking the Siegfried Line

Rhineland February 1945

Tim Saunders

Pen & Sword
MILITARY

First published in Great Britain in 2023 by
PEN & SWORD MILITARY
an imprint of Pen & Sword Books Ltd
Yorkshire – Philadelphia

ISBN 978-1-39905-528-4

A CIP catalogue record for this book is available from the British Library.

Typeset by Concept, Huddersfield, West Yorkshire, HD4 5JL.
Printed and bound in England by CPI Group (UK) Ltd, Croydon, CR0 4YY.

MIX
Paper | Supporting responsible forestry
FSC® C013604
FSC www.fsc.org

Pen & Sword Books Ltd incorporates the imprints of Aviation, Atlas, Family History, Fiction, Maritime, Military, Discovery, Politics, History, Archaeology, Select, Wharncliffe Local History, Wharncliffe True Crime, Military Classics, Wharncliffe Transport, Leo Cooper, The Praetorian Press, Remember When, White Owl, Seaforth Publishing and Frontline Books.

For a complete list of Pen & Sword titles please contact
PEN & SWORD BOOKS LTD
47 Church Street, Barnsley, South Yorkshire, S70 2AS, England
E-mail: enquiries@pen-and-sword.co.uk
Website: www.pen-and-sword.co.uk
or
PEN & SWORD BOOKS
1950 Lawrence Rd, Havertown, PA 19083, USA
E-mail: uspen-and-sword@casematepublishers.com
Website: www.penandswordbooks.com

Contents

Acknowledgements

This book, like its predecessor on the Reichswald, originated from a set of comprehensive battlefield study notes produced some ten years ago. The second COVID pandemic lockdown in the UK was an enforced opportunity to convert it into a book. The origin of some of the material is lost in the mists of time, but the obvious sources have been revisited and on at least one occasion have been referenced. Now that archives are open post-COVID, particularly The National Archives, Kew, which are back in business as normal, I have been able to add to the research with the help of the willing staff – many thanks. I must also acknowledge the help of the Army Library Service at Warminster Garrison (in my home town) and the incomparable Prince Consort's Library in Aldershot.

Having belatedly discovered the wealth of information available online in various forums, I must acknowledge their help in answering questions or simply giving me access to their corporate knowledge.

Among those who have given me unfettered access to their personal libraries, I would particularly like to acknowledge and thank my co-conspirator in many Second World War projects, Richard Hone. He has answered so many technical questions on orders of battle, tanks and equipment and has helped me with military German. I am also most grateful to fellow battlefield guide Andrew Duff for passing on to me an immense roll of Reichswald and VERITABLE planning maps and traces.

As always, I have to thank the Pen and Sword team for all that they have done to bring this project to print.

Tim Saunders
Warminster, 2023

Introduction

Originally conceived as a single volume covering Operation VERITABLE, the manuscript was getting far too large and had to be split into two volumes. Separate books now cover the fighting in the Reichswald and in the Kleve area, both in and around the great forest, in the early phases of VERITABLE in February 1945. The first volume covered the battle to break into the Reichswald and the fighting in the forest up to the defeat of XLVII Panzer Corps' counter-attack and the imminent breakout of the Guards Armoured Division onto the Maas floodplain to the south. This second volume concentrates on XXX Corps' main effort to break through the Siegfried Line to the north of the Reichswald with 15th Scottish and 43rd Wessex divisions supported by the tanks of 6 Guards and 8 Armoured brigades.

Operation VERITABLE was originally conceived by the First Canadian Army as a fast and fluid strike into the Rhineland across deeply frozen ground, but a thaw at the end of January condemned British and Canadian formations to fighting in appalling ground and weather conditions. Floods and saturated ground up to and beyond the vaunted Siegfried Line largely restricted armoured manoeuvre to roads and inhibited logistic resupply and reinforcement. Even so, with the Highlanders and Welsh fighting their way through the Reichswald, the 15th Scottish Division had broken through the Siegfried Line and beaten the Germans to the Materborn feature within thirty six-hours. In less than forty-eight hours, 43rd Wessex Division, despite rising flood waters and traffic jams, were in the outskirts of Kleve and poised to breakout into the Rhineland. However, that is when the hard slogging began as the Germans counter-attacked.

Many of those diarists, along with those who wrote their formation and unit histories, felt that the fighting in the Reichswald and around Kleve in the opening phases of VERITABLE was 'their worst experience since Normandy'. It was a struggle in which mud, blown-down trees and floods, as much the German soldier, his trenches and mines, were the enemy. All of which provided levels of 'friction' that even Clausewitz would have deemed impossible.

A delay in capturing the Roer dams and the Germans blowing sluices created floods that prevented the reinforced Ninth US Army from joining the battle as planned with Operation GRENADE delayed for over three weeks, leaving the Canadian First Army to fight the remaining German reserves in the west on their own. It was a bitter and costly battle.

Montgomery and Crerar were by no means friends, with Monty much preferring the British military heritage General Guy Simonds (left), who he believed should command the Canadian Amy. The field marshal had tried to sack Crerar in September 1944 for missing a planning meeting in favour of attending a commemoration at Dieppe, but Montgomery backed down. In return Crerar sought to have his army as an independent command but this was rejected and First Canadian Army remained under 21st Army Group for the rest of the war.

General Crerar wearing his signature duffel coat, with left, generals Horrocks, Barber (rear), Thomas and Ross.

Glossary of Terms

All wars produce their own lexicon. Therefore, it is no surprise that abbreviations abound in war diaries and accounts of the fighting. The main ones are listed here but, in an army, where combat training had priority over staff work, many non-standard and local variations were used. The following list will help.

2iC	Second in Command
A1 Echelon	Immediate replenishment of combat supplies
A2 Echelon	Further back planned replenishment of combat supplies
AA	Anti-aircraft
ADC	Aide de Camp
Adjt	Adjutant, Unit commanding officer's staff officer
Admin	Administration
Adv	Advance
AGRA	Army Group Royal Artillery, corps' artillery 'division', consisting of heavy, medium and field regiments plus anti-aircraft guns
AFV	Armoured Fighting Vehicle
Amn	Ammunition
AOP	Air/Armoured Observation Post
AP	Armour Piercing or anti-personnel
APCBC	Armour-piercing ballistic capped
APC	Armoured Personnel Carrier
APDS	Armour-Piercing Discarding Sabot (6- and 17-pounder anti-tank ammunition)
APIS	Air Photo Interpretation Section
Arty	Artillery
Assy Area	Assembly Area where troops regroup (e.g. tanks, infantry and gunners) for an operation prior to moving to the FUP
Aslt	Assault
A/Tk	(+ variants) Anti-tank
ARV	Armoured Recovery Vehicle
AVRE	Armoured Vehicle Royal Engineer
Axis	The central direction of advance
BC	Battery Commander
B Echelon	Entry point of combat supplies into a unit's logistic infrastructure
BCR	Battle Casualty Replacement
Bde	Brigade (British), equivalent to a US or German regiment
BK	Battery Captain

Bn	Battalion
Br	Bridge
Bty	Battery
Cas	Casualties
Casevac	Casualty evacuation
CCP	Casualty Clearing Post
CCS	Casualty Clearing Station
Cdn	Canadian
C in C	Commander in Chief
Civ	Civilian
CL	Centre Line or axis of advance
CO	Commanding Officer*
Co-ax	Coaxial machine gun mounted in tanks alongside the main armament
Conc	Concentrate, also Conc Area, where units assigned to an operation gather before moving forward to the assy area
Comd	Command
Coord	Coordinate
Coy	Company
CP	Command Post
Cpl	Corporal
CPO	Command Post Officer (artillery)
CRA	Commander Royal Artillery
CS	Close Support
CSM	Company Sergeant Major
D Day	The day on which an operation begins
Dem	Demolition
Dets	Detachments
DF	Defensive fire, pre-planned artillery, mortar or medium machine gun target areas on likely enemy approaches, etc.
DGNS	Dragoons
Div	Division
DP	Distribution Point (logistic)
DR	Dispatch rider, also 'Don R' or 'Don Romeo'
DZ	Drop Zone
Ech	Echelon, normally referring to fighting echelon and logistic echelons of a unit
Fmn	Formation, i.e. brigade, division, etc.
En	Enemy
Enfilade	Fire from a flank
Fd Regt	Field Regiment RA

*Today the distinction between CO and OC is well-defined, with the former commanding a unit such as a battalion and the latter a sub-unit such as a company, but in many British Second World War memoirs and documents they are transposed or used inconsistently.

FMC	Field Maintenance Centre
FOB	Forward officer Bombardment, naval gunfire
FOO	Forward Observation Officer (artillery)
FUP	Forming Up Place
Fwd	Forward
Gd	Guard, typically advanced, flan or rearguard
GOC	General Officer Commanding
GPO	Gun Position Officer
Gr	Grenadier
H Hour	The hour (time) at which an operation starts
HE	High Explosive
Inf	Infantry
Int	Intelligence
I Sec	Intelligence Section
JNCO	Junior Non-Commissioned Officer
KIA	Killed in action
KO	Knocked out
LAA	Light Anti-Aircraft
LAC	Light Armoured Car
LAD	Light Aid Detachment
LCA	Landing Craft Assault
LCpl	Lance Corporal
LCT	Landing Craft Tank
Ldr	Leader
Line	Field telephone wire
LVT	Landing Vehicle Tracked
LZ	Landing Zone
MG	Machine gun
MMG	Medium machine gun
MSR	Main Supply Route
O Group	Orders group, assembly of subordinate commanders for the issue of orders
OC	Officer Commanding
OP	Observation post
P Hour	Time of a parachute drop
PIAT	Projector Infantry Anti-Tank
Pl	Platoon
Posn	Position
Pt	Point
Pte	Private (rank)
Pz	Panzer
QM	Quarter Master
RAP	Regimental Aid Post
Rd	Road

Regt *or* Rgt	Regiment
REME	Royal Electrical and Mechanical Engineers
RHA	Royal Horse Artillery
RHU	Reinforcement Holding Unit
RMO	Regimental Medical Officer
RPM	Rounds per minute
RSM	Regimental Sergeant Major
RSO	Regimental Signals Officer
RV	Rendezvous point
SA	Small Arms
SB	Stretcher bearer
SBG	Small Box Girder Bridge
Sec *or* Sect	Section
Shelldrake	Appointment title for artillery
Shellrep	Report of enemy shelling, used to locate enemy batteries
Sgt	Sergeant
Sitrep	Situation Report
Sjt	Serjeant, the old form of Sergeant
SL	Start Line
Smk	Smoke
SNCO	Senior Non-Commissioned Officer
SP	Self-Propelled or support
Stand-to	'Stand to arms', fully man defensive positions; also a routine at dawn and dusk
Sub-unit	Company, squadron or battery sized unit
Sunray	Commander of any sized unit of formation
Sups	Supplies
Sqn	Squadron
Svy	Survey
Tac	Tactical, usually used in context of a tactical headquarters
Tac/R	Tactical reconnaissance by aircraft
Target	All guns within range when a '*xxxxx* target' was called (Mike = regiment; Uncle = division; Victor = corps; William = Army; York = AGRA)
Tgt	Target
Tk	Tank
Tp	Troop
Tpt	Transport
Unit	An infantry battalion or a British artillery or armoured regiment
Wef	With effect
WIA	Wounded in action
X Rds	Crossroads
Yd/yds	Yards
Yeo	Yeomanry

Chapter One

Autumn and Winter, 1944–45

Operation MARKET GARDEN in September 1944 had not succeeded in placing the Second British Army on the North German Plain, but with a firm hold on the banks of the River Waal at Nijmegen this was not the end of Field Marshal Montgomery's ambition to end the war in Europe by Christmas 1944. While 1st Airborne Division was being evacuated from the Oosterbeek Perimeter, staff officers in Headquarters Second Army were already planning to take another route across the Rhine and into the heartland of Germany, while the enemy was arguably still off balance. They proposed attacking east via a narrow manoeuvre corridor between the rivers Maas and the Waal and to cross the Rhine further upstream. The advantage was that, attacking from Nijmegen, they would avoid the stronger sections of the West Wall or Siegfried Line along Germany's border further south and they could cross the Rhine, Germany's last strategic barrier, where the river was confined to a single course. Clearing the eastern bank of the Rhine south towards the Ruhr without having to make a second assault river crossing had its obvious attractions. The disadvantage was that this narrow 10-mile neck of land was 'plugged' by the Reichswald forest and flanked by the floodplains of the rivers Maas and Waal.

This option had, however, previously been dismissed by Montgomery during a pre-MARKET GARDEN ground appreciation due to the narrow 5-mile frontage, forest tracks and only two decent roads. Having been blocked at Arnhem, needs must and an attack through the Reichswald Plug, Operation GATWICK/WYVERN, was planned. D Day for the attack by 43rd Wessex Division was scheduled for 10 October, but it was delayed and then cancelled by General Eisenhower, in favour of a resumption of his broad front strategy. For the Allied armies, closing up to the Rhine along its length was far from straightforward, as the 'Great Swan' from Falaise, across France and into Belgium had ground to a halt in a logistic crisis, largely because combat supplies were still being trucked forward all the way from Normandy. Despite the best efforts of the Red Ball Express and operations to open the Scheldt and the port of Antwerp, the result was that Eisenhower's armies could only mount offensive operations during the autumn of 1944 when they were allocated the necessary combat supplies in turn.[1]

Against the background of the logistic problems during the autumn months, Eisenhower was beset by his army commanders lobbying him one after the other. They argued why they should have priority over all others and presented

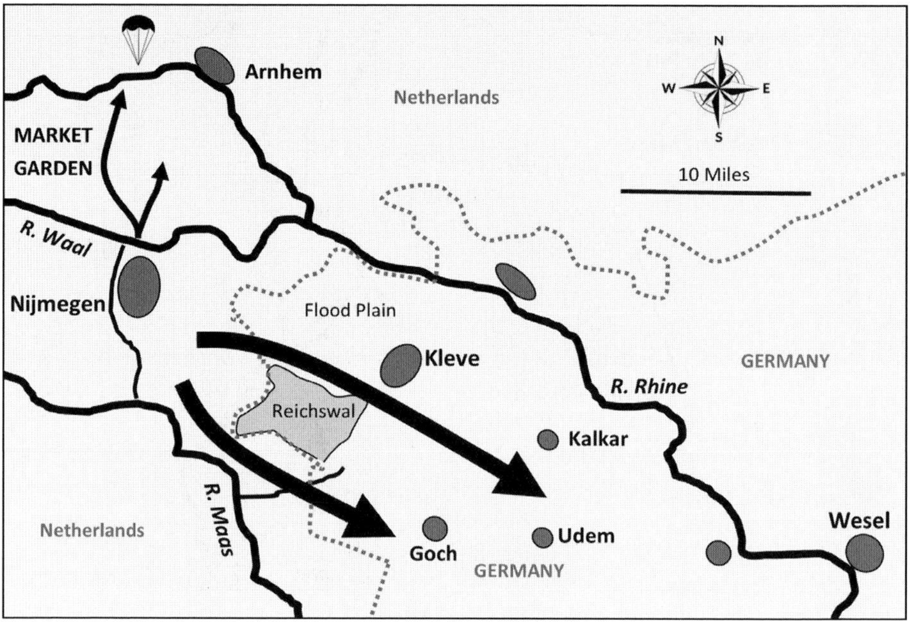

The situation at the end of MARKET GARDEN and the Reichswald option.

plans for delivering victory over Germany, in which, of course, they and their army would play the leading role! General Patton, for example, proposed that the Third US Army advance via Metz in a thrust across the Rhine, while Montgomery renewed his efforts to persuade Eisenhower of the practicality of an attack by the First Canadian Army through the Reichswald during November.[2] It was, however, Patton who received the combat supplies in one of the few set-piece battles he failed, with his army suffering heavy casualties and bogging down in the mud of Lorraine. Eisenhower rejected all the other generals' plans for lacking a strategic objective, being politically unacceptable or logistically unsustainable.[3] The result was rampant jealousy among the senior Allied commanders, born of personal ambition, which in turn led to levels of suspicion, discord and division between the Allies that was even noted in Berlin.

During November and into December, 21st Army Group's main effort was opening the Scheldt Estuary and the port of Antwerp for vast tonnages of combat supplies that were needed by the Allied armies of seventy-five divisions rising to ninety, numbering 4.5 million men. This task of securing the Scheldt approaches to Antwerp fell to General Crerar's First Canadian Army, which was already strung out along the Channel coast dealing with the various 'fortress' garrisons that had been left behind to deny ports to the Allies. Meanwhile, from Nijmegen southwards, General Dempsey's Second British Army, in a series of modestly resourced corps and divisional operations, strove to advance to the western bank of the Maas and clear some stoutly held enemy pockets.

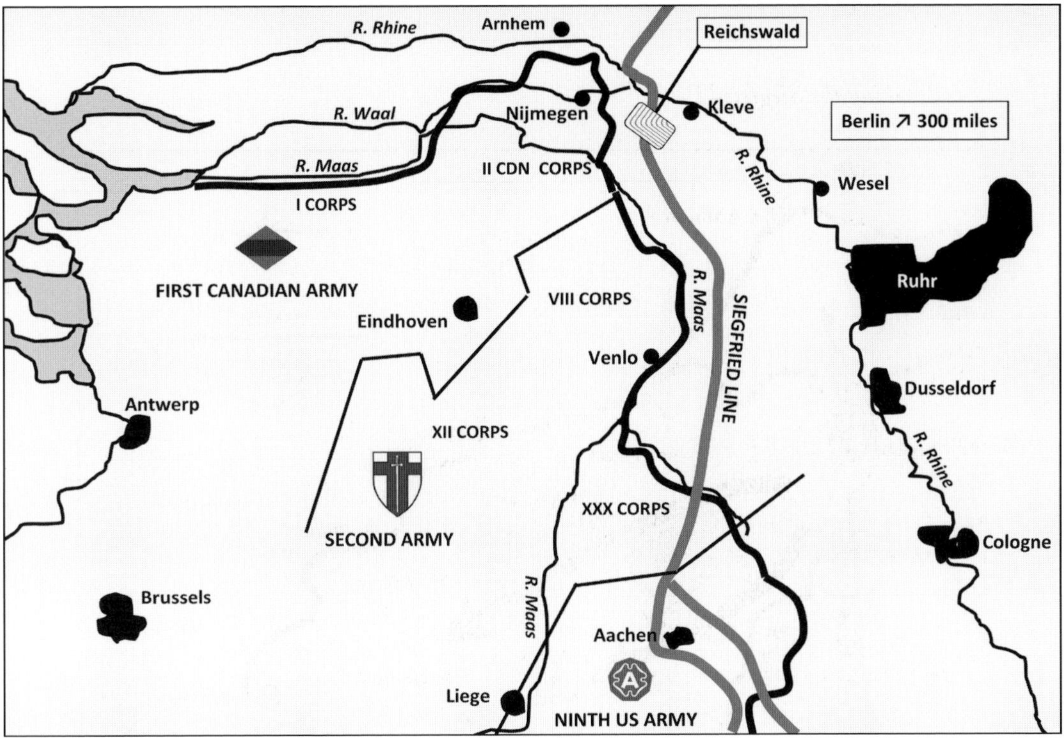

The 21st Army Group situation in the winter of 1944–45.

Following the remarkable German strategic recovery on the borders of the Reich, the Wehrmacht continued to demonstrate that they were far from defeated. As winter approached the Germans fought hard to contain the Allies in bitter battles in which they successfully prevented all but limited advances to the Rhine at the extremities of the front and the bulk of the 12th US and 21st Army Groups were held west of the Rhineland. As the weather worsened the Allies were only across the German frontier in a few places and only held a handful of toe-holds in the Siegfried Line. It was abundantly clear that there would be no repeat of the 1918 collapse of the German army.

Eisenhower's Strategy

When Eisenhower turned down Montgomery's latest proposal to attack through the Reichswald, the Field Marshal wrote a note that did not stand the test of time to General Crerar, who now had responsibility for the area south of Nijmegen, on 28 November:

> There is no intention of launching this operation now, and I have never expressed a wish to do so. All I want you to do is to examine it and put the planners on to thinking it out. It will NOT be launched till spring, i.e. March or later.[4]

Shortly afterwards, however, at a conference Eisenhower held with his army group commanders at Maastricht on 7 December, he announced his intention to resume the offensive as soon as January in order to maintain pressure on the enemy. Inter-Allied relations again came to a head during the conference, where Montgomery persisted with his demand for sole command of forty of the available seventy-five Allied divisions, with which to launch the single concentrated thrust to Berlin that he had espoused since the autumn. With Montgomery having again overplayed his hand, Eisenhower again rejected the 21st Army Group plan in favour of his preferred broad front strategy, but added that he favoured the northern route into the Rhineland and a formal crossing of the Rhine into Germany to the north of the Ruhr.

To deliver the Supreme Commander's 'assured northern crossing of the Rhine', Montgomery, the master of the set-piece battle, was allocated Ninth US Army, commanded by General Simpson, for the clearance of the Rhineland. The problem was one that was well understood by 21st Army Group: the obvious route via Venlo into the Rhineland was heavily defended and would also require a preliminary assault crossing of the River Maas. Therefore, the Reichswald, the 'plug' between the Maas and the Rhine, if forced quickly and cleanly, offered the field marshal an attractive option to deliver the northern arm of the attack into the Rhineland. Thus, a little over a week after dismissing an attack through the Reichswald it was again an active option and Montgomery rang General Crerar to discuss proposals for the attack through the Reichswald Plug!

The 21st Army Group Plan

In his directive of 16 December 1944 to generals Crerar, Dempsey and Simpson, Montgomery outlined his concept of operations for the forthcoming battles for the Rhineland and the Rhine Crossing:

> The future layout that we want to achieve is to face up to the Rhine ... on a front of two armies, Second Army being on the right and Canadian Army on the left. American formations are then to be included in 21 Army Group and, with the co-operation of strong airborne forces, the Rhine will be crossed.
>
> Before we can begin to develop successfully large-scale operations across the Rhine, we must clear the enemy completely from the west of the river and must join up with the American Ninth Army coming up from the south; we must in fact be in undisputed possession of all territory west of the Rhine from inclusive the general line Orsoy-Venlo northwards.

General Dempsey's Second Army was to clear the west bank of the Maas, simultaneously, in an operation now code-named VERITABLE, while the First Canadian Army would launch an attack from the north through the Reichswald Plug. Several days later, the Ninth US Army was to launch Operation GRENADE from the south across the River Roer. However, for a variety of reasons that will become apparent, Simpson lacked both sufficient divisions and resources with which to secure his envisaged starting positions by the time VERITABLE was launched. Having been squeezed out of the line by the advancing pincers of the Canadian and US armies, General Dempsey would prepare for his part in the assault crossing of the Rhine to the north of Wesel.

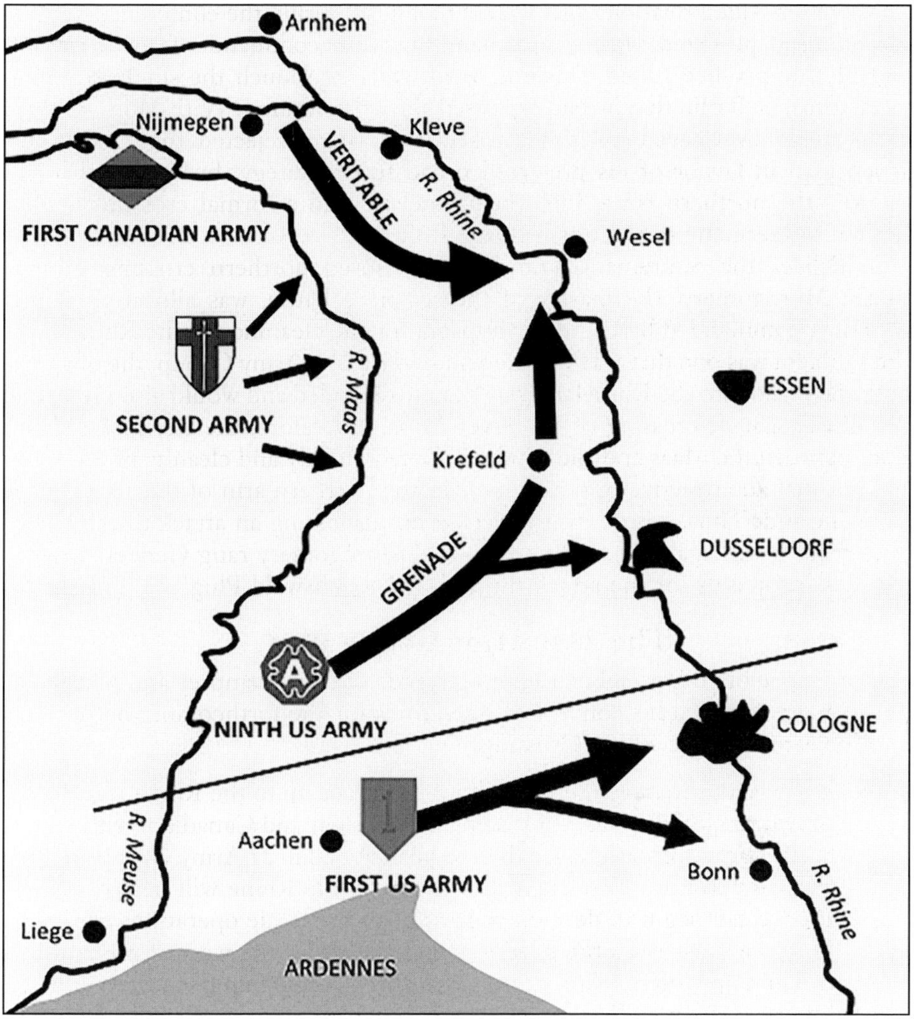

Field Marshal Montgomery's concept of operations for the Rhineland in 1945.

Coincidentally, the Germans launched a major Bulge offensive on the same day Montgomery issued his directive to the army commanders specifying January for the offensive. He, in common with other senior Allied commanders, believing that the Germans lacked offensive capability, wrote in his directive:

> The enemy is at present fighting a defensive campaign on all fronts ... at all costs he has to prevent the war from entering a mobile phase; he does not have the transport or the petrol that would be necessary for mobile operations ...

How wrong one can be!

General Harry Crerar, commander of First Canadian Army.

Believing that the Wehrmacht was incapable of offensive action, the Allies were rocked by Hitler's surprise attack before dawn on 16 December 1944. Twenty-eight German divisions were launched into battle in the Ardennes under the cover of poor weather, catching the First US Army ill-prepared for what developed into one of the biggest battles of the North-West European Campaign; the Battle of the Bulge.

With two panzer armies driving west and VIII US Corps in danger of collapse, and XXX Corps deploying south to provide a backstop on the River Maas, it was obvious that operations in the Rhineland would have to be postponed until the fighting in the Ardennes was resolved.

Eisenhower (centre) and his northern commanders. Montgomery (*left*) and Bradley (*right*). Rear rank (*left to right*), generals Crerar, Simpson and Dempsey.

The Third Reich's Geo-Strategic Situation

The Soviet's Red Army's dramatic advances on the Eastern Front during the summer months of 1944 and 21st Army Group's success in Normandy had been disastrous for Germany. Defeat to the east and west had forced Hitler's armies back to the borders of Germany. The Allies had, however, outrun their logistic support and gave the enemy armies a breathing space to mount the most remarkable strategic recovery during September and into the autumn of 1944. The Germans had succeeded in stabilising and strengthening the defences and began replacing their losses of manpower by combing men out from the military airfields and ports across Germany. Similarly, the huge amount of weapons and equipment lost during the year was being replaced by often ad hoc systems produced with whatever parts were available. This saw hastily reformed or assembled formations marching to the front as infantry. Not only were the Kriegsmarine and Luftwaffe raided for soldiers, but older men were directed into industry to release men of military age. In addition, the age of conscription was broadened from sixty down to just sixteen.

With the Nazis afraid of being 'stabbed in the back' as in 1918 by a civilian collapse, the German economy had only been gradually placed on a total war footing. However, the Allied bomber offensive mounted during 1943–44 had not reduced German war production, which as far as armour was concerned had peaked during that period. The dispersion, concealment and the construction of underground plants across Germany had defied the best efforts of the bomber barons. Nor had the bombing caused a collapse of German civil morale, as Churchill's scientific advisor, Professor Linderman, had calculated it would.

The dispersal of German output, however, had a weakness; it relied on the railway network for the delivery of parts and fuel. Consequently the bombers were diverted from striking centres of population to targeting oil supplies during the autumn of 1944. This had an immediate impact, creating difficulties in the supply chain and delivery to field formations. The impact of a lack of fuel for the Luftwaffe was disastrous. There was a reduction from a monthly delivery of 1,000,000 tons to just 350,000, which forced the Luftwaffe to stop training replacement pilots.

This lack of fuel meant that the Luftwaffe could only mount fifty night-fighter sorties per night and despite the presence of the Kammhuber Line, a system that enabled radar and night fighters to be integrated, the level of casualties to the aircrew and aircraft of RAF Bomber Command dropped from that suffered in 1942. In all, the Luftwaffe's paucity of fuel had increased the effectiveness of bombing of refineries and oil targets, which in turn reduced production of vital high explosives and synthetic rubber. Germany's ability to fight on was now being eroded, but Hitler was not going to give up while he still had hopes for the V weapons.

The impact of the strikes on the French road and rail system by bombers, resistance and the SAS had been so effective in choking off combat supplies to the German armies in Normandy that it was emulated during the preparatory phase of the Battle of the Rhineland. The German road and rail network connections

Allied bombers targeted German production and communications by day and by night.

to the VERITABLE and GRENADE areas were to be prioritised ahead of the strategic bombing offensive. For the British and US bomber leaders, Arthur Harris and Carl Spaatz, this was a diversion away from what they saw as their core business. However, the success of the switch of targeting to oil and transport was such that by the beginning of the battle German transport was working at a fraction of its previous efficiency. In short, General Eisenhower considered that the redirection of the bomber effort was having 'a definite influence upon the ground battle', despite the deployment of enemy jet fighters. Post-war analysis of the situation later proved that the drop was 'dramatic and significantly reduced the cost of the battles in Germany' through increasing difficulties in supply and redeployment.

The Red Army launched its expected winter offensive on 12 January 1945 with an overwhelming strength of five to one with some 200 divisions. Hitler calculated that the shock of his attack in the Ardennes and the rain of V1 and V2 rockets on the Allied logistic hub at Antwerp would prevent the Allies from resuming the offensive in the west, so the panzer formations were sent east to mount a desperate attempt to prevent a collapse that would take the Red Army to within striking distance of Berlin. This was, however, a vain hope as the Russians advanced nearly 200 miles from the Vistula to the Oder before they ran out of steam. While the Allies were still west of the Rhine, the Russians were within 40 miles of Berlin.

The Reichswald Problem

Having emerged as a key gateway to the Rhineland, staff officers of General Crerar's First Canadian Army studied the practicalities of mounting an offensive through the Reichswald on and off since the beginning of November 1944. The ground that they had taken over from the Wessex Division was known as the 'Reichswald Plug'. It consisted of the 10 miles of low ground between two of Europe's great rivers, the Maas and the Rhine. However, in the centre, forming a part of the German border, the Reichswald forest occupied 5 miles of slightly higher ground. Inside the wood's western and northern extremities there lay a low ridge that emerged from the forest, forming the broad Materborn feature. It was key terrain, overlooking the city of Kleve. If the Germans had time to deploy their reserves onto this high ground at the beginning of the battle, VERITABLE would become both slow and costly. Therefore the thrust by the 15th Scottish and 43rd Wessex divisions along the northern edge of the Reichswald that is the subject of this book was crucial to the success of XXX Corps' opening phase.

Flanking the north and south of the forest, two narrow strips of open floodplain were crossed by the only two decent roads east into the Rhineland. Of these manoeuvre corridors, the one from Nijmegen to Kleve, at just a mile wide, offered the best potential for seizing the Materborn feature, being on slightly higher and possibly drier ground. This road was to be General Horrocks' main effort for the attack on the Reichswald Plug. The disadvantage was that it was a difficult course

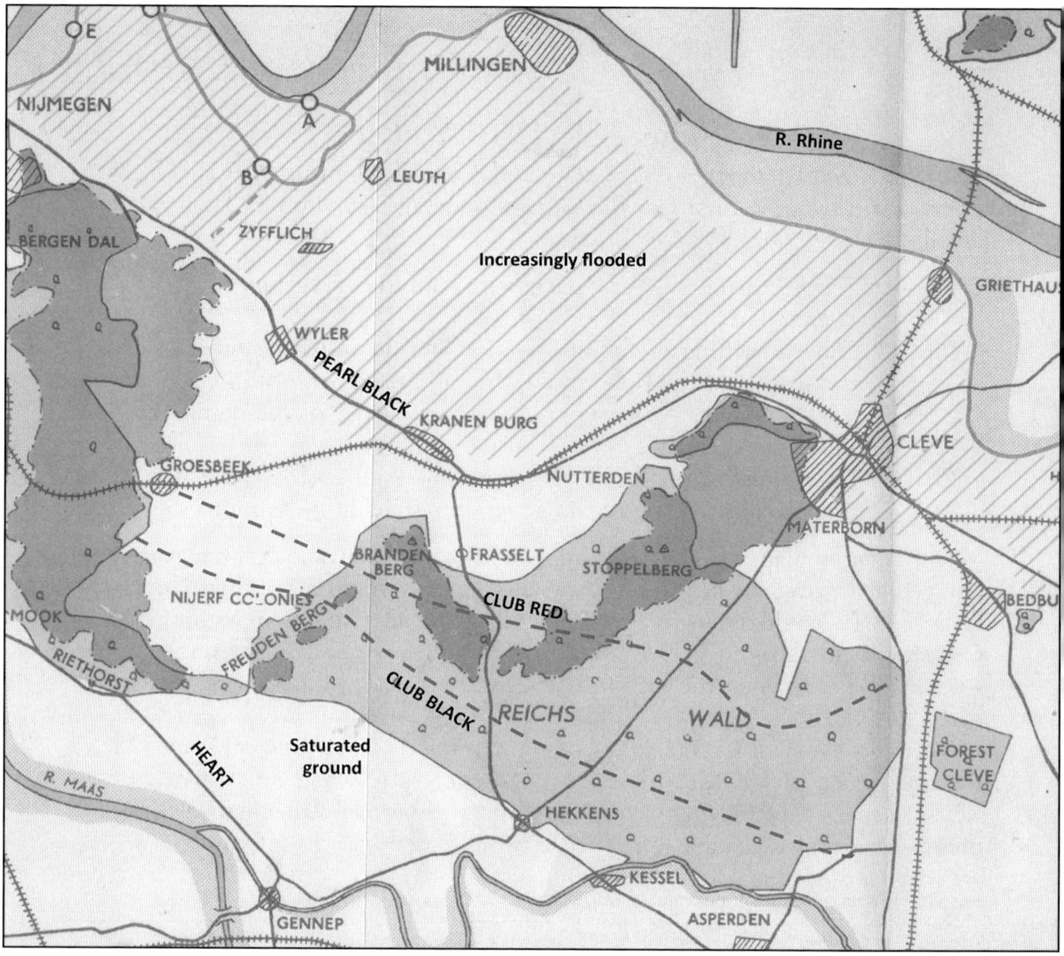

The ground between the rivers. In the centre is the 'Reichswald Plug'.

of action, as attacks to the south of the Reichswald on the Maas floodplain would be slower and in addition require a crossing of the flooded River Niers as well.

The problem of the floodplains was not confined to the expected heavy winter going but they could also be inundated to a depth that would make this 'no-go terrain' even for infantry. By breaching the Rhine dykes the Germans had already flooded much of the Betwe or 'Island' between Nijmegen and Arnhem. Thus it was confidently expected that they would breach the dykes of the great forest when the level of the Rhine rose as melt water filled the river. Consequently, the plain would be impassable except via the embanked roads or by amphibious vehicles. As the projected advance progressed beyond the Reichswald, the country for military manoeuvre between the two rivers widened out to 20 miles, but much of it was also floodplain. However, in the centre there was some higher broken but defensible ground, and the cities of Goch and Uedem, plus other large towns, all of which would become centres of resistance if the breakout along that narrow corridor north of the Reichswald was not secured by XXX Corps quickly, ideally in the opening hours of the battle.

The VERITABLE Plan

The campaign plan that generals Crerar and Horrocks drew up for VERITABLE was confirmed in the First Canadian Army directive issued on 25 January 1945. It fell into three phases:

Phase 1. The clearing of the Reichswald and the securing of the line Gennep–Asperden–Kleve.

Phase 2. The breaching of the enemy's second defensive system east and south-east of the Reichswald, the capture of the localities Weeze–Uedem–Kalkar–Emmerich and the securing of the communications between them.

Phase 3. The 'break-through' of the 'Hochwald lay-back' defence lines and the advance to secure the general line Geldern–Xanten.

Montgomery's plan was that once the area of Geldern and Xanten had been reached by Crerar, the Ninth US Army's advancing from the south in Operation GRENADE would be within striking distance of a junction with the First Canadian Army around Wesel. This would have completed the clearance of the Rhineland and opened the way for the Rhine Crossing, Operations VARSITY and PLUNDER.

Naturally General Crerar had planned that his II Canadian Corps would lead the first phase of VERITABLE but Montgomery so engineered matters that XXX Corps would inevitably replace General Simonds' Canadians in the first phase. This was, of course, an affront to the Crerar, but in subsequent phases,

General Crerar's plan for Operation VERITABLE.

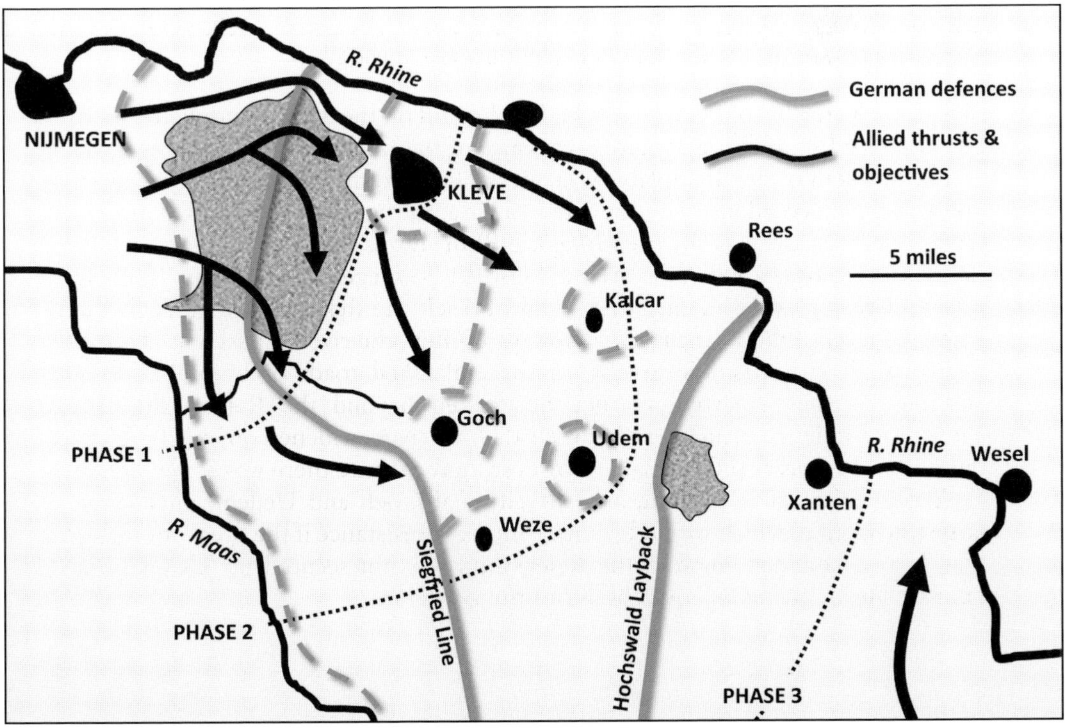

as the ground opened up, the II Canadian Corps to join the battle on the left flank adjacent to the Rhine. Such was the scale of the battle, however, that nonetheless the Canadians would play a significant role in clearing the Rhineland and fought some bitter and costly battles.

On their return from the Ardennes, General Horrocks and XXX Corps' staff took over responsibility for planning the initial assault on the enemy's forward positions out on the Groesbeek Heights. These had been greatly strengthened in the weeks since 43rd Wessex Division (XXX Corps) handed them over to the Canadians but with fighting through the Reichswald, and the capture of Kleve being the first major objective, they faced a considerable task. Crerar had optimistically expected that it would take around four days to clear the Rhineland. However, as ground conditions deteriorated, he briefed his commanders as late as 4 February that:

> If everything breaks in our favour, weather, ground, air support, enemy dispositions and reactions – I would not be surprised if armour of 30 Corps reached the Geldern–Xanten line in a few days. On the other hand, if conditions are against us, I see three 'set-piece' operations, one for each Phase, and the battle may well last three weeks …

General Brian Horrocks, commander of XXX Corps.

To deceive the Germans as to the true direction of the offensive, under the cover story of Dutch political pressure to liberate the rest of Holland, I British Corps'

> chief role was to 'implement and maintain' a cover plan indicating a prospective attack across the Waal and the Lek [Lower Rhine] directed on Utrecht, designed to liberate the northern Netherlands. It was hoped that the movement of British units from Second Army into the Canadian Army area might be interpreted by the enemy as related to this project.[5]

The historian of 44 Lowland Brigade described the process:

> An elaborate deception programme was carried out, of which the main purpose was to give the impression that the big attack was to be launched northwards across the Maas in the area of Breda and Tilburg towards Utrecht and Rotterdam. Bogus reconnaissance of the villages on the south bank of the Maas in this area were carried out by members of the Brigade, including the Dutch interpreters, who flaunted the Divisional sign, arranged billets, made useful contacts, and talked loudly of 'Utrecht' and 'Rotterdam' in the presence of the local population to advertise this entirely fictitious operation.[6]

These perhaps all too obvious measures did not deceive the Germans, nor did those by I Corps north of Nijmegen. They could clearly appreciate that a crossing of the Rhine further south would also cut off the northern Netherlands. German commanders' estimates indicated that the threat lay with the Second Army around Venlo and the US armies further south, and that any attack north of the Reichswald would be a feint.

Based on the contrasting ground states of mud or frost, General Crerar had instructed his planning staff to prepare two plans for Operation VERITABLE. If as throughout January the ground remained frozen hard, with rapid progress through the Reichswald Plug expected, he would unleash his armoured formations in order 'to disrupt and disorganise enemy resistance in the rear in the quickest possible time'. If, however, there had been a thaw and the ground became saturated then the second plan for a phased and inevitably slower attack would be used. In both cases it was stressed that, 'Should the enemy's resistance crumble, no opportunity was to be lost of exploiting favourable situations irrespective of which plan was in force.' Unfortunately, in the final days of January, there was a significant change in the weather away from dry, deep cold and clear conditions, with any firm ground disappearing when a rapid thaw set in on 30–31 January, followed by a wet February. The previously frozen, snow-covered tracks on the Groesbeek Heights quickly dissolved into mud with the passage of a single Canadian vehicle. With the dramatic change of ground conditions, beyond those that had been planned for, it is surprising that from Eisenhower downwards Allied commanders were determined that the operation should go ahead as soon as possible.

Field Marshal Montgomery and General Crerar.

The unexpectedly quick thaw also found many formations fully winterised, for example, the Churchill tanks of 34 Armoured Brigade were whitewashed and fitted with 700 tons of 'ice bar tracks'. These track extensions had prevented the build-up of ice on track shoes that in the snowy Ardennes had in the worst cases became so thick that turrets were lifted from the hull. In VERITABLE, instead of ice the Churchills would have to contend with thick glutinous mud that, along with tree branches, had the same lifting effect. Such were the conditions in and around the Reichswald that ploughs and other mud and ice stripper devices simply did not work.

Chapter Two

XXX Corps' Planning and Preparation

> Intention. 30 Corps will destroy the enemy between the River Maas and the River Rhine and breakthrough in a southerly direction between these two rivers. [*XXX Corps Op Instruction No. 47*]

Operation VERITABLE was the first occasion in which General Horrocks fought under the command of General Crerar. He wrote that once his plan was made:

> During the build-up period I had little to do, except to go around visiting troops. I had so far not come in contact with the Canadians, so I set out to try and get to know them better. I also saw quite a lot of their Commander, General Crerar, who, in my opinion, has always been much underrated, largely because he was the exact opposite to Montgomery. He hated publicity but was full of common sense and always prepared to listen to the views of his subordinate commanders.

Explaining his plan, General Horrocks wrote: 'We had to smash through this bottleneck before breaking out into the German plain beyond'; in other words, it was too be a frontal attack on the 10-mile frontage of the Reichswald Plug. His experience of MARKET GARDEN was another concern; the problems his corps encountered on Hell's Highway:

> I badly wanted the metaled roads [*sic*], which ran through it [the Reichswald] because I knew from experience how difficult it was to maintain a force, with all its manifold requirements, by a single road. So, I determined to use the maximum force possible from the outset and to attack with five divisions.

To maintain the advance Horrocks' staff selected four routes through the Reichswald battle area: two metalled roads, one on either side of the forest, and two stone-topped tracks that ran through it. The northerly Nijmegen–Kleve road had a hard top and is the route we are primarily concerned with in this book. It was designated 'PEARL BLACK' and the minor routes, little more than country roads and tracks across country and through the forest, were nicknamed 'CLUB RED' and CLUB BLACK'. The corps' secondary route, nicknamed 'HEART', was the macadam road to the south of the forest that ran from Mook east to Goch.

For the initial assault XXX Corps consisted of the following divisions: 15th Scottish, 53rd Welsh and 51st Highland and also allocated were Canadian

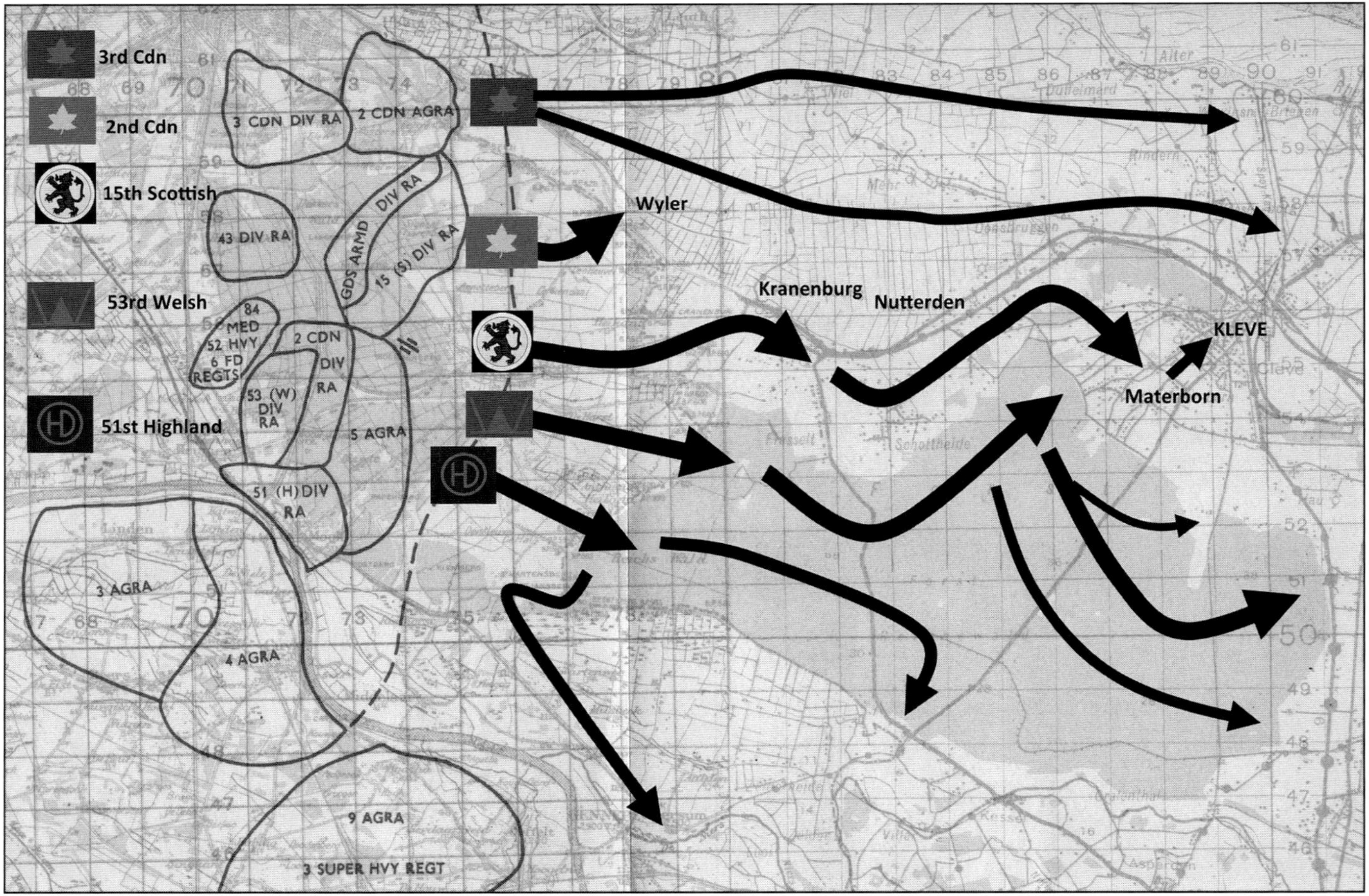

An outline of the XXX Corps' plan for VERITABLE's first phase and gun areas.

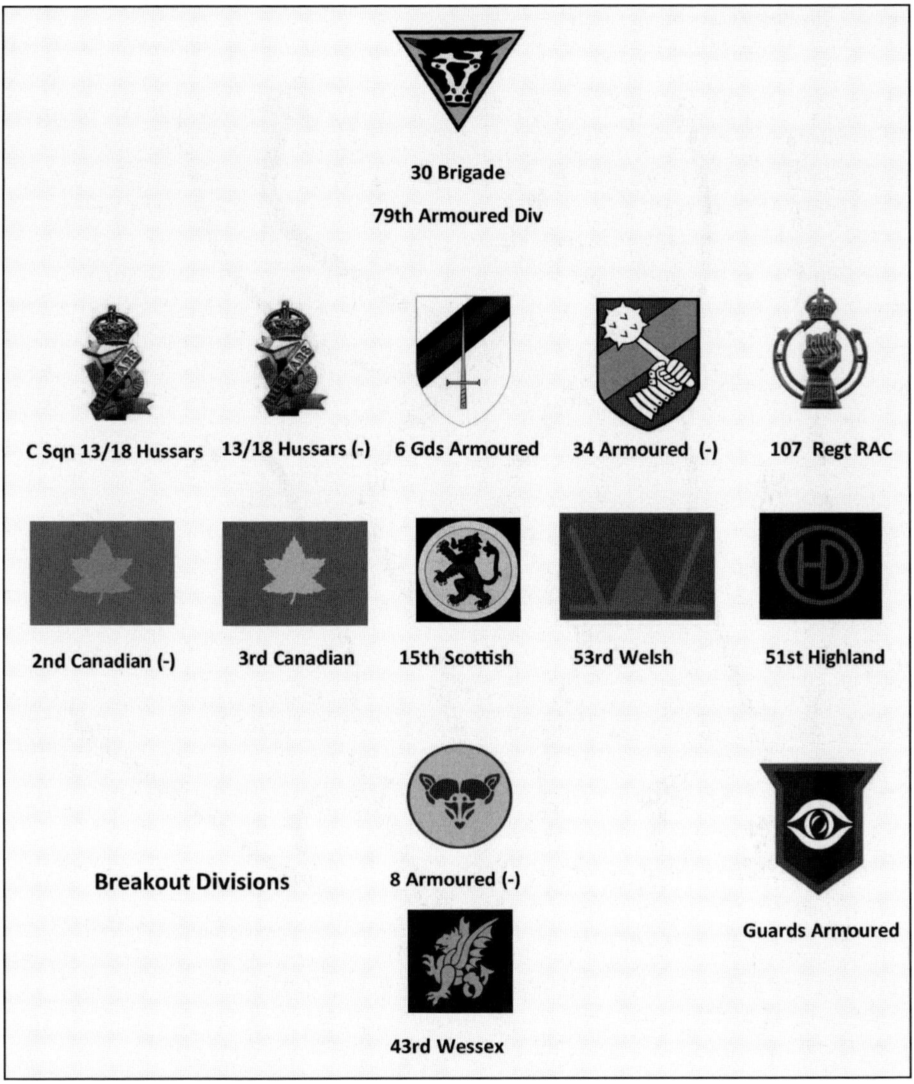

Attachment of armoured brigades and regiments to Operation VERITABLE's infantry divisions.

formations: a brigade from the 2nd Division and the 3rd Division. In the second phase, the Guards Armoured and 43rd Wessex divisions were ordered to be ready to exploit beyond the Reichswald into the Rhineland. Support for the assault was provided by three armoured brigades along with sundry units of assault armour from 79th Armoured Division. Two further British divisions were held as a reserve under the Second Army.

On XXX Corps' left the Canadians were to secure the first few miles of Route PEARL BLACK, the Nijmegen–Kleve road from Wyler and then clear the

Rhine floodplain. Alongside them the 15th Scottish Division and the Churchills of 6 Guards Armoured Brigade, holding the corps' main effort, were to fight through the forward German defences into that narrow piece of higher ground between the floodplain and the Reichswald, and break the Siegfried Line beyond Kranenburg. Once through these defences the Scots and their tanks were to dash and seize both the Materborn feature and Kleve. The 43rd Wessex Division and the tanks of 8 Armoured Brigade, waiting in Nijmegen, were to conduct a passage of lines and break out into the Rhineland in the direction of Goch.

On XXX Corps' right flank the two divisions that were to attack through the Reichswald were the 53rd Welsh Division and the 51st Highland Division, supported by 34 Armoured Brigade. Their task was also to fight through the enemy's forward defences and then break into the Reichswald and advance to the Siegfried Line. Once that had been achieved, the Highland Division was to swing south out onto the Maas floodplain, clearing defences and securing crossings of the River Niers. Finally, when the bridges and routes on this flank were secure, the Guards Armoured Division would be released into the Rhineland.

XXX Corps' Order of Battle

(See Appendix I for the Phase One groupings)

The three British and Canadian divisions and their supporting armour that fought on the northern flank of the Reichswald came from diverse backgrounds; many were Territorial Army soldiers or the Canadian equivalent the militia, others were members of war-raised units. Of the latter, the 1st Worcesters and 2nd Argylls, despite their regular battalion numbers, were replacement battalions for those that had gone into captivity in Singapore and Tobruk. Thus, they were to all intents war-raised units as well.

15th Scottish Infantry Division

Attacking on the northern flank of the Reichswald was the 15th Scottish Infantry Division, which had originally been raised as a New Army division in the First World War and was re-raised for the Second World War, as recorded in the divisional history:

> On 2 September 1939 the 15th Scottish Division was reborn. It had been begotten by national necessity out of 52nd Lowland Division.[1]
>
> The business had started that spring, when, with a wave of his magician's wand the Secretary of State for War had duplicated the Territorial Army. Unfortunately, Mr Belisha had omitted to duplicate with the same gesture the Territorial Army's equipment, accommodation and training facilities.

As hostilities broke out, existing territorial battalions provided cadres for new units, as volunteers flocked to the colours in a manner reminiscent of 1914. Many were old soldiers, whose military experience eased the problems of training. Initially the 15th was based in towns scattered across southern Scotland.

Initially the divisional badge worn on the sleeves was a white letter 'O', the fifteenth letter of the alphabet, but following an inspection by King George VI in 1940 the Lion rampant of Scotland was inserted into the centre of the badge.

However, by the end of September the division was concentrated in the Borders, living in old mills in Galashiels and Hawick. In October, 'essential workers' taken back by the Ministry of Labour and men not meeting new medical standards were replaced by English recruits from the Midlands 'who [apparently] soon became Scottish as the Scots'.

As the Battle of France in 1940 reached its climax, 15th Scottish moved south to the Essex coast, where they prepared to face the expected invasion. As the threat to the UK receded, the emphasis swung to training but, like many formations, the 15th's organisation and tactics went through numerous changes, and in 1943 the division joined VIII Corps. The Scots were soon taking part in increasingly complex exercises in Yorkshire that all suspected were preparations for the 'Second Front'. Suspicions that the division was to take part in the coming campaign grew when General Montgomery visited them and addressed units from the bonnet of a jeep. In common with other invasion troops, the King and Mr Churchill also visited 15th Scottish Division. In April 1944, the 15th moved south to begin the process of waterproofing and final training. The division began to arrive in Normandy on 13 June and prepared for its first battle, Operation EPSOM.

The weather-delayed EPSOM was a brutal introduction for the division to the cost of war, heavy infantry casualties totalling 5,500 men, and the requirement for numerous replacements became the hallmark of the fighting in Normandy. The division, however, prospered and developed into a fine fighting force, performing particularly well in the British part of the western breakout, Operation BLUECOAT.

6 Guards Armoured Brigade

Supporting the Scots in Operation VERITABLE was the 6 Guards Armoured Brigade.[2] In 1941 the infantry battalions of 30th Guards Independent Brigade were converted to tanks and adopted the RAC black beret but retained their regimental badges. Redesignated as a 'tank brigade', the guards tank units were organised and equipped to support infantry divisions in offensive operations with their more heavily armoured and slower Churchill tanks. As casualties mounted with the progress of the war, the Household Division pressed for the return of their battalions. This was resisted by the Prime Minister and they remained with tanks.

During the Normandy Campaign the 6 Guards fought with VIII Corps and as such had established a good working relationship with the 15th Scottish, contributing significantly to success in BLUECOAT and subsequent operations.

The shoulder patch of 6 Guards Armoured Brigade and cap badges of the Coldstream, Grenadier and Scots guards.

Between October 1943 and January 1945 the brigade fought in Holland, particularly at Tilburg, Overloon, Venraij and Meijel, before joining XXX Corps for VERITABLE.

43rd Wessex Infantry Division

The 43rd Wessex Division was formed as a part of the Haldane reforms in 1908 from well-established West Country volunteer and militia units and had been reformed as a part of the Territorial Force after the First World War.

The almost exclusively Territorial Army 43rd Wessex Division was one of the few fully equipped formations in the UK in the aftermath of Dunkirk and formed a part of the GHQ mobile reserve north of London. The 4th Dorsets' historian provides a flavour of the time:

> There were roadblocks and machine-gun posts to be sited, constructed and manned during the hours of darkness: occasionally there were crashed enemy aircraft to be guarded and enemy airmen to be captured; patrols had to be organised to investigate reported cases of light signals and parachute landings, an operational commitment that decreased as the national spy-fever abated.[3]

With the reduction in the invasion threat during 1941, the division was spread out across Kent and into Sussex, where it could concentrate on training in local areas and assembling for larger exercises in the wooded hills of Stone Street inland from Folkestone.

In March 1942, General Thomas took command of the Wessex Division and instigated a notoriously austere regime of camp life and training, overseeing the division's transformation from a coastal defensive formation into one of the best infantry divisions that was to fight in the North-West European Campaign. He earned a reputation as a tough and innovative trainer of troops with extremely high standards. Little escaped his eye and he impressed on all those under his command his intended tactical methods.

Taking his que from Montgomery's briefings in early 1944, according to Brigadier Essame, Thomas:

> ... rightly insisted on the elimination from active command of all officers whose battle-worthiness was in the slightest doubt and introduced the

King Peter II of the Yugoslavian Government in exile inspecting a guard of honour provided by 4th Dorsets.

Major General Ivor Thomas, commander of 43rd Wessex Division.

> realistic and rigorous training that alone offered any prospect of success. Efficiency for battle therefore overrode all other considerations.[4]

Despite wearing breeches and boots of a former age, General Thomas 'conceived warfare in terms of speed – speed of thought and decision – of rapid issue of orders and effective communication'. He was a tough and driving commander in battle and his aide-de-camp, Captain Pat Spencer-Moore, recalled that: 'Many officers feared a confrontation with the GOC more than they did the enemy!'

Sharing a trait with many successful commanders, he had a tough streak and was prepared to commit troops to potentially costly operations. However, in common with most British commanders who had fought in the First World War, he did not squander lives needlessly. His nickname, 'Butcher Thomas', predated the casualties incurred in his division's battles and had more to do with his character and the robust manner with which he dealt with those who failed to meet his standards.

As a part of XII Corps, the 43rd took part in Exercise BLACKCOCK in Yorkshire between September and November 1943. In this exercise, the division already familiar with the methods that had been developed over the previous years, practised the procedures and tactics it was intended to use in north-west Europe alongside XII Corps' other fighting formations.

The Wessex Division's introduction to battle in its first major action on Hill 112 was as brutal as the 15th Scottish's and the level of casualties transformed the Territorial Army nature of the division at a stroke. Nonetheless, the Wessex emerged as one of Montgomery's fighting divisions, spending most of its time under command of XXX Corps from Operation BLUECOAT to MARKET GARDEN and to the forming of the backstop on the River Maas during the Battle of the Bulge.

8 Armoured Brigade

The 8 Armoured Brigade was a highly regarded desert formation that, like other armoured brigades, had undergone some reorganisation on their return to the UK in late 1943, mainly in order to balance experience of battle. The 8 Armoured had served with XXX Corps since landing its DD tanks on GOLD Beach as the first assault wave on D Day. General Horrocks, in the forward to the brigade's history, wrote:

> During practically all the subsequent successful fighting, the Fox and the Pig (30 Corps Sign) were together. On occasions, I am afraid I have had to ask the 8th Armoured Brigade to undertake some very unpleasant tasks, but they were all carried out magnificently, and on no single occasion can I recall the slightest hesitation.
>
> There have been times in this war when, in the heat of battle, the atmosphere between the Infantry and Tanks has become somewhat strained. But this has never happened when the 8th Armoured Brigade was present; if you want to know what the Infantry Soldier thought of the Fox you have only to ask the men of such famous Divisions as 43rd (Wessex), 51st (Highland) or 50th (Northumbrian), and I have no doubt as to the favourable and enthusiastic answer you would get.

In January the brigade returned north from the fighting in the Roermond–Geilenkirchen area to re-join XXX Corps and come under command of the Wessex Division in the breakout phase of VERITABLE that was to see the two familiar formations striking into the Rhineland.

The traditional Wessex Wyvern badge of 43rd Infantry Division (*top left*). The Fox's mask shoulder flash of 8 Armoured Brigade (*top right*) and the 'Pig' of XXX Corps (*bottom left*). The badge painted on the vehicles of 79th Armoured Division (*bottom right*).

79th Armoured Division

Any commander looking at the tactical overprint maps of the Germans' forward defences on the Groesbeek Heights and the Siegfried Line north of the Reichswald would have concluded instantly that the assault armour of 79th Armoured Division would most definitely be required. As a matter of routine early in the process of planning, officers from the 79th were on hand to both advise on the most effective way to use the various pieces of assault armour and to ensure that they were not misused. Those units attached to Brigadier Duncan's brigade of flail tanks (30 Armoured Brigade), were the crocodiles of 141 (The Buffs) Regiment RAC and the 2nd Fife and Forfar Yeomanry, plus the Armoured Vehicle Royal Engineers (AVREs) of 6th and 42nd assault regiments RE.

The assault armour was heavily committed to breaking into the enemy's forward defences, with General Hobart's assault armour clearing the way. Flail tanks would deal with the mines and (AVREs) would lay small box girder (SBG) bridges across the anti-tank ditches and take on defences with their petard demolition guns. Once through the enemy's forward positions, 79th Armoured Division's vehicles would help the fight through the Siegfried Line.

Fire Support

By this stage in the North-West European Campaign the artillery support was lavish and, as Horrocks noted, 'was very carefully worked out and was on the most massive scale I ever remember'. He had under his command no fewer than five British and Canadian army groups Royal Artillery (AGRA), which were in effect artillery brigades, in addition to each infantry division's seventy-two 25-pounder guns, which brought the artillery total to 1,050 guns. In addition, a regiment of super heavy 8in guns and the launchers of the 1st Canadian Rocket Battery. There were 446 guns, mortars and machine guns allocated to firing PEPPERPOT shoots.[5]

The Rocket Unit's 'Land Mattress' was fired by a battery of twelve projectors, each having thirty-two launch tubes, which in terms of throw weight made each launcher the equivalent of ten rounds fire for effect by a complete field artillery regiment. The rockets were fired on a ripple system to avoid collisions in the air and impacted in an area of approximately 400 yards square. A total of 4,608 rockets were available for the opening stages of VERITABLE, which would be fired in salvoes at fifteen targets across the corps' front. The five divisions submitted bids for this fire and thirteen targets were included in the fire plan between 0500 and 1400 hours during 8 February. As the warhead's effect was mainly blast rather than splinter, the targets were to be engaged, as far as safety limits permitted, just before the infantry arrived in the target area. It was found that following the rockets with 25-pounders achieved even better suppressive results, as the enemy were invariably still stunned and had their heads down when the infantry arrived.[6]

Officers inspecting one of 1st Canadian Rocket Battery's launchers.

The Army Groups Royal Artillery (AGRA)

The idea of the AGRA was conceived as a result of the anti-invasion exercise BUMPER during 1941. This was organised by the First World War gunner officer General Alan Brooke, who was at the time C in C Home Forces, with his chief umpire being the then Lieutenant General Montgomery. The exercise developed the mass fire-based First World War practice but modern communication technology enhanced command, control and above all flexibility. AGRAs were formally established in 1942 and were to be found in all British theatres of war.

The AGRA was a medium artillery brigade, with its own headquarters, which was generally affiliated to one of the corps but, as in the case of VERITABLE, they were grouped for massive fire effect under XXX Corps.* Each of the army AGRAs normally consisted of six or seven artillery regiments, a headquarters, signals company ammunition supply companies and REME light aid detachments. The Army AGRAs each had a self-propelled regiment of Sexton 25-pounders, and four medium regiments, plus a heavy regiment of 7.2in guns.†

With a slightly different organisation, the 2nd Canadian AGRA included a heavy anti-aircraft regiment, and the 21st Army Group's 9th AGRA had a single 'super heavy' regiment of 8in and 240mm guns.

Five AGRAs were grouped under the overall command of CRA First Canadian Army to support the Opening phases of Operation VERITABLE. In addition to the Canadians' own AGRA, three were attached from Second Army and there was the 21st Army Group's AGRA. Their role in the battle was to fire the crushing three-hour-long opening bombardment followed by the creeping barrage that covered the advance. The 5th AGRA had a particular responsibility for firing counter-battery engagements. Again, in the case of VERITABLE, with the difficulty of getting divisional gun groups forward, the medium and heavy guns of the AGRAs were usually able to provide fire with their longer range, thanks to an extremely flexible command and control system.

Once the battle was underway the guns of the AGRAs were to continue with their fire plans, but in the event of the inevitable German counter-attacks that their doctrine demanded, guns could be diverted to join the 25-pounders of the divisional artilleries in breaking these up. Thanks to the good communications and inherent flexibility it was possible to mass fires according to the scale of the threat.

MIKE	Regimental shoot by twenty-four 25-pounders.
UNCLE	Divisional shoot by seventy-two 25-pounders.
VICTOR	A shoot by all guns under command of a corps in range.
WILLIAM	A shoot by all guns under command of the Army in range.
YORK	A shoot by all guns of a particular AGRA.

When a Forward Observation Officer called for instance 'Mike target, Mike target, Mike target', especially regimental or divisional shoots, the procedure was usually to drop everything, 'shoot first and ask questions later'!

* For example, 3rd AGRA normally supported XII Corps and 5th AGRA XXX Corps.

† ORBATs had varied considerably in the early days of the North-West European Campaign but by the end of 1944 had settled into more or less standard establishment.

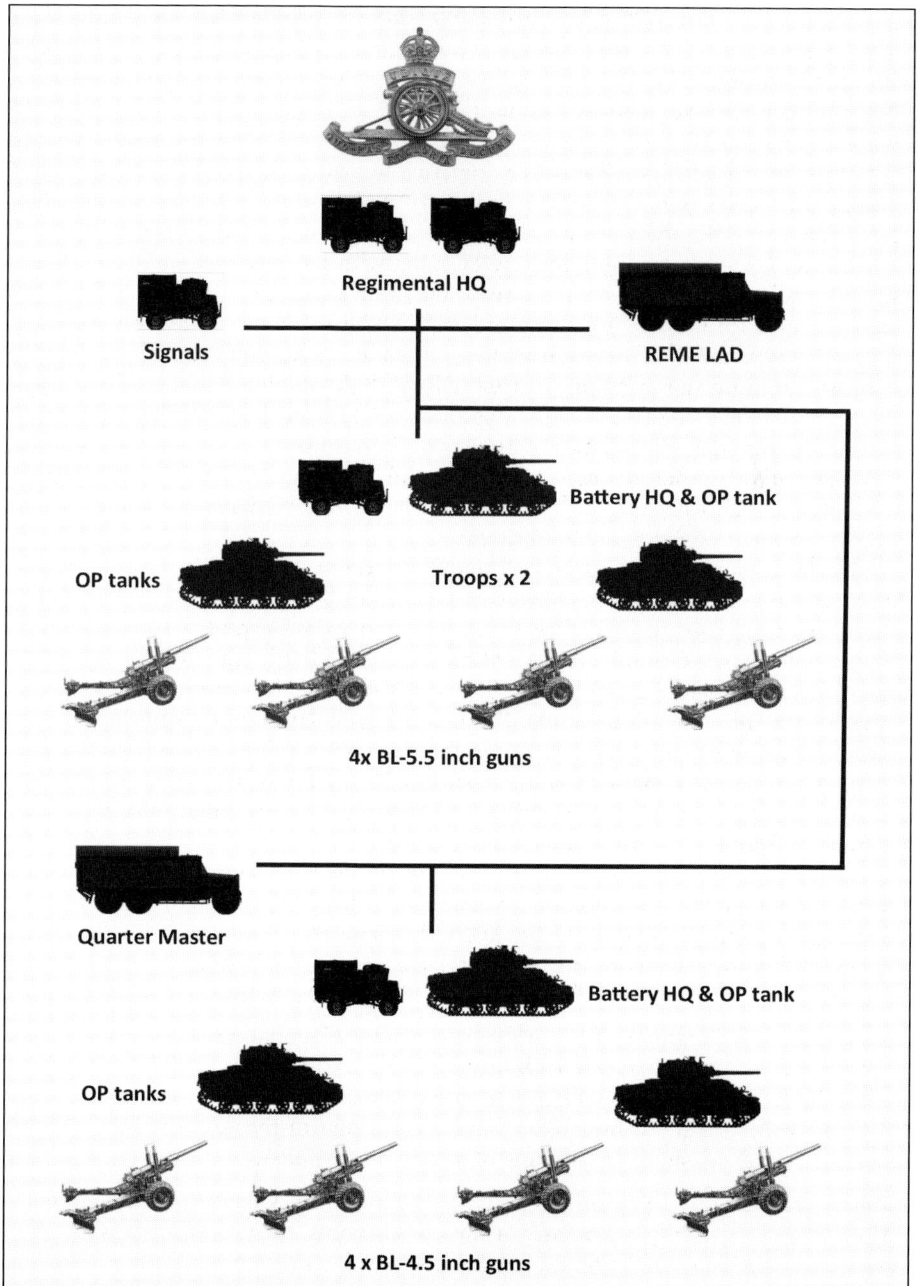

The organisation of a medium regiment, including armoured observation post tanks, as found in the Army Groups Royal Artillery that supported offensive operations throughout the North-West European Campaign. Not all medium regiments had 4.5in guns.

Logistics

The opening of the Scheldt and the port of Antwerp had by mid-December transformed the logistic situation of the Allies. In contrast, the reduced amount of combat supplies reaching the German army was placing them in an increasingly parlous position. Despite V weapon bombardment of Antwerp, the amount of combat supplies available for Montgomery's next offensive was more than adequate but with deep frost followed by rain, a major commitment by the Royal Engineers was required to get the supplies to the dumps being established behind the front line on the Groesbeek Heights.

It required fifty companies of British and Canadian engineers and twenty-nine companies of pioneers to repair and maintain hundreds of miles of roads before the move of supplies could begin. Most of the routes were not designed for heavy military traffic and there were also choke points that required removing or bypassing. To take the heavily laden trucks and transporters, some seventy bridges had to be built, including five across major rivers, one of which was a railway bridge, across the Maas. Of these, the record-breaking Ravenstein 'high-level' pontoon bridge, known as the QUEBEC Bridge, was 1,280ft long.[7]

Despite all the labour committed to route maintenance, as described in a 21st Army Group Summary of Operations, 28 January–4 February 1945, difficulties persisted:

> During Jan the roads had been universally ice-bound. Just prior to the time when movement was to reach its peak, from 3 Feb onwards, came the thaw with all its attendant troubles. Many roads deteriorated rapidly and eventually ruts developed to a depth of 18 inches to 2 feet – and others collapsed completely at various points. Diversions were extremely difficult to improvise as the surrounding country in most places became water logged. The very carefully planned forward movement from staging areas to concentration areas and onwards across the R. Maas had to be recast daily in the light of existing road conditions. That final assembly was completed by the right time in spite of these abnormal and most difficult conditions says much for the high standard of staff work of the traffic staffs, and the superhuman efforts of the traffic control personnel and the RE concerned with road maintenance.[8]

Despite the demands of the Battle of the Bulge, supplies were being dumped in the Canadian Army's rear area and with the Supreme Commander's intent that VERITABLE would take place by 25 January, they were being trucked into the forward area at a rate of 7,500 tons per day.

Artillery ammunition for the 1,050 guns was by far the largest commodity to be moved forward in both weight and volume. As an example, every 25-pounder gun was allocated 1,677 rounds of ammunition for the battle, which was dumped at gun positions, and held on first- and second-line unit transport, or kept back at army dumps. To keep a 25-pounder in action, each gun required eight truckloads

A convoy of Canadian vehicles being led through a badly damaged village.

of ammunition to be brought forward to gun positions in 3-ton trucks that could carry 180 rounds at a time. Lieutenant George Blackburn, of 4th Field Regiment, RCA, wrote:

> To the gunners, the size and importance of an operation is best indicated by the build-up of ammunition, and no one has seen such mountainous deliveries of shells since Normandy. All of it has to be on gun positions before dawn February 3 so that the roads will be free for guns, tanks, and troops to move up on the last four nights before the attack. And it seems the deadline is met.
>
> In less than two weeks more than three-quarters of a million shells have been accumulated at gun positions – 633,160 of them just to take care of the opening tasks … ranging from 20-pound missiles to 360-pound monsters.

Royal Army Service Corps soldiers stacking ration boxes.

With XXX Corps numbering 200,000 men and with II Canadian Corps poised to join the battle, the First Canadian Army had accumulated 2,319,222 rations in its maintenance areas. These supplies and much more required 25,000 vehicles to bring them forward prior to and during the battle, which in turn consumed 1,300,000 gallons of fuel.

Due to both security and a lack of space in the Nijmegen area, 15th Scottish Division's ordnance field park unusually supplied all three phase one British assault divisions.

Operational Security and Observation

To preserve surprise, Field Marshal Montgomery insisted that every Op Sec measure be taken and rigidly enforced, and with the mass of combat supplies being brought forward the potential for providing the Germans with a major intelligence indicator was ever present. Canadian Lieutenant George Blackburn noted that 'all moves were carried out within the hours of darkness, with vehicles required to be off the roads and hidden by dawn, strict traffic control was enforced'. Trooper Smith, of C Squadron, 141 (The Buffs) Regiment, RAC, records a visit while they were in the assembly area in the outskirts of Nijmegen:

> An officer looking very important came marching down the street and demanded to speak to the Troop Sergeant. The newcomer explained that he was officer I/C camouflage XXX Corps, and that when flying over the area that morning he had had no difficulty in distinguishing our tanks. He was quite pleasant about it and asked us to improve our camouflage more as a request than a command. As we could not remember seeing any German aircraft since New Year's Day it did seem more cautious than perhaps was necessary but we promised that we would do the best we could within the limits of being able to work on the tanks. This seemed to satisfy the officer. He went away and we returned to [repairing] our wheel.[9]

Meanwhile, XXX Corps released from operations further south, the divisions and brigades regrouping with them moved into concentration areas up to 60 miles from the Groesbeek Heights from mid-January onwards. From there they also moved forward by stages at night, only reaching their assembly areas in the woods behind the in-place Canadian divisions during the nights before VERITABLE's D Day. General Horrocks explained:

> By day the normal amount of transport for the two Canadian divisions already in the area used the roads freely and no change was made, so that the Germans would not become suspicious, but from dusk to dawn the roads were packed with transport, moving nose to tail, and before it became light, almost like magic the units would disappear into their concealment areas.

With the Germans having a very good electronic warfare capability, it was vital that the same level of radio communication was maintained during the moves forward as had existed before that phase of preparations began. Consequently, all movement was conducted under radio silence, with no fewer than 1,600 military policemen controlling road movement between hides en route forward. In the forward area, however, 'more important than anything else was the control of reconnaissance'. General Horrocks continued:

> ... literally thousands of officers and NCOs had to be given a chance to study the ground over which they were to attack. The Germans, who had become used to seeing very little movement on the wooded hills held by the Canadians in front of them, would suddenly have seen these same hills almost covered by figures wearing a different-coloured khaki battledress (the Canadian battledress was darker than ours), studying maps, using field glasses, and so on. There is an old Army saying, 'Time spent in reconnaissance is seldom wasted', and this unusual amount of movement could only mean one thing – an impending attack. We therefore had to impose the

> most rigorous control on any movement in the area occupied by the 2nd Canadian Division, and a reconnaissance report centre was established in the Dutch barracks at Grave, where everyone wishing to view the battlefield had to report. The staff at this centre would then control the number of people entering any particular area, by a system of passes, allowing them access to a certain view-point, for a definite period. They were then fitted out in a suit of the darker Canadian battledress. A series of sentries were posted at intervals, to whom the passes had to be shown.

Inevitably the burden of hosting visitors fell on 2nd Canadian Division's artillery units. The war diary of 4th Canadian Field Regiment for 5 February recorded that regimental headquarters 'really needed a revolving door to accommodate the horde of representatives from the advance parties of the formations coming to join us for the impending shenanigans'.

The most important of 4th Field Regiment's observation posts was the Groesbeek Windmill, which had first been used by 82nd US Airborne Division during the fighting on the heights back in September. Lieutenant Blackburn wondered why it was still standing:

> Why the Germans left that windmill intact will always be a mystery, for obviously it was the best observation post in the countryside. Certainly, had

The Groesbeek Windmill still stands today although the village, now a town, has expanded around it.

> they known what was going on there during the last weeks of January and the first week in February, it would not have been left standing. During that period, it was filled with officers from generals down to subalterns each day planning Germany's destruction.

A troop commander of A Squadron, 107 Regiment, RAC, Lieutenant Foley, was one of those who took his NCO tank commanders forward to an observation post overlooking the heights and the German forward positions:

> It isn't often one can get a grandstand view of a potential battlefield, and when I took Five Troop along to have a look at it, they found it hard to believe that the harmless-looking fields and cottages were deserted except for German listening posts covering the mines which were undoubtedly thickly sewn ...
>
> From the front of a large wood to the west of the Reichswald we stared through our binoculars at Germany. The ground between was low-lying and looked boggy. Here and there derelict gliders of the Arnhem battle dotted the landscape and the burned-out remains of vehicles told of the battles which had already been fought over this stretch of land.
>
> Tony Cunningham asked: 'Is that the anti-tank ditch, that white thing zig-zagging across by the group of red houses?'[10]
>
> 'That's it,' said Ian. 'But the funnies are going to get us over that.'

In spite the scale of the preparations for VERITABLE and visits to the forward area by recce parties, thanks to the effectiveness of Horrocks' Op Sec measures at the end of January situation maps in German headquarters still marked XXX Corps as 'Whereabouts unknown'.

XXX Corps' Concentration

The 15th Scottish Division spent two weeks in the Tilburg area resting, taking in replacements and training with Guards' Churchills that were to fight with them in the coming battle. Infantry battalion drivers were also sent for instruction on the newly issued small amphibious vehicle, the Weasel.

The movement of thousands of trucks, artillery pieces and tanks into their assembly areas immediately behind the First Canadian Army's rear via the choke points on the River Maas at Grave and Mook required the engineers' efforts to keep the roads open to be extended further forward. Now the thaw had set in roads broke up under the stream of night-time convoys, and tanks that were making the last leg of the journey forward on their tracks carved deep ruts around corners and created flooded dips that needed constant filling.

The 44th Lowland Brigade's history describes a typical night move from the concentration area to their assembly area 50 miles forward, where they were joined by the supporting arms:

> On the evening of 6th of February the Brigade moved out from Tilburg in convoy and by a devious route without any lights, reached Nijmegen in the

Royal Engineers building a class 60 Bailey Bridge.

early hours of the morning and went into billets. The whole town was one great armed camp, with thousands of soldiers, tanks, guns and vehicles of all kinds concealed in the shattered streets. Unfortunately, the cold spell of weather had broken and had given way to slush, mud, floods, rain – which augured ill for the forest tracks in the Siegfried Line. Anxious eyes scanned the sky during the 7th of February, but it was dull and damp and gave little promise of dry weather to come.

The Supreme Commander's Decision

General Eisenhower, no doubt with the surprise of Hitler's offensive in the Ardennes foremost in his mind, maintained his policy of closing up to the Rhine in order to reduce the possibility of the Germans launching another counter-offensive in the west. He explained:

> In the situation facing us in January, the German enjoyed the great advantage of the Siegfried defences in the area northward from the Saar, inclusive. As long as we allowed him to remain in those elaborate fortifications his

> ability was enhanced to hold great portions of his long line with relatively weak forces, while he concentrated for spoiling attacks at selected points. This meant that a large proportion of the Allied Force would be immobilized in a protective role, with only that portion on the offensive that could be maintained north of the Ruhr. In that single zone of advance, we could not logistically sustain more than thirty-five divisions.[11]

When Montgomery returned north from the Bulge on 16 January, General Crerar presented his plans for Operation VERITABLE, and a week later the 21st Army Group plan for VERITABLE and GRENADE, along with Second Army's operations to clear the remaining German pockets west of the Maas, were in principal approved by the Supreme Commander. The target dates for VERITABLE's D Day were set as 8 and 10 February.

There was, however, a problem: in mid-January 12th US Army Group was still pushing the Fifth and Sixth Panzer Armies out of the Ardennes Bulge. Consequently, Eisenhower could not give Montgomery his final authority to launch the Battle of the Rhineland. He persisted in hoping that pressure by the First US Army would result in a German collapse in the Ardennes/Eifel that would take General Hodges' divisions to the banks of the Rhine. This was a legitimate exploitation of success, and he would have been on safe political ground with the US media, but the First US Army, after six weeks of fighting, had lost momentum and was soon halted by the Germans. Consequently, it was not until 28 January that Eisenhower finally gave authority for VERITABLE to go ahead as planned on 8 February, but that was not the end of the delays.

Anglo–US relations were at a new low following Montgomery's lack of tact and a degree of wilful US misunderstanding following a 7 January press conference on the conduct of the fighting in the Ardennes. It resulted in any willingness to cooperate between Bradley and Montgomery evaporating and when ordered to break off the fighting in the Ardennes on 21 January, Bradley prevaricated and failed to regroup some of First Army's divisions to Simpson's Ninth US Army, arguing that water released from the Roer dams in his area would stop GRENADE's attack across the river below the dams. He, of course, aimed to keep hold of these divisions for his own projected 12th US Army Group offensive, and also keep hold of the Allied main effort. In short he had not secured the dams for the furtherance of his own aims. Eisenhower was forced to issue a direct order to Bradley on 1 February to release the divisions as directed to General Simpson.

The result of Bradley's and Hodges' failure to capture the dams, until after the Germans had so badly damaged the gates, prevented Simpson from crossing the River Roer until 23 February. This condemned General Crear's army to fighting on its own without the Ninth US Army's southern pincer for a full two weeks, rather than the planned two days. There is no doubt the wilful delays cost thousands of casualties. It also undermined 21st Army Group's intent to envelop and destroy German forces west of the Rhine, allowing them to withdraw across the river with losses but in relatively good order and live to fight another day.

(*Left*) General Omar Bradley, commander of 12th US Army Group. (*Right*) Lieutenant General Courtney Hodges Commander First US Army.

General Crerar's message to the troops of First Canadian Army that were to take part in Operation VERITABLE.

[illegible]BRUARY 1945 — FIRST CANADIAN ARMY

PERSONAL MESSAGE
From the
ARMY COMMANDER

Six months ago, almost to a day, history was made by formations of this Army in their Southward drive which broke the "CAEN hinge" and closed the "FALAISE pocket". The same, and other formations shall again record great achievements in the days ahead by breaking through the "REICHSWALD pivot" and turning this key sector of the Siegfried Line.

The operations which we are about to undertake are of the greatest possible importance. Indeed, the result of them can lead to speedy and complete Allied victory. The assault will be launched in great strength and with most powerful fire support. Whatever the difficulties of ground and weather, the forward thrust through the enemy and his defences will be pressed without respite. He must be given no time or opportunity to collect his thoughts or his resources. The opportunity is at hand. Let us see to it that it is firmly seized and decisively exploited.

(H. D. G. Crerar) General
GOC-in-C
First Canadian Army

Chapter Three

The Siegfried Line and the Defenders of the Reich

Prior to the Battle of the Bulge, Field Marshal von Rundstedt had been reinstated as Commander in Chief West after being sacked at the height of the battle for Normandy. He, however, had very little power to actually influence events that were being increasingly directed by Berlin, but he was regarded as a competent commander and was the architect of the German battle for the Rhineland, loyally supporting Hitler's decision to fight west of the Rhine despite his own reservations. In the command structure below von Rundstedt, there was little agreement as to where the Allies would attack or in the Wehrmacht's capacity to defend the Reich.

Von Rundstedt believed that the Americans would attack to the south, in the area of the Aachen salient, while the British would launch an assault crossing of the Maas around Venlo some days later. This was an estimate that General Blaskowitz, the newly appointed commander of Army Group H, concurred with, arguing that the direct route to the strategically vital Ruhr industrial area was the most likely Allied option. Having taken over from General Kurt Student, Blaskowitz was responsible for holding the northern front from Walcheren on the coast south towards Aachen, where the bulk of his reserves, principally General von Lüttwitz's XLVII Panzer Corps, were deployed to cover the southern or Venlo flank. In the aftermath of the Battle of the Bulge, von Lüttwitz could only muster about ninety panzers across his weak corps to support General Schlemm's First *Fallschirmjäger* Army.

Hitler's vision of the West Wall or Siegfried Line was of an impregnable belt of steel and concrete, but von Rundstedt, however, reported unfavourably on its strength to Berlin. General Blumentritt recorded that:

> Rundstedt alluded very critically to the West Wall in a report to the German Supreme Command and described it as a mousetrap – this drastic report about the West Wall aroused Hitler's deepest displeasure. He called it positively insulting and gave it as his opinion that the enemy would tremble before these 'fortifications'.

General Straube, commander of LXXXIV Corps, was also critical of the defences in his area, which were 'a farce ... It wasn't a wall, it was an idea.' The Allies may not have 'trembled' but breaching the Siegfried Line most definitely featured in their calculations.

Field Marshal von Rundstedt, C in C West.

General Blaskowitz, commander Army Group H.

General Schlemm had taken over command of the First *Fallschirmjäger* Army when its erstwhile commander General Student had been promoted to briefly command Army Group H during the autumn. Schlemm also disagreed both with Hitler's view of the strength of the Siegfried Line and the likely direction of the forthcoming Allied offensive. His own estimates concluded that the Allies were most likely to attack south from the Groesbeek Heights between the rivers Rhine and the Maas. He argued that with the Germans still controlling the Roer dams and its potential flood waters, an attack from this direction could not be the main Allied effort. He further argued that the British would not commit themselves to an assault crossing of the Maas when they could attack from Groesbeek between the two rivers. Despite the work on his defences of the Reichswald, and the good going for armour on the direct approach to the Rhine from the Maas at Venlo, Schlemm still concluded that the Reichswald represented a 'side door to the Ruhr' and this was where the Allies would attack. He had deployed 7th *Fallschirmjäger* Division in reserve positions, with several *kampfgruppen* that could intervene in the battle within six to eight hours, a crucial factor if tasked promptly. A report on Schlemm's post-war questioning reads:

> Schlemm claims that Blaskowitz at Army Group and Rundstedt, the C-in-C West, believed the next big Allied move would be an American offensive

> launched from Roermond together with a British attack across the river at Venlo. This was opposed to Schlemm's personal view, who expected the big blow to come south through the Reichswald as it eventually did. He advanced this view to his seniors but was constantly assured that there was no evidence of large concentrations in the Nijmegen area. The worst that could be expected there was a holding attack launched by two or three Canadian Divisions, he was told.

The fact that the 'armed camp' in Nijmegen had not been identified points to the weakness of the Luftwaffe's recce capability and the Allies' effective operational security.

Schlemm's formation responsible for the majority of the layered defence of the Rhineland south of Nijmegen, including the Reichswald, was General Erich Straube's LXXXVI Corps. Straube, who did not believe in his commander's Reichswald estimate, was competent but slow to make decisions, often becoming bogged down in minor detail to the great frustration of his staff, who nicknamed him the Little Watchmaker. His view was that the floodplains of the Rhine and Mass and the bulk of the Reichswald were entirely unsuitable for large-scale operations, and he therefore believed that any attack through the 'side door' was

General Alfred Schlemm.

General Erich Straube, 'The Little Watchmaker'.

likely to be diversionary. Despite Schlemm's repeated requests, with few reserves available to Blaskowitz the only reinforcements Straube received were a handful of decidedly second-rate police, stomach and ear battalions.

The Defences

Following the destruction of much of the Seventh Army in the Falaise pocket and the headlong retreat east during September 1944, along with continued fighting in the autumn, the Wehrmacht was occupying the West Wall or Siegfried Line covering Germany's borders. Its northern extremity from the Reichswald to the Rhine had not been completed during the line's pre-war construction and throughout its length much of its armaments, fixtures and fittings had been removed and used in the Atlantic Wall. As a result, most of the concrete bunkers and casemates, many of which were not big enough to take the larger guns of 1945, were used as shelters for the surrounding field positions, which were dug to thicken up the line to an appreciable depth.

General Schlemm, believing that the Allies would attack the weakest section of the Siegfried defences, planned his defences in depth, laying out three main lines: the Forward Line, the Siegfried Line and the Hochwald 'layback'. In addition, there were intermediate entrenched positions, while the larger Rhineland towns were ringed with defences, creating strongpoints around which armoured reserves could manoeuvre.[1]

The Forward Line was in reality a strong outpost position, consisting of an anti-tank ditch and a complex double-layered trench system, occupied by six weak battalions each on a frontage of approximately 1,500 yards, with depth from the outposts to the rear companies of some 2,000 yards. Here a second line was dug inside the western edge of the Reichswald for the reserve companies. Unlike the defences in the open farmland, which had been mapped by the Allies using aerial photography, detailed intelligence of trenches inside the forest was limited, as photo reconnaissance was, of course, blinded by the tree cover.

Much of the labour to dig the field defences was completed by Soviet prisoners of war and forced labour, including local people working on the defences of their town. The principal features were anti-tank ditches, which were believed to be normally 12–15ft wide at the top, narrowing to 6ft at the bottom and were 8ft deep, containing 1–4ft of water, depending on the height of the water table. To save labour wherever possible the numerous drainage ditches that already existed were enlarged. In front of the ditch, minefields had been laid and trenches dug from which infantry could cover the whole obstacle belt with overlapping and interlocking arcs of fire. Communication trenches had also been dug, allowing the defenders to redeploy rapidly from one side of the obstacles to the other as well as laterally.

Somewhat over 2 miles to the rear, the Siegfried Line defences cut through the Reichswald from Tuthees on the edge of the Rhine's floodplain, south to Hekkens, then crossed the River Niers and ran south-east inside the German frontier and east of the Maas. The Reichswald sector that XXX Corps was to

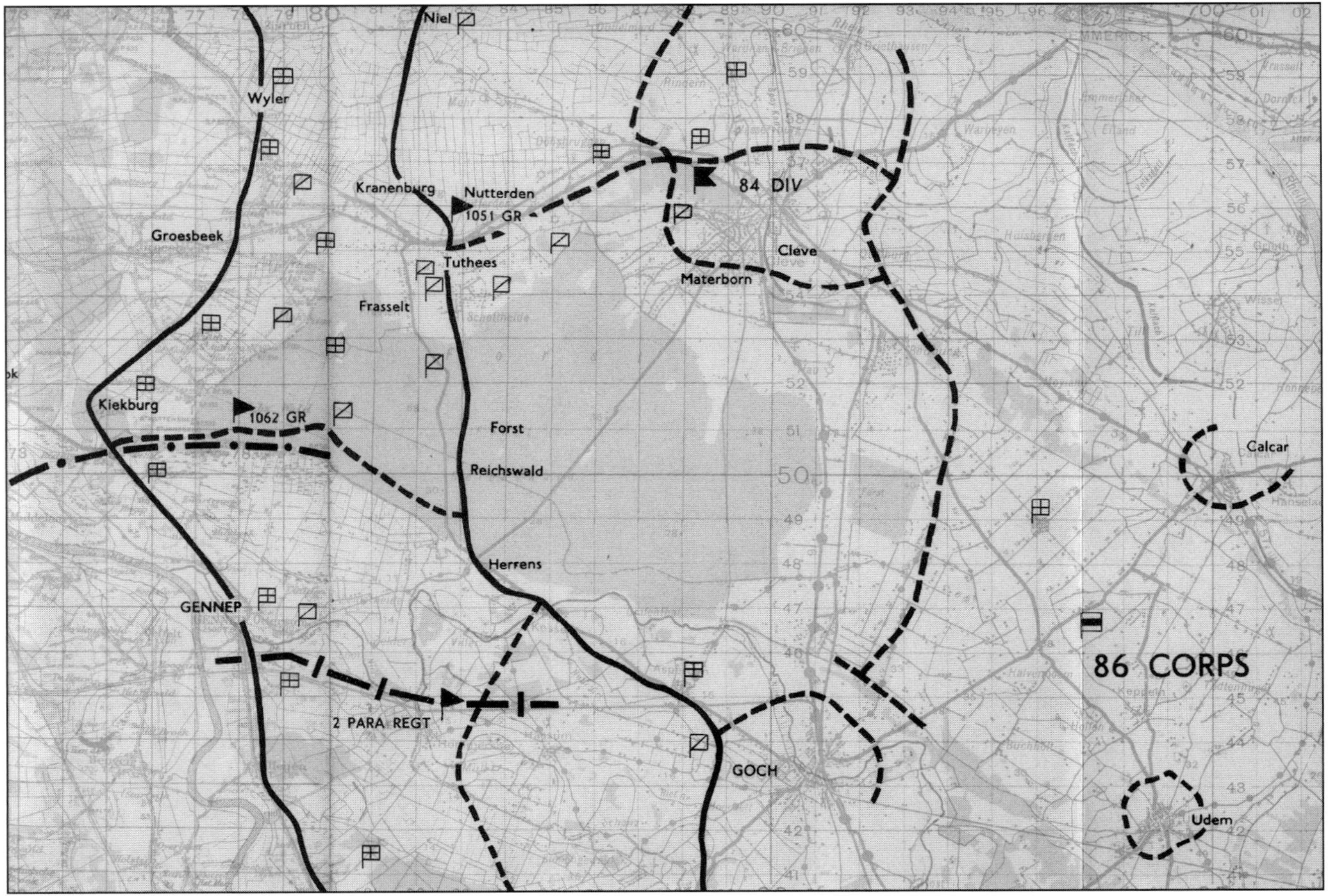

The First *Fallschirmjäger* Army's layered Rhineland defences. Map extract from, BAOR, *Battlefield Tour Operation VERITABLE* (BAOR, 1947).

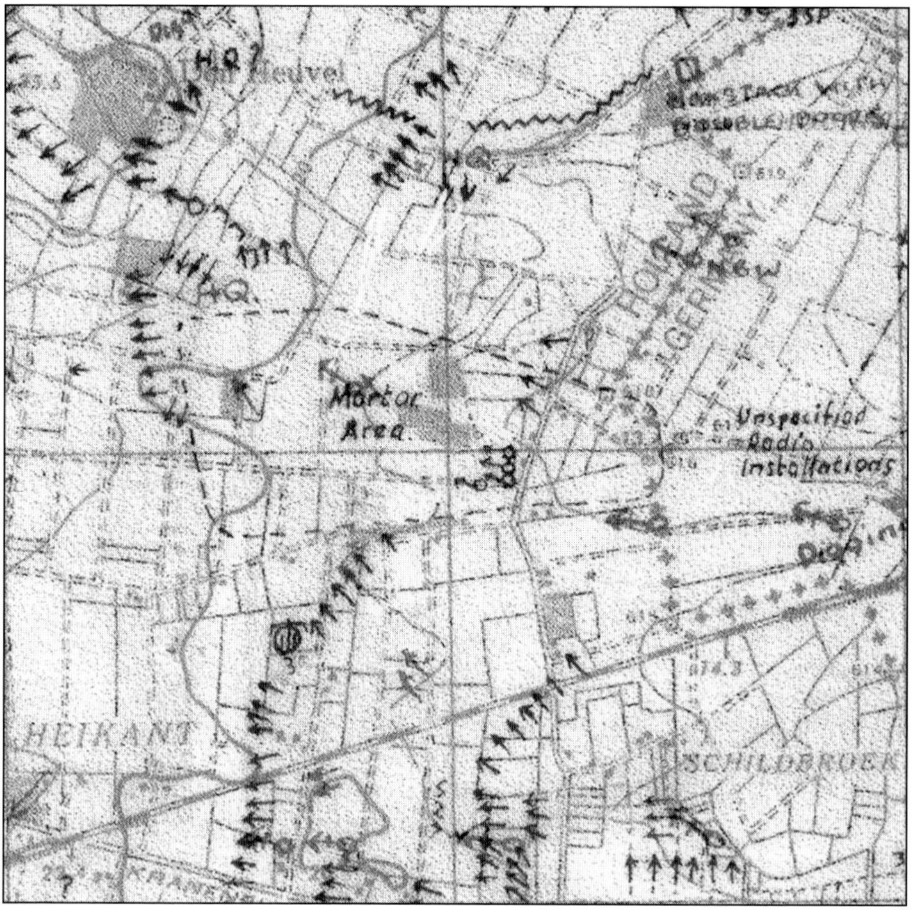

Extracts of the Defences Overprint maps. (*Above*) A 2km square section of the Forward Line west of the Reichswald on 15 October 44 (prepared by the 43rd Wessex Division). (*Opposite*) the same area in front of 15th Scottish Division on 2 February 45. The map extracts taken from Defence Overprint Sheet B (Rhine) Edition of 15 Oct 44 – 1:25,000. Defence Overprint, Groesbeek North Edition of 2 Feb 45 – 1:25,000.

attack, other than the seven identified large bunkers, lacked the formidable network of concrete casemates that Ninth US Army would encounter further to the south, but such concrete as existed was surrounded by similar field defences as were to be found in the Forward Line.[2] Tree cover again prevented detailed intelligence being developed but the stretch of Siegfried Line running 1½ miles from the north of the Reichswald out onto the Rhine floodplain, which 15th Scottish Division was to attack, was well documented.

The whole of the Reichswald was considered by the Allies to be 'a self-contained centre of resistance', but beyond the eastern edge of the forest there were significant pre-prepared defences on the high ground of the Materborn

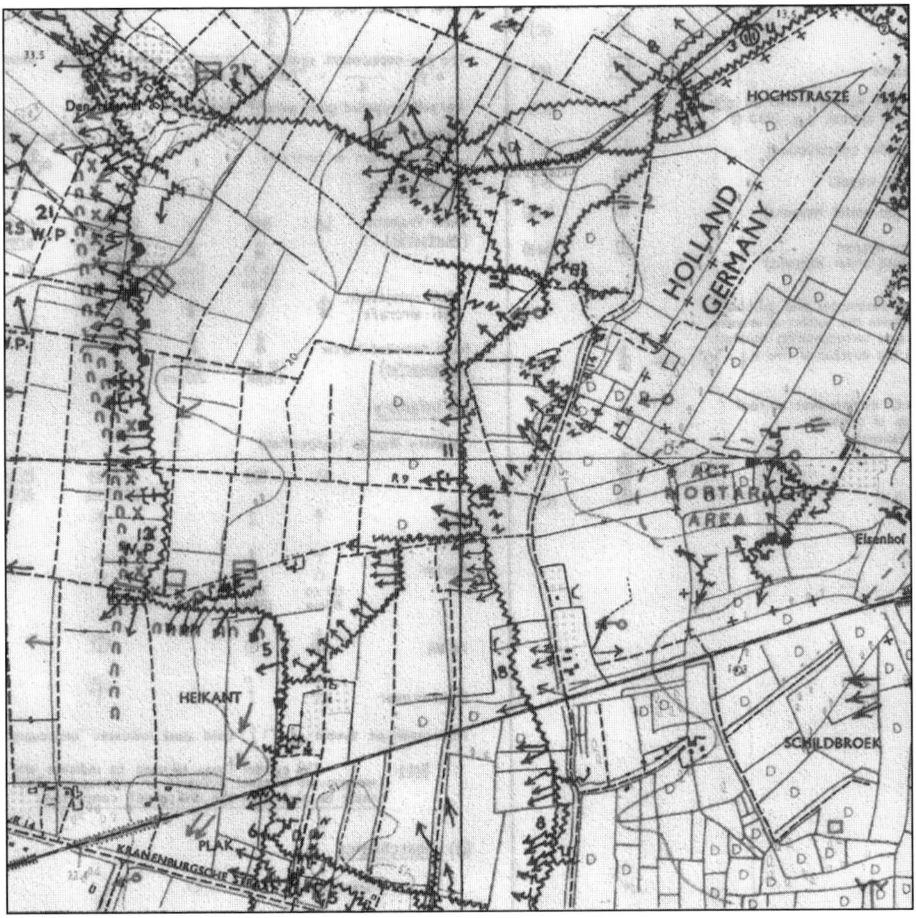

feature. Overlooking the city of Kleve, if fully occupied, this broad plateau would potentially need another deliberate attack before XXX Corps could break out into the Rhineland. Of the defended towns beyond the Reichswald and Kleve, General Horrocks wrote:

> ... the small Rhineland towns had been turned into fortresses prepared for all round defence. I was told that the houses of all these German frontier towns had been specially constructed for battle; with loopholed concrete basements they were capable of all round defence. In war, as in most things, the Germans certainly are thorough ... The chief enemy resistance came from the cellars in the villages.[3]

A further 5 miles south-east lay the defences of the Hochwald 'Layback', which covered the approaches to the Rhine around Xanten.

German civilians digging an anti-tank ditch in the Rhineland during January 1945.

On the Rhine floodplain, there were few formal defences, as the ground was wet, flat and intersected with drainage ditches and old river channels. During most winters the numerous dykes contained the Rhine floods. VERITABLE's planning staff were, however, aware that as a result of the thaw and the Rhine's increasingly high-water levels, the Germans, by blowing these dykes, would inundate most of the floodplain, potentially creating a major obstacle several miles wide.

Defenders of the Reichswald Plug

At a naval Conference at Kiel in July 1939, Hitler briefed his audience of senior officers that Germany would not be ready to resume what he referred to as 'the struggle' until 1943 or 1944. Despite this the Wehrmacht seemed impressive but there was little depth or resilience in its structures for a long war. Initially, from 1939 until the end of 1941, the German army was almost universally successful but Hitler's gamble in invading Poland had committed Germany to a war that by his own estimate the country was not ready for. With mounting losses following Stalingrad, Tunisia and Kursk in 1943, Germany's capacity to fight was becoming heavily constrained and it was by late 1943 well and truly on the back foot. Add further losses during 1944 on the Eastern Front, Italy and Normandy, and by the autumn of that year the situation for the Reich's defence, in terms of manpower, equipment and weapons, was critical. The Wehrmacht's capacity to defend the Reich was further and fatally undermined by Hitler's Ardennes offensive, thanks to a heavy consumption of fuel and ammunition, along with further losses of men and armour that Germany could ill afford.

Views of the German senior chain of command on the likely location of the Allied attack

Field Marshal von Runstedt
(C in C West) –
Venlo

General Blaskowitz
(Army Group H) –
Venlo

General Schlemm
(First *Fallschirmjäger* Army) –
Reichwald

General Straube
(LXXXVI Corps) –
Venlo

Major General Fiebig
(84th Infantry Division) –
undecided

Typical of German formations fighting in the west in early 1945 was the 84th Infantry Division, deployed facing XXX Corps' attack. The division had been formed from the *Erzatzheer* (Reserve Army) during 1943 and deployed to the Fifteenth Army in the Pas de Calais during February 1944. When the invasion finally took place in June, the 84th had moved west to Rouen but was only released to march to Normandy in July, along with most of the rest of the German infantry divisions in the Pas de Calais. Being harried by Allied fighter-bombers, they made slow progress, and were forced to conduct marches in the short hours of mid-summer darkness. On arrival the division joined LXXXVI Corps on 4 August, by which time the Seventh Army was struggling to contain the US breakout. The division fought at Vire and during the Mortain counter-attack before being encircled in the Falaise pocket, where the 84th's divisional commander, General Menny, was captured and only a single regiment and supporting arms escaped destruction.

Having suffered losses of 5,500 men, the remnants of the division fell back to the Somme and subsequently marched back across northern France to the borders of Germany. During MARKET GARDEN, the 84th fought to contain the Guards Armoured and 82nd US Airborne divisions in the Groesbeek Heights and Nijmegen area during September 1944. General Heinz Fiebig took command of the shattered division.

In 1939, at the outbreak of war, Major Heinz Fiebig commanded an infantry battalion during the Polish campaign. By August 1944, he had held various regimental, staff and training appointments and as a colonel he briefly commanded a division in Russia and then for a short period he led the 712nd Coastal Division in Belgium. Having taken command of the 84th Infantry Division, Fiebig was responsible for its reconstitution back in Germany to the *Aufstellungswelle* 32 order of battle with men from the recruitment wave 32 of late 1944. He was promoted to *Generalmajor* in December 1944 and established his headquarters in the northern suburbs of the city of Kleve some 10 miles behind his division's front line.

General Fiebig was 6ft tall and described as being 'striking and usually debonair'. His post-war British interrogators, however, described him as 'a charming fellow to have at a party; the last man to lead a division in the field'.

The division was initially rebuilt with two regiments each now being organised with two battalions, but a third, the 1062 Grenadier Regiment, joined the division in December. There was also an independent fusilier battalion, which with a paucity of vehicles and fuel were mounted on bicycles for mobility, with recce and 'fire brigade' roles. The two police battalions of dubious quality were attached to the division as reinforcements along with the battalions referred to above, which were made up of men that were incapacitated in two ways: there was an ear or *ohern* battalion of men who were hard of hearing and a stomach or *Maggen* battalion. The total bayonet strength of the reinforced 84th was by January 1945 approximately 4,000 infantrymen, plus around 1,500 attachments. It should be borne in mind that the infantry, though few in number, retained much of their firepower, with a plentiful allocation of automatic weapons including the *Sturmgewehr* 43, but volume of fire could not replace the reduction in quality of the soldiers. The divisional artillery had been similarly reduced to seven batteries each of four guns across three battalions, but to compensate companies consisting of four 120mm mortars each were established in the three infantry regiments.

The usual divisional troops such as pioneers and artillery had been similarly cut to weak battalions or companies totalling approximately 4,200 men. Along with reductions in infantry manpower, the German infantry division progressively dropped in overall strength from a total of 18,000 men in 1939 to 10,279, and even then few divisions were up to their establishment.

Order of battle of the 84th Infantry Division

84th Fusilier Battalion (bicycle recce)

1051 Grenadier Regiment

I Battalion

II Battalion

1052 Grenadier Regiment

I Battalion

II Battalion

General Fiebig

1062 Grenadier Regiment

I Battalion

II Battalion

184 Artillery Regiment

I Battalion

II Battalion

184 *Panzerjäger* Battalion

Two companies of 75mm *panzerjäger* and one of 37mm flak.

2 *Falschirmjäger* Regiment (wef 6/7 February)

I Battalion

II Battalion

III Battalion

280th Ear Battalion

176th Stomach Battalion

Munster Security Battalion

The *Sturmgewehr* 44, the first true assault rifle, was emblematic of late-war German infantry battalions.

In the division's infantry regiments, the effective but time-consuming and resource-intensive Pak 40 75mm anti-tank gun had by early 1945 been almost completely replaced by handheld weapons including the *Panzerschreck* 43/54 (eighteen per battalion) and a continuing plentiful supply of the shorter-range *Panzerfaust*.

Although the 84th Division was not titled a '*Volksgrenadier* division', as many others had been during the autumn, it was reconstituted with a mix of rear-area units; a *Landwehr* fortress battalion, redundant Luftwaffe and Kriegsmarine personnel, along with conscripts. It broadly conformed to the same *Welle* 32 establishment, but every division differed in detail thanks to shortages and weapons being issued in lieu of those that were unavailable. This makes the

The *Panzerfaust*.

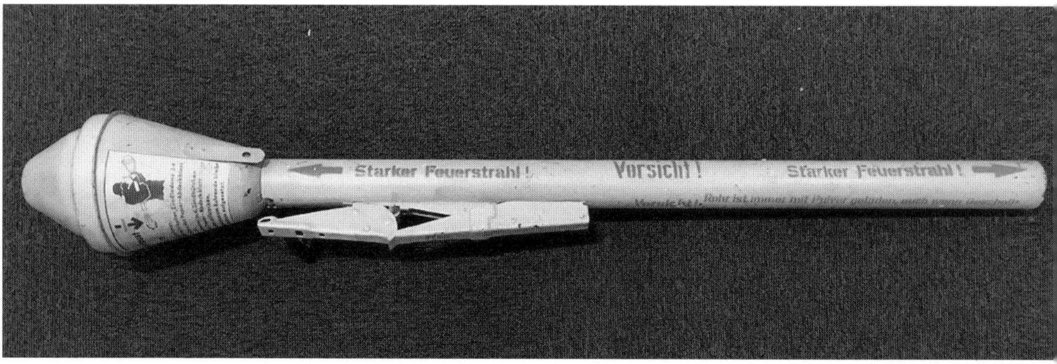

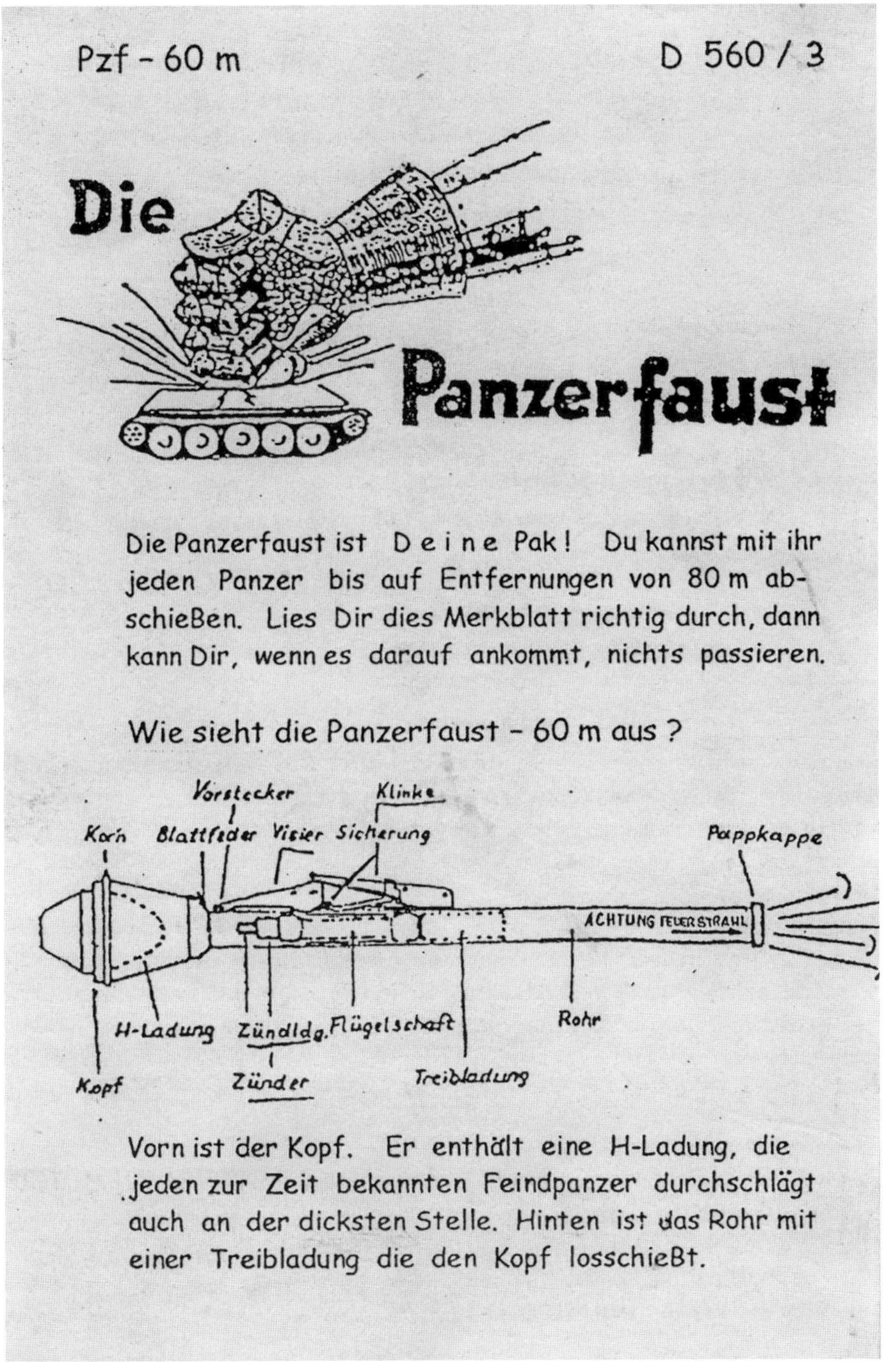
Pzf - 60 m D 560 / 3

Die Panzerfaust

Die Panzerfaust ist D e i n e Pak! Du kannst mit ihr jeden Panzer bis auf Entfernungen von 80 m abschießen. Lies Dir dies Merkblatt richtig durch, dann kann Dir, wenn es darauf ankommt, nichts passieren.

Wie sieht die Panzerfaust - 60 m aus?

Vorn ist der Kopf. Er enthält eine H-Ladung, die jeden zur Zeit bekannten Feindpanzer durchschlägt auch an der dicksten Stelle. Hinten ist das Rohr mit einer Treibladung die den Kopf losschießt.

The *Panzerfaust*: the front page of its very simple manual.

The *Panzerfaust*: a sketch of how to fire the weapon.

divisions exact order of battle hard to tie down, as well as its variety of units; police, stomach ear battalions and along with *Volkssturm* units, which were attached from the surrounding Rhineland cities and towns.[4]

The divisional *panzerjäger* battalion now had just a single company of nine towed Pak 40 guns and a company of self-propelled anti-tank guns (StuG III, StuG IV or Hetzer). There was no longer a flak battalion, with a company of nine 37mm *Flakvierling* now being a third company in the *panzerjäger* battalion.

Post-war British operational analysis examined the Germans' increased reliance on handheld anti-tank weapons. They concluded that armoured losses to these weapons in Normandy was just 6 per cent but later in the North-West European Campaign, when the number of 75mm anti-tank guns dwindled, this figure increased to 34 per cent.

It is clear from the number of *panzerjäger* and artillery pieces faced by XXX Corps during the first two days that General Fiebig had under his command some LXXXVI Corps assets. When it was accepted that XXX Corps' attack on the Reichswald was not a feint, General Schlemm was able to dispatch reserves and further army troops, which included *Schwere Panzerjäger Abteilung* 655. This heavy unit consisted of a company of the highly effective *Jagdpanthers* and two companies of *Jagdpanzer* IV,[5] with which to bolster the division's crumbling defences. The 655 *Panzerjäger* was reported to have a strength of thirty-six vehicles at the time of the Bulge but this had probably been reduced to some twenty operational vehicles by late January 1945.

The *Jagdpanther* mounted the same Pak 43/3 as the Tiger II.

German Intelligence

Thanks to XXX Corps' operational security measures during the move north from the shoulder of the Bulge, plus the Germans' own convictions that the Allied blow would fall further south, they lacked useful warning of the offensive through the Reichswald Plug.

General Straube, though not sharing his commander's views on the likelihood of the Reichswald being subjected to the main Allied attack, throughout January regularly dispatched patrols as deep as 6 miles into Allied territory. Lying up for two to three days observing, these patrols only reported seeing the vehicles of 2nd and 3rd Canadian Divisions and soldiers wearing the distinctive green-coloured Canadian battle dress. This was nothing to be concerned about but following a rare day of Luftwaffe reconnaissance flights on 6 February (D-2), the Germans spotted indicators of Allied concentration and preparations for an offensive. Camouflaged supply dumps were identified and what had hitherto been reported as dummy artillery positions were occupied by men and guns. The forward dumping programme had begun on 26 January but by 6 February the number of troops and weapons and the vast dumps of combat supplies were increasingly difficult to conceal. This fact was acknowledged by General Crerar at a conference on 4 February. 'From D-3 onwards, it will be increasingly difficult to conceal from the enemy the necessary forward assembly, in the Nijmegen area, of the large assaulting force.' He wrote in his campaign report:

> . . . up to 6 Feb it was pretty clear that the enemy had no specific knowledge of my intentions in the Reichswald. On that day, however, I had to assume that his aircraft, flying over the Army area on tactical reconnaissance, had

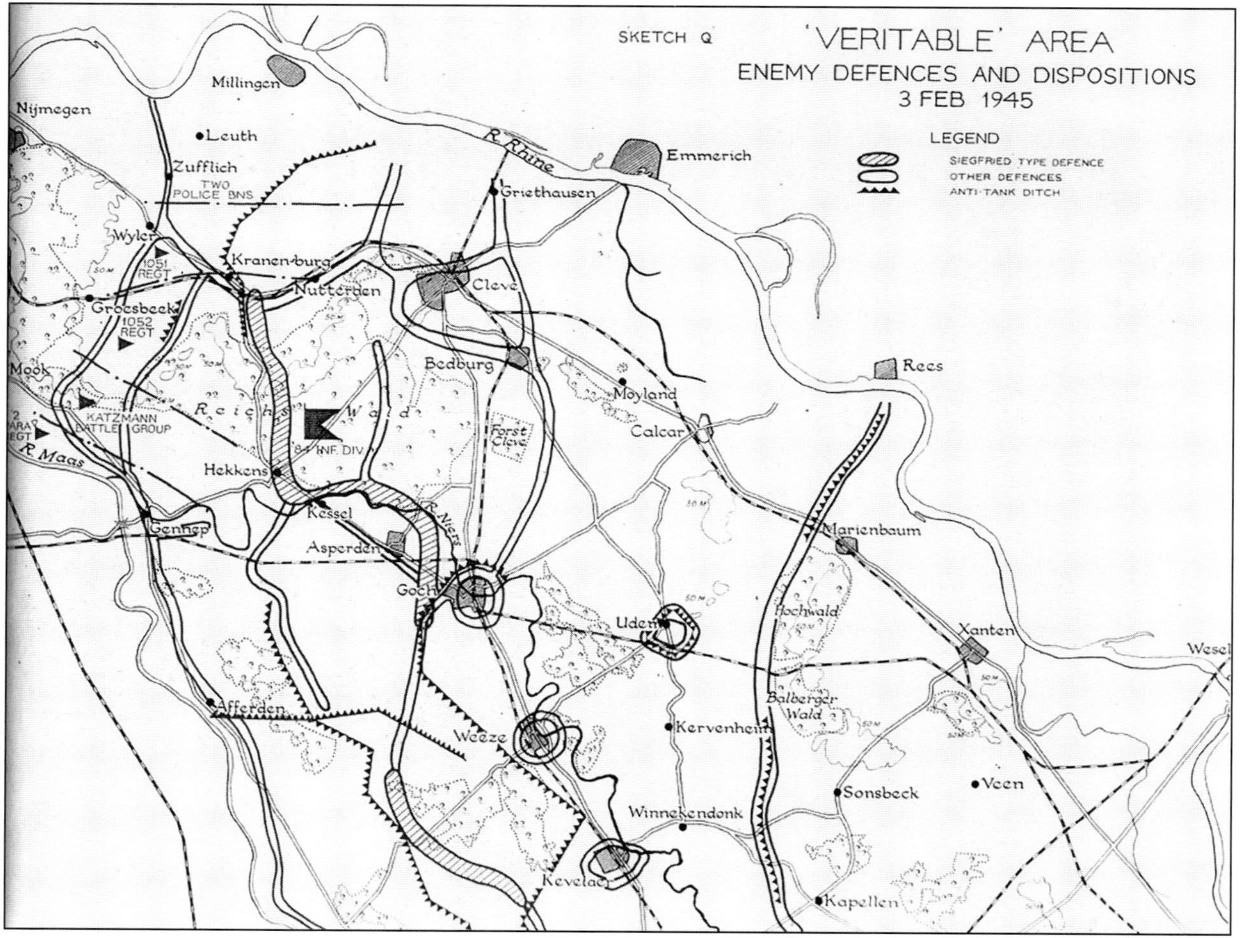

The German defence of the Rhineland was based on a series of defensive positions that First Canadian Army would have to fight through. Not all, however, were fully developed and XXX Corps' fight through the Reichswald and the Siegfried Line north of the forest was but the first phase.

The Junkers Ju 188 light bomber and reconnaissance aircraft was one of the types capable of taking high-altitude photographs of the Nijmegen area.

> observed the unavoidable signs of our enterprise, especially in the district between Grave and Nijmegen, where the many hundreds of vehicles and tanks, many of them impossible to conceal as the only hard standings were roads and streets, could hardly have escaped the vigilance of the camera. General Student [*sic*] must have now had a shrewd suspicion that I was going to attack in the Reichswald sector. He could not rule out an attack north of the Maas, but his reconnaissance was so widespread as to give him an accurate comparative view of activity along the whole of our front. But in surveying the enemy's problems and possibilities, I decided that there was little he could do to improve his situation as it then stood. Most of von Rundstedt's available forces were required either to remain in the south to meet the American threat from Roermond to the Ardennes, or to move to the east to fight the Russians.

Though still not entirely convinced that the impending attack would be anything more than a diversionary affair, Blaskowitz was prevailed upon by Schlemm to redeploy a regiment from the Twenty-Fifth Army to bolster the 84th Division in the Reichswald. What this reinforcement of just 2,000 men lacked in numbers it made up for in both the quality of men and weapons. As a part of the original *fallschirmjäger* division, 2nd *Fallschirmjäger* Regiment had retained much of its quality and by 3 February it was positioned around the south-west tip of the Reichswald, where it proved to be the toughest of the defenders to overcome. The presence of the *fallschirmjäger* reinforcements was, however, revealed to intelligence staff by three deserters brought in by a Canadian patrol.

A *Falschirmjäger Feldwebel* wearing the late-war camouflaged jump smock, with two small pockets on his right sleeve to carry what appear to be flare pistol cartridges. He wears leather jump boots with side laces, and is holding a standard stahlhelm, not the FJ pattern. His weapon is the late pattern FJ 42 with wooden butt and modified pistol grip. The bayonet, usually attached facing backwards under the barrel, is missing. It may, however, have been screwed into its fighting position below the muzzle.

Chapter Four

The Opening Bombardment

> The preliminary artillery bombardment began at 0500 hours. Targets included enemy forward positions, headquarters and communications with a min of six tons directed on each target. The success of the assault was later attributed largely to this fire support. [*21st Army Group VERITABLE report*]

The opening stage of Operation VERITABLE was launched on a very narrow front of just 5 miles, and it was to be a frontal attack. Therefore, General Horrocks needed one of the heaviest opening bombardments of the war to blast his way through the German defences. To be fully effective the Army and corps artillery commanders insisted that they needed both time and daylight for accuracy and, of course, the liaison officers from the Second Tactical Airforce argued the same point for air support. Artillery commanders estimated that they needed a clear three hours of daylight to complete a fire plan, consequently, H Hour would not be until 1030 hours.

The outline plan consisted of the following:

(a) a five-hour period of artillery preparation including a deceptive smoke-screen along the entire front;
(b) a standing barrage containing both smoke and H.E., lasting for about an hour to enable the infantry to form up on the start line;
(c) the thickening of the barrage for half an hour reaching its climax at 1030 hours when it was to start moving forward.[1]

In two weeks, almost exclusively during the long cold winter nights, gun positions were prepared and camouflaged and then the 1,050 guns were brought forward from the concentration areas by stages, finally reaching their pre-dug pits during the nights of 2–4 February. The guns remained camouflaged and silent, with no daylight movement permitted, but inevitably with so much equipment and man-power in the forward area, the Germans reported that an increasing number of positions were manned. Fortunately, despite General Schlemm's concerns, Blaskowitz dismissed these as preparations for a diversionary attack.

This was far from the case, as the numbers and scale of the planning recorded by the BAOR historian demonstrate:

> Over one thousand guns, not including anti-tank and Bofors guns, were in support of the attack and initially it was primarily an artillery battle [author's emphasis]. In planning the operation, it had been decided to take full

The Mk II 25-pounder field gun was the workhorse of the British and Canadian divisional artillery in North-West Europe. A total of 408 guns from the six divisions' artillery took part in the bombardment: 360 towed guns from five infantry divisions and forty-eight SP and towed guns from one armoured division. In addition, there were differing numbers of 25-pounders, mainly SP in the AGRAs.

> advantage of the great superiority in artillery and have a heavy preliminary bombardment. The Corps Commander accepted the resultant loss of surprise for the initial attack but stressed the need for reducing as much as possible the time taken to complete the pre-H-Hour programme ... It was hoped to saturate the enemy positions to such an extent that local reinforcement, ammunition supply and movement would be really difficult. As the initial attack was being carried out simultaneously by four divisions, each on a narrow front, both its support and the artillery preparation were planned by the CCRA [Corps Commander Royal Artillery] with the active co-operation of divisions at all stages. Any special tasks which divisions wanted to engage were passed to Corps for inclusion in the programme.[2]

Artillery planning on the scale of VERITABLE required additional manpower at both Army and corps level. The BAOR historian continued:

> Extra officers and draughtsmen were employed on the RA Corps staff for the production of this plan and a Royal Engineer reproduction section was attached. The planning team was divided into two, one portion doing the plan, the other dealing with the operation orders, moves, assembly and briefing. Another officer was responsible for the ammunition. Barrage and smoke screen traces were issued on 5 February whilst the bombardment traces and task tables followed a day later. The CCRA's final conference was held on 4 February which was rather late. It would have been easier if the deadline for alterations to the fire plan had been a day earlier. An overprint 1:25,000 map showing the fire plan, code names for groups of targets and target

numbers was produced and issued down to company commander level. These maps proved very valuable.

Not since D Day had mapping and tables been so freely circulated down to battery and company commander level but on the eve of the attack, Lieutenant Blackburn visited his battery's gun position and complained about the late dissemination of plans:

> The command posts are still completing a mountain of work. The details of the fire-plan for many concentrations and a barrage, including overprinted maps and traces, accompanied by all sorts of complicated timing-schedules and scales of fire, were only received by command post staffs at 7:30 P.M., and the strain of deciphering the meaning of it all and working out the fire-plans for the guns has put everybody in a foul mood. They all pose the obvious question: If they could build roads and bridges, and move up thousands of tons of ammunition in the sixteen days since Monty gave the order for the push, why the hell couldn't the arty brass have completed their plans for the guns sooner?

Included in the preliminary bombardment were PEPPERPOT shoots at specific targets requested by divisions, and it was not just field artillery gunners that worked on their fire plans. In these shoots all the Bofors, the main armament of tanks, anti-tank guns, mortars and machine guns that were not required on other tasks were to engage specially selected targets with indirect fire. The resulting deluge of fire lasted ten minutes on a single target as each PEPPERPOT was fired in turn. The aim was to neutralise key points in the enemy's defences and to undermine the defenders' morale. A typical divisional machine gun battalion had 7 million .303 rounds for their seventy-two Vickers guns and thousands of 4.2in mortar rounds ready for PEPPERPOT shoots during the course of 8 February.

The XXX Corps' artillery plan briefed by the CRA at a conference on 26 January was complex, but the outline for the preliminary fire plan lifted from the corps' artillery operation order reads:

> Prior to 0500 hrs: No fire except normal activity by 2 and 3 Cdn Divs.
> 0500–0730 hrs: Artillery Preparation. Bombardment including counter battery, counter mortar and PEPPERPOT.
> 0730–0740 hrs: Deception smoke screen covering the Corps front.
> 0740–0750 hrs: Silence. Sound ranging and flash spotting detachments detecting active enemy hostile batteries and mortars.
> 0750–0915 hrs: Artillery preparation as above.
> 0915–1300 hrs: Smoke screen north-west edge of REICHSWALD.
> 0920 hrs: Intense Counter-battery on the results of information gained earlier. Opening line of barrage (mixed HE and smoke). Rate of fire very slow.
> 1000–1030 hrs: Thickening up of barrage.
> H Hour and first lift of the barrage. Smoke screen on 2 Cdn Div left flank.

One of the Vickers machine guns that fired tens of thousands of rounds in the indirect fire role during PEPPERPOTS as well as thickening up the barrage. Note the number of empty MG belts.

Control of counter-battery fire was vested in 5 AGRA and the ten-minute check fire or 'silence' was designed to make the Germans believe the attack had started, which it was hoped would prompt the enemy to fire their mortars and artillery defensive fire targets. This enabled the detachments of two survey regiments,[3] which were deployed to each division on the Groesbeek Heights, to use sound-ranging equipment and flash spotting to plot German artillery positions. In addition, the emerging technology of mortar-locating radar was to be used. The resulting data from both systems was to be rushed to HQ 5 AGRA and the waiting artillery staff would then plot the location of enemy batteries, including ones that had up to that morning remained masked. At 0920 hours, with the locations of enemy gun positions circulated to the AGRAs, medium batteries would open a heavy counter-battery fire for forty minutes. In the event, no fewer than forty-five enemy batteries and nineteen mortar positions were identified or confirmed and targeting these contributed to a much-reduced German response when the attack did begin. A prisoner of 2nd Battalion 184 Artillery regiment reported that six out of twelve guns had been put out of action by counter-battery fire before the battle started.

A 5.5 inch gun belonging to 2nd Canadian AGRA.

On the gun positions during D-1, beneath camouflage netting gunners worked on unpacking their shells for the initial serials of the fire plan. Behind them lay the logistic chain necessary to feed the guns with the prodigious amount of ammunition the battle was forecast to demand. Some 750,000 rounds of assorted ammunition had already been dumped in the woods and hedgerows around Groesbeek and convoys of trucks stretching back via corps maintenance areas, to the Army roadhead and beyond to Antwerp were ready to roll forward.

After a short night's sleep, the gunners awaited 0500 hours and the preliminary fires. Among them was Lieutenant Blackburn:

> It's now drizzling rain, cold and miserable – a rotten morning for the gun crews, all of whom have been at their guns for some time now completing the preparation of ammo for the big shoot, taking shells out of their cases, removing safety caps, and stacking them in piles handy to the guns. And as you slosh through mud and stumble up and down over incredibly deep water-filled ruts left by the trucks and quads pulling and winching guns into position around here during the night, you feel for the poor late-arriving British gunners, and most especially for their command post staffs. It must be wicked trying to set up under such wretched conditions for a shoot of such magnitude.
>
> As you pass behind 26th and 14th [battery] positions, and in front of other British field and medium regiments that have been slotted into spaces behind

> and beside them during the night, you can see very little in the windy, wet darkness, but there are faint sounds of voices calling out orders, and brief, glowing flickers of subdued light from hooded lamps-electric hovering over dial-sights of guns getting a final check of their 'parallelism' – making sure all are perfectly on line.
>
> Silhouettes of gun muzzles poke up against the night sky where previously there were only scrubby pines. Unseen hordes of gunners, dripping with rain, are now standing to their guns as they carry out last-minute tasks. By the time you make it to 2nd Battery, ghostly faint voices from Tannoy speakers in gun pits are calling 'Take Post,' an order presently being given on scores of positions. You try to visualize 9,000 gunners arranging themselves in customary gun-drill positions behind their weapons awaiting H-hour, five minutes away.
>
> Until firing gets under way you decide to stay out of the hair of Lieut. Jack Bigg, who is in charge of Baker Troop guns this morning in place of the GPO [gun position officer] Doug MacFarlane, who is up in the Groesbeek windmill, one of twenty [Canadian] forward observers ...[4]

Lieutenant Blackburn, having discussed the likely effect of the bombardment on the ground with the command post officer, recalled:

> At 0459 hours, with only a minute to go, you leave Hutch starting the countdown over his two phones to the troops and go outside to see what you can see. For a few seconds there is deep silence, broken only by the slight rustle of wind and rain lashing the surrounding trees and bushes, covering up the sounds of nearby Tannoy speakers that must now be carrying voices of countless GPOs counting down the seconds to their gun sergeants.
>
> One faint, distant voice yells, 'Fire!' and for a split second, there's a rising chorus of urgent voices on all sides yelling 'Fire!' before the night is overwhelmed by furious, flashing, roaring waves of sound and concussion, rending and tearing the darkness with monstrous, theatrical effects such as only 1,500 guns, mortars, and rockets can unleash when deployed in overlapping concentrations on a narrow front – a dreadful stimulant that causes you to shiver as with a chill, even as you begin to perspire.

At the time of the normal winter stand-to at dawn, the infantry in their assembly areas were awakened by the opening crash of the bombardment rolling through the woods. Private Warke, of the Glasgow Highlanders, recalled:

> As always before an attack I had a fitful sleep but at least the night was long in February. The noise of the guns woke us all and I sat up looking at the sky above us through the trees that was bright with continuous flashing of the firing. I tried to roll back into my blanket and greatcoat but I couldn't go back to sleep. Half awake, my mind wandered with thought and fears of the morning's battle. Sergeant McGee prodding me with his foot and saying 'Get ready for stand-to' was a relief.

A 25-pounder Battery RA and RCA deployed for action

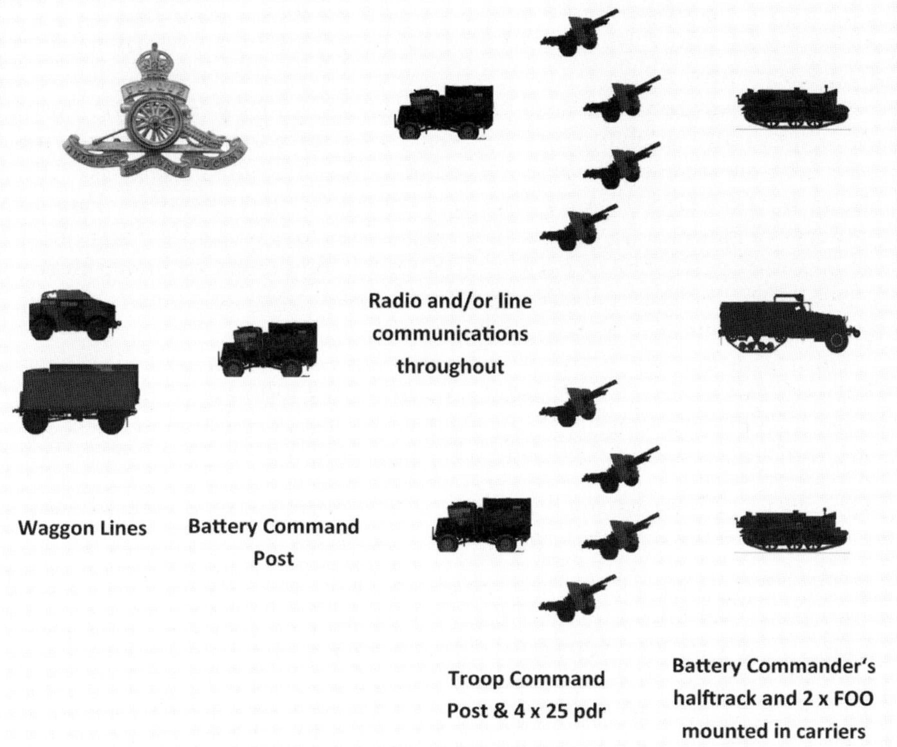

The 25-pounders in a troop were normally deployed about 20 - 30 yards apart in a curved line, mainly for the best anti-tank defence.

Troop gun positions were occupied to present less of a counter-bombardment target. Thus a field regiment of three batteries deployed in six separate troop positions.

The battery commander was usually co-located with the CO of the unit being supported.

The battery captain (BLK) ran the Battery CP. In the troops the senior officer was the Froward Observation Officer (FOO) and the troops' other officer were the gun position officer (GPO) and the Command Post Officer (CPO).

The BAOR historian explained the targeting:

> The preliminary bombardment for each phase was to follow the principle of hitting known enemy localities, headquarters and communications as often as possible in the time available. Each locality was to be subjected to an increasing intensity of fire until the morale of the enemy had been shattered. Five bombardments were to be carried out between 0500 hours 8 February

Cap badge of the Royal Canadian Artillery and the Glasgow Highlanders.

> and 0100 hours 9 February and each target was to receive a minimum of 6 tons of shells. 2 Cdn Div, which had been holding the sector for some time, air photographs and defence overprints supplied the information from which targets were selected and grouped. To make control more easy bombardment groups were formed for each target area.

As the sky lightened a Canadian Historical Section officer described the scene:[5]

> The weather promised to be fair, and the sight of the airbursts and tracer in the sky, against the yellow light of the rising sun was very impressive. There was continuous roll of heavy gunfire that was punctuated by staccato bursts of MG fire from all sides …
>
> A few birds were still flying across the sky in a bewildered manner, as the artillery took up their theme again, and the tempo accelerated as the full weight of 1,000 guns was brought to bear against the enemy. Beyond the occasional airburst, and the odd round over a wide area, there was little reply from the enemy and, at this stage, the spectator was left with the impression that hostile positions were being simply smothered. The gaunt trunks and torn branches of trees, ruined farm buildings, and the smoke and cordite fumes that swept across the area all contributed to the strange and fascinating panorama of war.[6]

Prisoners later questioned by First Canadian Army confirmed that the bombardment was very effective, with many being stunned by the hours of *trommelfeuer*. Anti-tank gun and machine gun crews could not reach their weapons pits until the barrage lifted; 'communications were totally disrupted':

> The Germans had the impression of overwhelming force opposed to them, which, in their isolated state, with no communications, it was useless to resist. On the other hand, prisoners generally agreed that casualties from the

A medium 4.5 or 5.5in gun in action before dawn.

Bofors anti-aircraft guns with Canadian gunners unpacking rounds and clearing empty cartridge cases during a PEPPERPOT shoot.

bombardment were not high, on a rough average only 5 per cent. Equipment suffered more than personnel. Counter-battery fire seems to have prevented very much enemy shelling during the attack. During the day well over half a million rounds were fired ...

German Reaction

Reports of the preliminary bombardment reached the headquarters of 84th Division in Kleve before 0600 hours on 8 February 1945. General Fiebig, sharing the broad German opinion that the attack would be further south, believed that a Canadian operation of any scale was very unlikely because of the difficult going both in the forest and to the flanks. Thanks to the number of Allied troops appearing on the Groesbeek Heights, a diversionary attack on the Reichswald was, however, not unexpected and initially LXXXVI Corps did not consider it to be a serious matter. Consequently, it was only at 1045 hours, when reports arrived that the forward defences had been penetrated, that any lingering doubts General Fiebig may have had that this was the Allied main effort were dispelled, but by then it was too late to commit the scant reserves immediately available to best effect.

In his headquarters near Rees, General Schlemm, nearly 20 miles from the Reichswald, was awakened by the sound of the Allied guns and was immediately convinced that the expected offensive had begun. As was customary for German commanders, Schlemm drove forward to Headquarters 84th Infantry Division at Kleve to assess the situation for himself, while his staff at First *Fallschirmjäger* Army headquarters rushed to their desks, received reports and passed on information to Army Group H. Everything Schlemm was told by General Fiebig confirmed his belief that this was the main enemy attack, although one of the Army Group liaison officers, reflecting Blastowitz's view, voiced the opinion that it could be a deception. On his own initiative Schlemm ordered 7th *Fallschirmjäger* Division to concentrate for a counter-attack at Gennep, and returned to his headquarters to personally brief Army Group H by telephone and request the immediate allocation of XLVII Panzer Corps to his command. Despite the scale of the bombardment and the attack, General Blastowitz was cautious and ordered 7th *Fallschirmjäger* Division back to Venlo.

Due to effective operational security during the preparatory phase, German intelligence had been unable to locate XXX Corps since it left the line in the Ardennes/Liege area and they, with justification, were also concerned that General Simpson's Ninth US Army would attack further south. At this stage Blastowitz stuck to his estimate and was not prepared to act, telling Schlemm that he must 'consider the possibility of a British attack via Venlo' and not redeploy his reserves until 'it is clearly established that the bulk of the British forces are in the Kleve area'. Consequently, the army group commander rejected Schlemm's request for the deployment of XLVII Panzer Corps.

Blastowitz's firm view that 21st Army Group's offensive would come in the British Second Army's sector around Venlo bought valuable time for generals Crerar and Horrocks to fight their way through the Reichswald Plug. If they were able to break into the forest and force the Siegfried Line defences before German reinforcements arrived, VERITABLE would be making a promising start.

Air Support

In the clear cold weather of January, RAF officers from Headquarters 84 Group, planned lavish air support for Operation VERITABLE by the Second Tactical Air Force. The detail of tasks was planned in conjunction with Crerar's Army Headquarters and XXX Corps. However, due to the unpredictability of February weather and the twenty-four hour limit on forecasting of the day, it was originally proposed that D Day could be delayed in the case of poor weather by a day to ensure air support. On 1 February, however, SHAEF ordered that VERITABLE was to start on 8 February whatever the weather conditions.

In addition to RAF heavy bombers, medium bomber aircraft were also available from No. 2 Group and the USAAF's Ninth Air Force. The plan for their use was:

> **Before D Day** – Road and rail interdiction against railways, bridges and ferries leading to the battle area. In this case care was to be taken not to give any indication of the point of attack. Selected ammunition, petrol and stores dumps were also to be attacked.
>
> **D-1** – Focal points leading to the main battlefield [Kleve, Goch, etc.] to be attacked by heavy bombers with further interdiction on the main North and South routes in the battlefield area.

Night of D-1/D Day – Villages and towns selected by Intelligence [Uedem, Kalkar, etc.] to be attacked but care to be taken to avoid heavy cratering.

D Day – The main task was the destruction and demoralisation of the enemy in the NUTTERDEN and MATERBORN defences. Isolation of the battlefield was to be achieved by armed reconnaissance and intruders by night. Artillery was to be silenced by attacks by fighter-bombers controlled by a Forward Control Post (FCP). Military headquarters and telephone communications were to be attacked but not at the expense of close support.

Night of D Day/D+1 – All approaches to the battlefield area to be covered to prevent the arrival of enemy reserve formations. These routes were to be selected as a result of information received from tactical reconnaissance and armed reconnaissance on D Day.

D+1 – All roads and railways leading to the battle area and *all* the RHINE crossings to be covered by armed and tactical reconnaissance in order to maintain an effective disruption in the possible arrival of enemy reserves.[7]

In addition to these planned sorties, a RAF Forward Control Post (FCP) was to be co-located with Headquarters XXX Corps in order to best coordinate air support to the battle by speedily processing requests from the divisions for strikes by a wing of 84 Group's fighter-bombers. The aircraft in a cab rank circling to

Conditions at Canadian airfields in Holland were scarcely better than at the front.

A Spitfire of 440 Squadron RCAF at a 2nd Tactical Air Force advanced landing ground. The compressor to the left is recharging the air bottles that operated the guns pneumatically.

the west of the Maas were dispatched by the FCP, which had in support an experimental Mobile Radar Control Post that in the event of poor weather could assist in directing aircraft to target areas.

Further forward, once control of the attacking aircraft was handed over by the FCP, a system of contact cars that had been developed in Normandy came into play. Pilots on the ground speaking direct to the aircraft by radio, using language understood by airmen, would direct the fighter-bombers to their target or recce area. Four such 'cars', normally tanks or armoured cars with suitable radios, were available for deployment as the advance progressed through the enemy position.

A system of continuous replacement at a rate of four aircraft every five minutes was planned to ensure that there were sufficient aircraft airborne at any one time to support the four and later five divisions in action.

Initial fighter-bomber targets were, however, planned to be in depth, beyond the artillery bombardment, with interdiction sorties to attack movement of enemy reserves, in particular reinforcement of the Nütterden and Materborn features, which were key to the early breakout from the confines of the Reichswald Plug.

H Hour

At 0915 hours, as the final phase of the barrage began, a smokescreen was fired across the frontage of the attack to cover the moves forward of the assault troops of the infantry divisions from their assembly areas in the woods. The infantry, tanks and assault armour threaded their way through the defensive positions of

2nd Canadian Division on marked and recce routes and deployed in their FUPs waiting to cross the start lines at 1030 hours. A Canadian historical branch officer watching 15th Scottish Division move forward wrote:

> As H-hr approached, if anything, the noise increased, and a new note was added by the sound of armour moving forward and planes passing overhead. The combined effect produced a vivid picture of a war of machines – a war of calculated and terrible efficiency. A wounded soldier, with face covered by a field dressing, was directed to a nearby RAP, as pockets of smoke began to fill the contours in the ground. The historical officer and war artist were compelled to shout at each other in order to make themselves heard above the noise. Carriers rattled by, with red cross flags prominently displayed, and a tp of Cromwell tanks that had been camouflaged with straw against the walls of a demolished barn added their guttural roar to the din of battle.
>
> Churchill and Sherman tanks began to move east along the draw in square 7556, through the scattered debris of gliders that remained from the airborne attack of the previous September. At 0950 hrs the barrage, which represented the climax of the preliminary bombardment, was observed to be beginning. Capt Hunter and Capt Pepper proceeded down the draw to observe the armour and specialized assault equipment moving forward. Besides the orthodox types of tanks, there were Flails, Crocodiles, AVREs all with their fluorescent panels (for identification from the air) glowing like red hot plates against the dull background. A tank officer enquired anxiously about minefields but could not be satisfied. The armour lurched forward with all vehicles stripped for action – one tank still had a frying pan dangling from the back of the turret. An Air OP flew slowly overhead, and smoke

2nd Argyll and Sutherland Highlanders moving up to join the Churchills of the Scots Guards at the start line.

> shells continued to drop a short distance in front, as the deafening noise increased. Some enemy rounds dropped about 300 yards distant, and personnel took cover but the armoured advance went on without hesitation. There was an air of urgency and tense expectation evident everywhere as H-hr approached.

The advance from the start lines across no-man's-land was preceded by a barrage 450 yards in depth, 'consisting of three lines of field artillery 100 yards apart and two lines of medium artillery superimposed, also 100 yards apart'. Rather than creeping forward it would move in blocks of 300 yards every twelve minutes. To allow the infantry commanders to control their advance:

> ... a minute before the end of firing on each block all guns on the front line ceased firing high explosive. One gun per troop then immediately fired one round of yellow smoke indicating that no more high explosive would land on that line and that the barrage would lift ...

This proved to be effective and 'the lift of 300 yards enabled troops to make a tactical advance between lifts and made unnecessary the demoralising plod forward behind and at the speed of the normal barrage'.

Sherman 75s and Fireflies of the Sherwood Rangers Yeomanry taking part in the bombardment.

British and Canadian Medium Artillery

British and Canadian medium regiments were grouped into Army Groups Royal Artillery (AGRA) along with sundry other field, heavy and anti-aircraft regiments. AGRAs were normally affiliated to a corps but could be grouped as required for a major offensive such as VERITABLE.

The workhorses of the medium regiment were the 5.5in and 4.5in guns. They were superficially similar but the guns had different characteristics. The main similarity was that the carriage of the two guns was almost exactly the same but the differing calibres gave the guns overlapping but complementary capabilities.

BL 5.5in gun. By 1945 the gun was provided with 82lb high-explosive shells, which with Charge Super gave it a muzzle velocity of 1,950ft per second and a range of 18,100 yards. As far as VERITABLE was concerned, the other ammunition used extensively was the 100lb smoke shell. In addition to HE and smoke ammunition there were illuminating rounds and several types of chemical shell. The normal HE fuse for the shell was the pre-war percussion, impact No. 117 fuse but by the time of VERITABLE the T100 proximity fuse was becoming available.

BL 4.5in gun This gun specialised in counter-battery work, having a longer barrel, which gave the greater range of 20,400 yards using Charge Super for its 55lb shell. Its nickname was 'The 10-mile Sniper'.

5.5in shells dumped ready for use.

A British BL 5.5in gun in action.

The prime mover for both 4.5 and 5.5-inch guns was the 4 × 4 AEC Matador truck.

Smorenhoek
Zyfflich
Berg
Wyler
Kamp
Groesbeek
Schildbroek
Hettsteeg
Horst
Bruuk
Knapheide
Breede weg
Grafwegen
REICHS

Chapter Five

VERITABLE Begins

> The infantry attack which went in at 1030 hours was unique in that four divisions moved forward simultaneously on a 6-mile front between the Nijmegen-Kranenburg-Kleve road and the River Maas near Mook.
>
> [*CMHS report No. 155*]

As was his custom, General Horrocks had gone to the forward area and was looking out over the open country and the German defences between the wooded Groesbeek Heights and the Reichswald beyond, across which the leading units of his corps would advance:

> In the early hours of 8 February, I climbed into my Command Post for the battle; it had been constructed for me by the Royal Engineers and consisted of a platform half-way up a large tree. From here I could see most of the valley in front, and I was connected by line with a group of small scout cars below me at the bottom of the tree, each of which was tuned in on the same wireless link with a similar vehicle at the advance HQ of each of the divisions taking part. From my viewpoint I could follow the progress of the attack by the lifts in the barrage. Everything seemed to be going according to plan, though units began to complain (over the air) more and more about the state of the going ...

The barrage was likened to a 'wall of fire'. It was some 4,500 yards wide and 450 yards deep falling across the front of the advance of the Welsh, Canadian and Scottish divisions. With some simple maths, Lieutenant Blackburn calculated that about 6,500 shells were detonating in every grid square per hour. A Canadian war artist recorded:

> At 10:29, as a line of yellow smoke-shells indicated the final minute before the barrage lifted, infantry and tanks began to pass through the 2nd Cnd Division's forward defensive line on that grey, drizzly morning, to advance into Germany. It soon turned out that the weather had taken side with the enemy, in the form of a wet, that unavoidably slowed down progress of what should have been a fast thrust by a highly mechanized force to a mud begrimed crawl. Operation Veritable unavoidably began to run behind schedule.

The weather at daylight had been promising, allowing aircraft to get away to a good start on what was hoped would be a full day's programme of air strikes:

> Successful sorties were flown by the tactical groups with the object of disrupting communications between HOLLAND and GERMANY at

General Horrocks up on his OP platform shortly after dawn on 8 February 1945.

TERBORG, ZEVENAAR and ARNHEM. KRANENBURG, where the enemy had an ammunition dump, was attacked but the weather soon deteriorated . . .

Despite the fine start to the day and the successful air strikes, as the morning progressed drizzle set in. General Horrocks commented that it made 'life even more unpleasant, if possible, for the unfortunate infantrymen and preventing any support from the air'. Strikes scheduled for later in the day on Kranenburg and the Nütterden and Materborn features were among those cancelled.

The move to the forward assembly areas on the wooded Groesbeek Heights behind the Canadian defences began in the early hours of 8 February. The 15th Scottish Division's historian wrote:

The eastern sky was still glowing red with [German anti-aircraft fire] and shot with tracer. On the Right the 46th Brigade, with the Tank Coldstream Guards and its shar of 'Funnies' in support, moved up to the woods by Groesbeek, where the forward battalions, the Glasgow Highlanders and the Cameronians, established their aid posts. The 227th Brigade on the left, with the Tank Scots Guards and more 'Funnies' in support, started rather earlier to move up to the Nederriksche woods west of Hooge Hof. Already the roads – or tracks rather – to the front were packed with vehicles.

Still before dawn, while the gunners worked their way through the fire plan, the armour was moving from Nijmegen. Trooper Smith, a radio operator in a Crocodile of 141 Regiment, RAC, recalled that:

The streets were still dark. The sky was black in contrast to the flashes of exploding shells which silhouetted the trees and housetops. Infantry plodded beside us at the edge of the road. A column of Carriers was stopped at a cross-roads to let us by. A scout car made vain attempts to pass the tanks in front. An officer was standing on the pavement and shaking his fist at us.

It was getting light by then; a grey, cold, misty dawn with the smell of rain. Now we were out in a wasteland of gorse, blackberry brambles and coarse rank grass with here and there a cluster of stunted trees and bushes. On both sides of the track was dispersed a regiment of Sexton SP guns, muzzles lifted in expectation. The farthest fired, and flame and pale smoke rippled down the line. We passed near enough to hear the clang of breech blocks opening and ejecting spent cases and the shouts of the gunners.

During the move forward there were some anxious moments:

when vehicles became temporarily stuck in the mud in the narrow tracks. However, all battalion groups arrived complete but with a shrewd idea of what conditions would be like on the tracks in the valley beyond the start line. This caused considerable anxiety because the success of the initial assault largely depended on the ability of the flails to gap the enemy

A Churchill Crocodile of 141 RAC training at Eastwell Park prior to the invasion.

> minefields … If the gaps were not made quickly then the infantry would not catch up the barrage.[1]

Having reached forward assembly areas the infantry and tank crews had breakfast and made final preparations for the advance. With the troops fed, the BAOR historian described the final move forward out of cover to the FUPs:

> To the accompaniment of the noise from the artillery fire which increased in volume as H Hour approached, the attacking formations moved forward to form up behind their respective start lines. In order to deceive the enemy the front line had been held and was still held by two brigades of 2 Cdn Div and it was in the area immediately behind these two brigades that the Scottish [Canadian] and Welsh brigades, with their supporting armour, waited to advance. Some doubt had been felt as to whether, in view of the wet conditions, the attack should be made with all the allotted armour. Trials had been carried out the day before but as a result no alterations were made to the plan. The smoke screen protecting the troops as they advanced from the wooded area down the forward slopes at GROESBEEK to the start line was effective. The enemy was not by this time prepared to retaliate …

At the same time as the 51st Highland and 53rd Welsh divisions crossed their start lines and advanced on the forward enemy positions, to their left, two of the other three divisions under command of XXX Corps had also begun their advance at 1030 hours. What faced 2nd Canadian and 15th Scottish divisions was open farmland dotted with farms bisected by drainage ditches and country tracks, with the odd stand of trees. That going for both infantry and armour across sodden ground was going to be slow, was not in any doubt.

Major Stothers, of the Royal Regiment of Canada, had a grandstand view of the battle as the assault troops moved through his defensive position to the FUP and began their advance:

> The tanks open up with their machineguns. All buildings on the immediate front – houses and farms strung out along the road leading out of Groesbeck all the way to the German border are aflame or smoking. The infantry keep up a steady advance, and the tanks move up to join them. Masses of armour now move up in a steady stream.

General Horrocks was soon receiving reports that thanks to the artillery barrage, it was apparent that:

> The enemy was completely bemused, and very little resistance was encountered; our worst enemies that day were mines and mud. The continual rain [that started later] turned the terrain into a quagmire. Mud and still more mud must be the chief memory of anyone who fought in this battle.

2nd Canadian Division

With two of its three brigades deployed as the in-place force, Major General Mathews' 2nd Canadian Division nonetheless had a vital if limited role in VERITABLE's opening phase, the capture of a triangle of ground including the defended village of Wyler. This straggling village was regarded as 'the northern anchor of the enemy's front line'. The village was located at the foot of the slope down from the Groesbeek Heights and controlled the vital Nijmegen–Kranenburg–Kleve road and the floodplain across which their fellow Canadians of 3rd Division would advance later that day. Of more immediate concern,

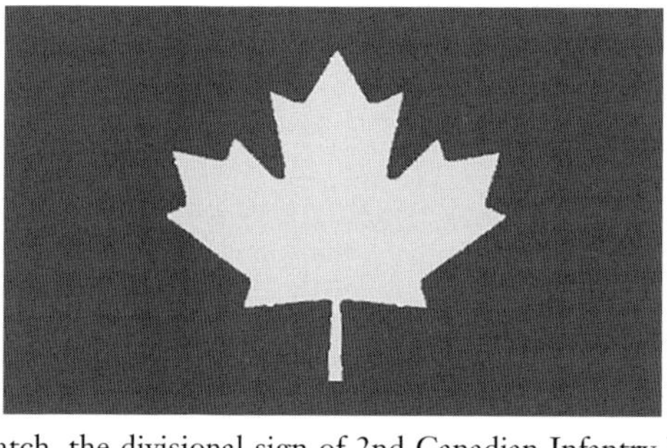

A grey patch, the divisional sign of 2nd Canadian Infantry Division.

however, was that a battalion of 1052 Grenadier Regiment positioned at the top of the slope facing south could enfilade the advance of 15th Scottish Division.

The Shermans of the uncommitted Sherwood Rangers and 4th/7th Dragoon Guards of 8 Armoured Brigade took part in shoots on the Canadian front with their 75mm or 17-pounder main armament firing high-explosive shells. Lieutenant Colonel Christopherson, commanding the Sherwood Rangers Yeomanry, recorded in his diary:

> The first stage of the operation was called PEPPERPOT during which the tanks of the Regiment were to be used as artillery, which was wrong in principle, in order to augment the existing artillery on the Canadian division front. Each tank in the Regiment was allocated 220 rounds of high explosive.

Brigadier Megill's 5th Canadian Brigade was supported by the Shermans of C Squadron, 13th/18th Hussars (8 Armoured Brigade) and, from 79th Armoured Division, a troop of flails of the 1st Lothian Yeomanry and a troop of AVREs. In addition to their own field regiment RCA, the brigade had the fire support of 4th Canadian Medium Regiment's 5.5 and 4.5in guns.

1st Canadian Rocket Battery's Land Mattress system being loaded. The battery provided support as a part of PEPPERPOT shoots across the corps' frontage throughout the day.

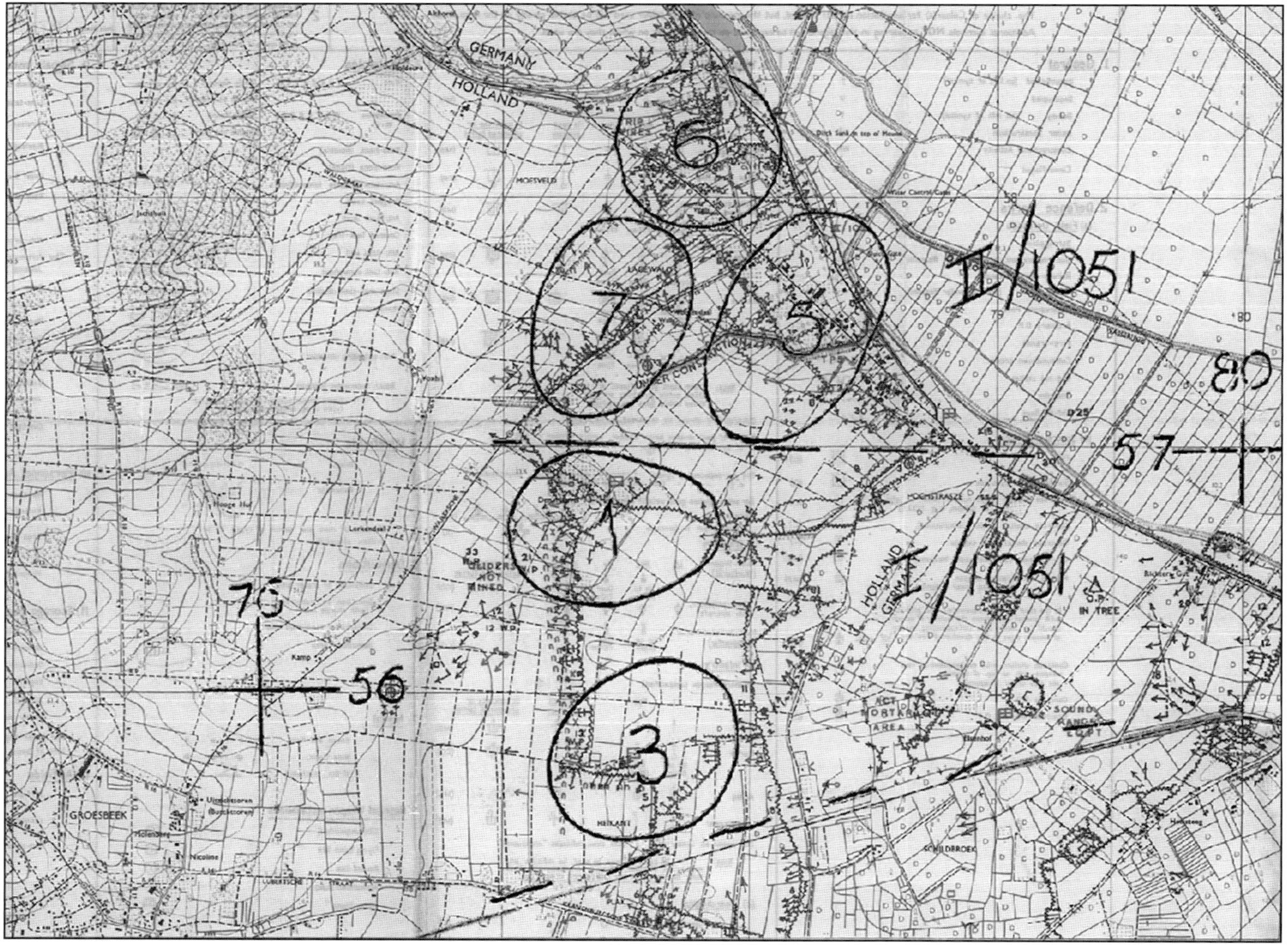

Five enemy company positions facing 5th Canadian Infantry Brigade had been located.

As the morning of 8 February dawned, a 'Niagara' of shells fell on the enemy's forward positions, all but drowning out the Calgary Highlanders' pipers as the infantry made their way forward to their FUPs. Lieutenant Powell, the battalion's intelligence officer, commented on the sights and sounds of the barrage, in particular the impact of 1st Canadian Rocket Battery:

> I never saw anything like that in my life. The ground just rocked ... That was the first time I saw those multiple rockets fired. There was a farm and a grove of trees down near Wyler ... that place just disintegrated, all in one smack.

The Toronto Scots, the division's machine gun battalion, joined the PEPPERPOT shoots and: 'On that one day they fired thousands of mortar bombs and hundreds of thousands of rounds of [.303] ammunition, burning out almost one hundred machine gun barrels.'

Attacking from Nederrijksche Woud north of Groesbeek, 5 Brigade advanced across the northern extremity of the open Groesbeek Heights, with two battalions forward, le Régiment de Maisonneuve and the Calgary Highlanders. In front of the Maisonneuves, the Allied artillery had 'crushed the enemy's forward defences'. Brigadier Megill reported that:

> Keeping right up to the line of the barrage, the two battalions attacked across country to cut the highway south-west of Wyler, thus surprising the enemy who, it appeared, had expected the main thrust along the obvious route along the road from Nijmegen through Berg en dal (7459). With the help of grenades, the first localities were cleaned out very quickly, but *Schü-mines* caused some casualties to the attackers.[2]

Making use of the yellow smoke rounds indicating that the barrage was about to move on, the Maisonneuve were able to keep very close to the bombardment and were on the Germans in Den Heuvel before they could recover from the numbing effect of the shells. In one instance, however, their advance had been so quick that several dugouts were passed without being cleared by the leading platoons. The enemy duly appeared and engaged the Canadians from behind. In response Company headquarters signaller Private Lefebvre charged one of the bunkers, firing his Sten gun as he went, grenaded the entrance and bravely went in to clear it, appearing with four prisoners. He was awarded a well-deserved Military Medal. In this attack, Lieutenant Fontaine also received a notable award. The citation for his Military Cross describes his actions:

> When his company came under fire from a cleverly sited machinegun post which threatened to delay the advance and cause numerous casualties Lieutenant Fontaine with one man set off to destroy the post. Under continuous enemy fire they managed to get to a position close to the machinegun post and with determination and great gallantry rushed it and killed three occupants.

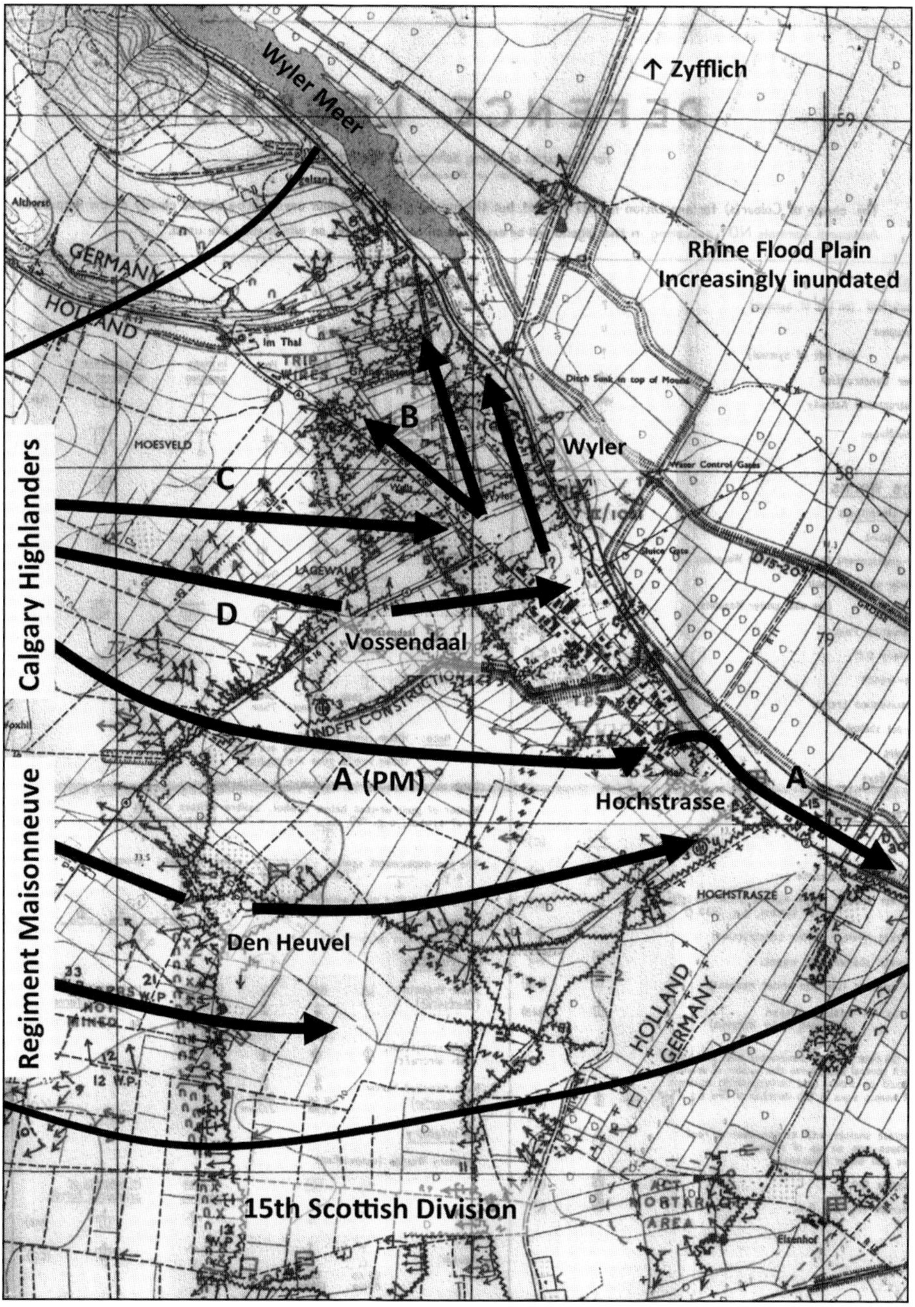

The 5th Canadian Brigade's attack on the Wyler Triangle.

At 1123 hours the Maisonneuve reported Den Heuvel secure. As they reorganised an officer paused to count forty-six German dead in the shattered ruins of the hamlet alone, before the French Canadian soldiers pressed on to Hochstrasse, on the Kranenburg road, which they reached at 1320 hours.

The Calgary Highlanders on the brigade's left flank had from the outset greater difficulties, including crossing their start line twelve minutes late. The advance was led by A and C companies, right and left forward respectively. C Company followed in support, while B Company brought up the rear as the battalion reserve. Their regimental history records that:

> A Company attacked a few minutes late and moved down a secondary road toward the hamlet of Vossendaal. About 1.2 kilometres from their start line, at about 1100, they came under mortar and machinegun fire and found themselves in an area heavily sown with *Schü-minen*. Within minutes virtually all the men of the lead section were wounded. Lance Corporal McMahon, in command of the section, saw that the machinegun fire was coming from two houses at the edge of Vossendaal. He manoeuvred through the minefield, rushed the two houses, silenced the guns, and single-handedly took twenty-three Germans prisoner. He feared the Germans would try to overpower him, so he knocked the one man he thought was leader (he turned out to be an officer) to the ground, then ushered the rest back to the Canadian lines, forcing them to carry Canadian wounded through the minefield.

Having reached the Kranenburg road and enveloped Wyler to the south, the Calgary Highlanders avoided a frontal attack on strong German positions to the north-west of Wyler on the more direct and obvious route. At this point the Highlanders' fight for the village began in earnest when Lieutenant Colonel Ellis ordered C and D companies to swing north and fight their way towards the village, attacking it from the rear. C Company, however, soon found itself involved in heavy fighting, during which the company commander and a platoon commander were killed. 'To keep the operation moving the Commanding Officer committed B Company, and after artillery and mortar fire had been called down on the objective . . .' B and D companies fought their way along the escarpment, clearing buildings en route to Wyler. Brigadier Megill commented that: 'There was some delay but after stiff fighting, supported by artillery and 4.2-inch mortar fire, the village was finally reported cleared by 1830 hours.'

During the afternoon, the Calgary's fourth company, A Company, was released from reserve to advance south down the Kranenburg road 'with relative ease'. Meanwhile, to the north of Wyler the Sappers of 7th Field Company RCE were working to open the vital stretch of road from Berg en Dal to Wyler (PEARL BLACK) but: 'The Sappers, working for some time without infantry protection, were delayed by thickly sown minefields.' The road through Wyler should have been open by 1600 hours; consequently, 15th Scottish Division's priority traffic was not moving south along the first stretch of PEARL BLACK

The *Schü-mine* 42 (*Schützenmine 42)*

The mainly wood construction *Schü-mine* 42 was introduced by the Wehrmacht for several reasons. Firstly, to be less easily detectable than standard metal-cased mines and, secondly, it was cheap and easy for German industry to make in large quantities.

The case was a simple wooden box with a hinged lid containing a half-pound block of explosive and a detonator. When stepped on the lid depressed, releasing a retaining pin, which in turn released a striker that initiated the detonator.

As a minimal metal mine, the head of the mine detector had to be swept across the box if any reaction was to be heard in the earphones. In ground that had been shelled and polluted by shell fragments, the *Schü-mine* 42 was very hard to detect electronically. With probing being a very slow process in VERITABLE, it was planned that the infantry would cross minefields via lanes swept by the flail tanks.

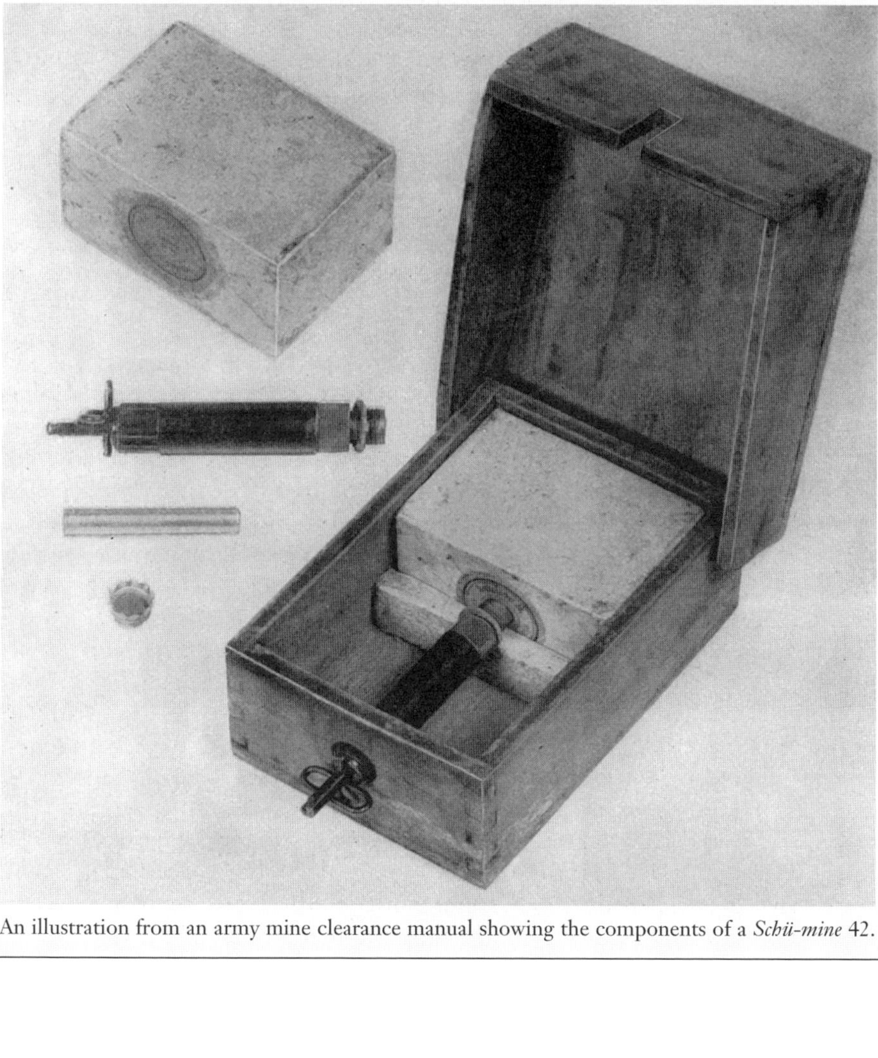

An illustration from an army mine clearance manual showing the components of a *Schü-mine* 42.

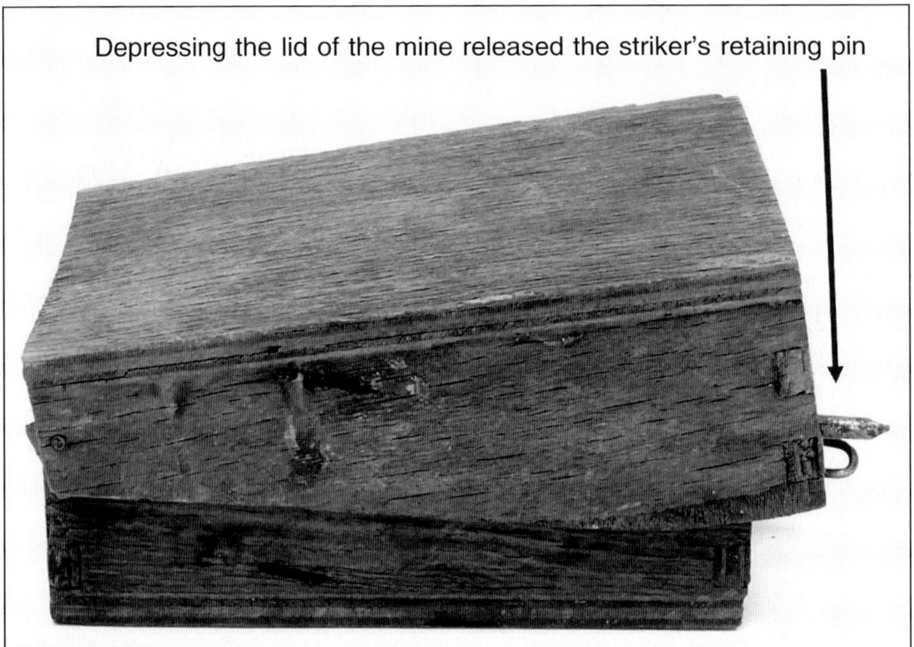

Initiation of the *Schü-mine* 42.

until 2100 hours. This delay in opening the route through the Wyler triangle was to have a knock-on effect on the development of the division's subsequent operations.

The Calgary Highlanders suffered a total of sixty-seven of the brigade's eighty-five casualties but during the day, a total of 322 prisoners were taken by 5 Brigade, almost all from the two battalions of 1052 Grenadier Regiment.

The Canadian Historical Section report stated that 2nd Canadian Division were the first formation to report reaching their objectives and that: 'Keeping right up to the line of the barrage, the two battalions attacked across country to cut the highway southeast of Wyler, thus surprising the enemy who, it appeared, had expected the main thrust along the obvious route along the road from Nijmegen through Bergendal.'

15th Scottish Division

Major General Barber's 15th Scottish Division held XXX Corps' main effort in the first phases of Operation VERITABLE, which had been conceived hoping that the ground would still be frozen hard as a rapid thrust along the narrow stretch of slightly higher ground north of the Reichswald to seize Kleve. From there it was planned that the 43rd Wessex Division would fan out into the Rhineland. Similarly, Guards Armoured Division following the Highland Division would join the Scots in the breakout to the south of the Reichswald. In General

Brigadier Megill, commander 5th Canadian Infantry Brigade, photographed during a visit by Field Marshal Montgomery and General Crerar prior to VERITABLE.

Horrocks' optimistic words, between them they would 'with any luck seize a bridge over the Rhine'. In the event, with the rapid thaw, a battle of a very different character faced the Scottish infantry and their supporting arms.

As the HQ BAOR battlefield historian wrote, the division faced the same wet ground and a lack of good routes into Germany as the other divisions:

> The initial attack to be undertaken by 15 (S) Div, which would take it up to the SIEGFRIED position, did not present any great difficulties except for the lack of axes. A good deal of accurate information had been obtained concerning the defences, minefields and troops manning the German forward line. The attack was to be supported by very heavy artillery fire and provided the flanking formations were able to capture their objectives, there was every reason for the task being successfully completed. But it did involve crossing a

Soldiers of 2nd Argyll and Sutherland Highlanders marching to their FUP.

> very wet valley, in which the only road – a country road at that – petered out after the first 2 miles. From this point until the SIEGFRIED position was reached and for any additional axes, the division had to rely on the farm tracks which were unlikely to stand up to motor traffic in wet weather. An alternative was to open the railway line to KRANENBURG as a road.

The 15th Scottish and its supporting tanks of 6 Guards Armoured Brigade were not only confronted by poor ground conditions but a potentially difficult tactical problem; they had to break through two successive defensive positions including the Siegfried Line and then to dash a further 5,000 yards to seize the Materborn feature overlooking Kleve. All this they had to achieve before the enemy could occupy the vital ground of the feature. General Barber's plan was that in GILBERT, the first phase of the Scots' attack, two brigades were to break through the forward German defences and seize Kranenburg. This was to be completed by 1600 hours and the second phase, SULLIVAN, with the aid of Monty's Moonlight (movement light)[3] would be undertaken during the night of 8–9 February by a single brigade group, which would break through the Siegfried defences and secure the Nütterden feature. In phase three, code word LAYTON, the first two brigades were to pass through the Nütterden position and secure the Materborn area and go on to clear the ruins of the city in phase four (JOHNSON). If the situation allowed, i.e. a German collapse, the division was to 'Dispatch strong patrols to capture ... UEDEM and KALKAR and to clear the west bank of the Rhine ...'

The divisional operation order detailing the phase one tasks for the two brigades reads:

> Phase I: Codeword GILBERT
> To be completed by 1600 hours D Day. Two Brigades up.
> *Right*: 46 (H) Inf Bde Gp with tasks:
> (a) To seize high ground between AUF DEM HOVEL 810544 – KRANENBURG 8055.
> (b) To secure line of FRASSELT rd 8153 within own bdys in order to cover Start Line of 44 (L) Inf Bde Gp in Phase II.
> *Left*: 227 (H) Inf Bde Gp with tasks:
> (a) To capture KRANENBURG.
> (b) To secure built-up area about 818553.
> (c) To block approach from North by rd 806563.

The 2nd Argyll and Sutherland Highlanders' (2 A&SH) war diary recorded details of the move forward to the FUP and the problems encountered before the attack started:

> Reveille was at 0300 hours and the bn moved off on tanks to FAA [Forward Assembly Area] at 0500 hours where the troops had breakfast. Remounting their tanks, the bn was filmed by Gaumont-British as they moved down to the FUP. The barrage was terrific and the thunder of the guns unbroken. Bofors and MMGs fired 'pepper pot' tasks. Leading coys detanked and deployed and negotiated the first obstacle – our own minefield which lay on our side of the start-line.

Fortunately, most of these were US anti-tank mines that had been largely surface laid under enemy pressure during MARKET GARDEN. The Argylls' historian continued:

> The tanks had some bad luck. The Scots Guards [Churchill] tanks got through alright but the Flails, Crocodiles and AVREs on which so many hopes had been built, were delayed first crossing a stream and then a series of boggy patches, and they were never able to catch up with the battle. What was worse, all the carriers stuck in the narrow gap in the minefield, already churned up by the Churchills, so that when the tanks and infantry moved forward at 1030 hours, they went without any of the sapper or pioneer stores necessary for gapping the minefield or expected wire obstacles.

Thus, the plan for the funnies and the infantry to arrive in a co-ordinated manner at the forward edge of the German minefields largely miscarried.

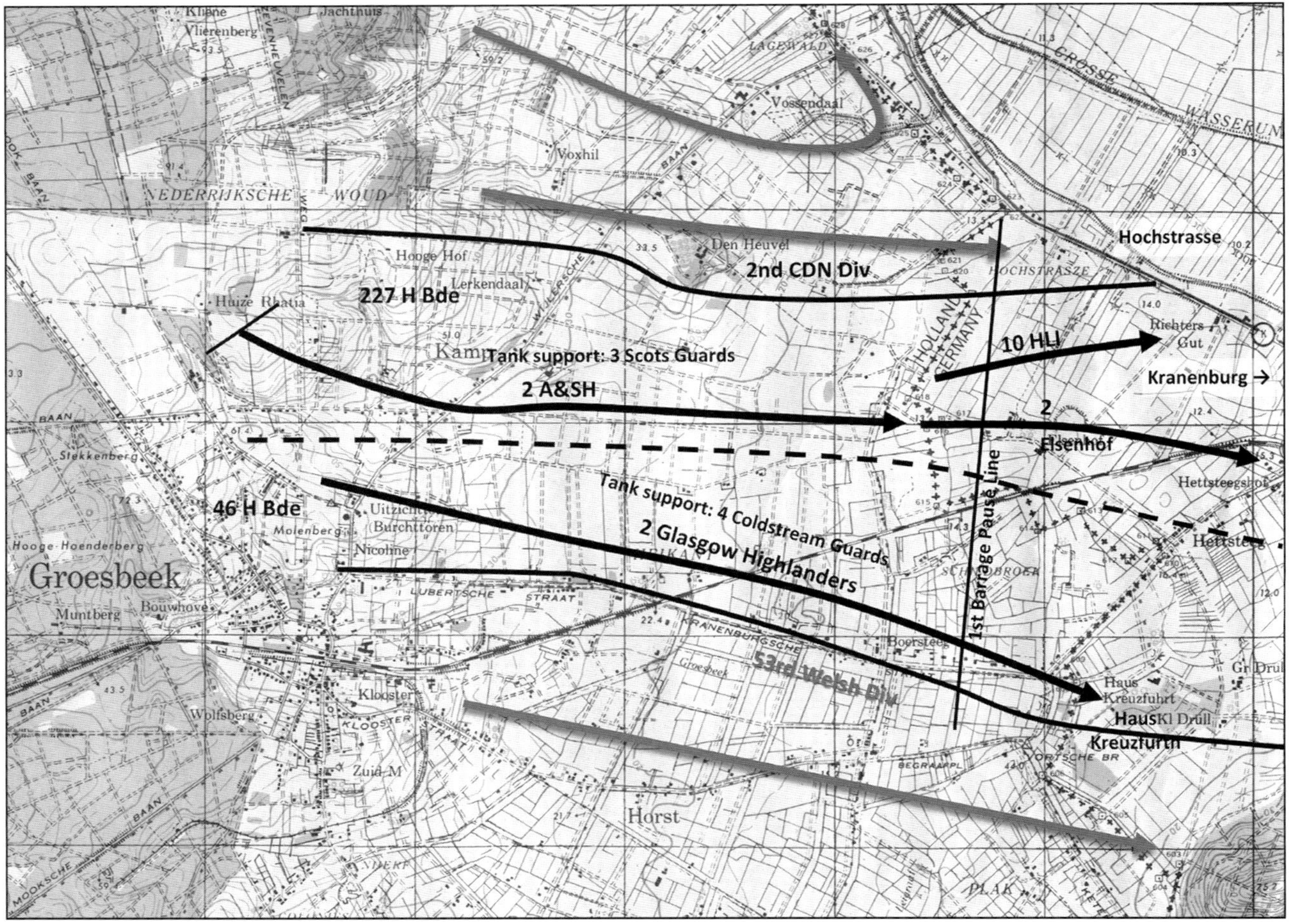

15th Scottish Division's attack on the forward German position, 8 February 1945.

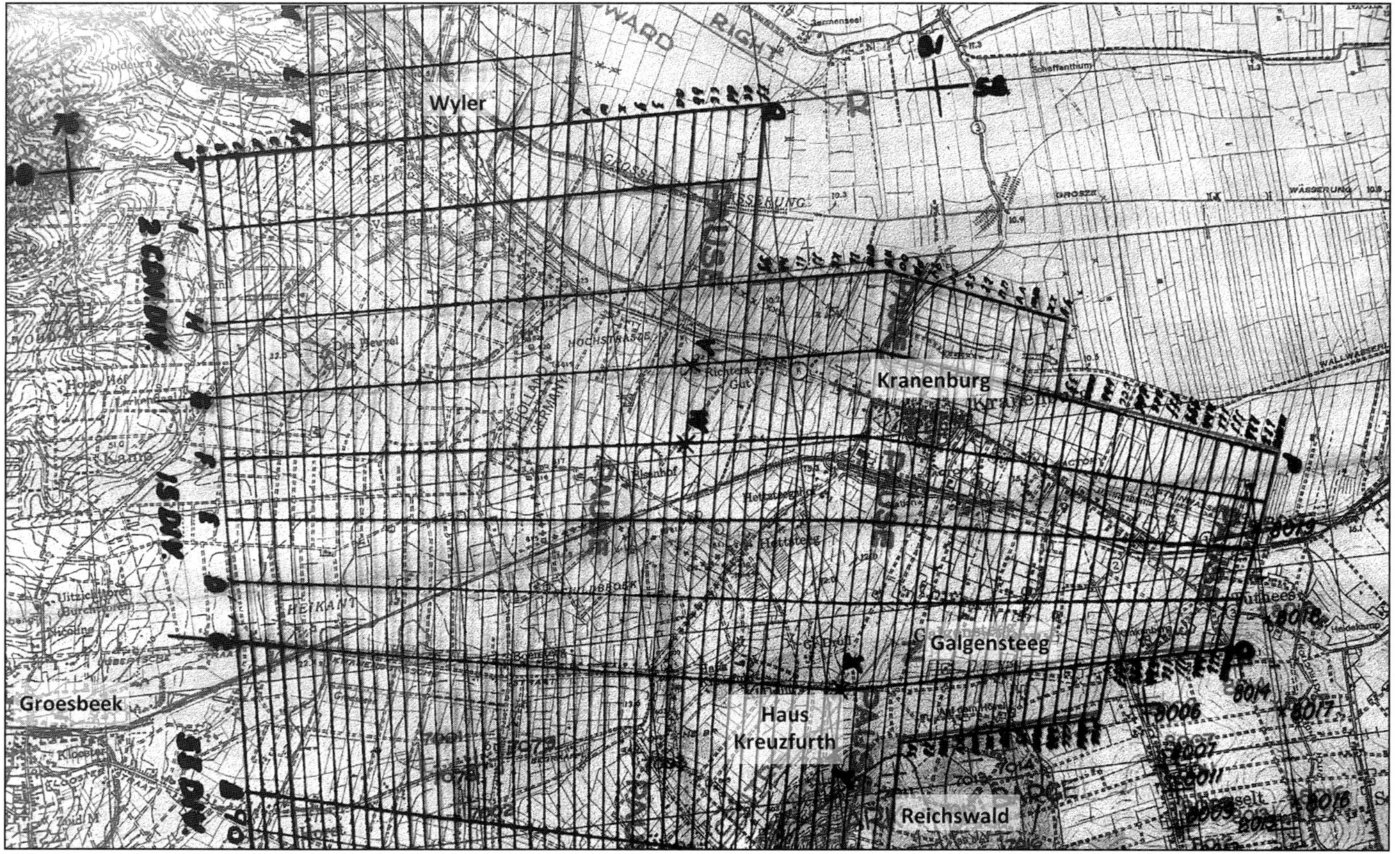

A 1:25,000 map of the battle area with the gunners' barrage overlay showing the lifts ahead of the advance.

46th (Highland) Brigade

The 2nd Glasgow Highlanders led 46 Brigade's attack along with 4 Tank Battalion, Coldstream Guards. They were to advance with their right flank on the Lubertsche Straat (the beginning of Route AYR) to their objectives, the hamlets of Haus Kreuzfuhrt and Hettsteeg, a distance of some 2,000 yards. At 1010 hours the infantry and armour left their separate FUPs to cross their start lines in order to arrive on the enemy's front-line defences at the same time. But, as already indicated, plans appeared to have miscarried. The BAOR battlefield historian noted:

> As soon as the Flails and supporting tanks started to cross the start line it became clear that it was touch and go whether they could reach the minefield before they became bogged. The going seemed to be worse on the left and progress there was very slow. By 1040 hours the Flails on the right reported that they had completed a gap. At the same time the Flails on the left reported that they were completely bogged down. Only one gap was therefore available.

Lieutenant Hammerton was commanding one of the two troops of B Squadron, 22nd Dragoons, that were to create a pair of gaps through the 100-yard deep minefield. His task was to breach it near the railway crossing at Heikant and, having heard reports of a German self-propelled gun, he began his advance:

> We emerge from the cover of the trees and buildings at a fair speed and start down the slope. Geoff [troop corporal] reports a large crater, unseen from the start line, which he manages to avoid, but we go straight into it. Bas Frost

The 22nd Dragoons' cap badge.

Lieutenant Hammerton on commissioning into the RTR before being transferred into the war-raised 22nd Dragoons.

immediately goes into reverse, but it is no use. I decide to let them get the tank out in comfort so ... I take over his [another] tank and crew and we speed up to get close to Geoff again, both his guns and mine trained to the right, our gunners' eyes trying to spot that SP before it catches sight of us. There is movement behind a haystack. We both fire HE – and some startled chickens flee in a shower of hay.

We reach the edge of the minefield and I give the order: 'Start flailing, now!' One-and-a-half m.p.h. feels slower than ever. Forward we creep, chains throwing up mud and grass, yard by slow yard, the engine racing and creating a gale through the turret — but not a single explosion. On, and on, so slowly that the Infantry and an Army cameraman start to walk past my tank. 'Silly fools!' I think. 'When we hit mines they'll cop it from the shrapnel! And where's that SP? Why doesn't it fire at us?'

Then I see Geoff stop. He reports that he's reached our objective and that there are Germans with their hands up in a nearby trench ... I tell him to call the Guards and tell them to come on – we've opened a mine-free lane for them. They don't budge ... They must think it's too narrow, so we both turn back to the start line, widening the lane by another two tanks' widths – a perilous operation because we are both presenting our least armoured backsides to the enemy. Still there is no fire from any quarter, but the infantry are dealing with the chaps with their hands up. As we complete the wider lane, the Guards tanks move towards us and carry on through to their objective.[4]

Meanwhile, the Glasgow Highlanders' A Company had already followed the barrage through the minefield, but on the left a platoon of C Company sustained

A technical drawing of the Sherman Crab.

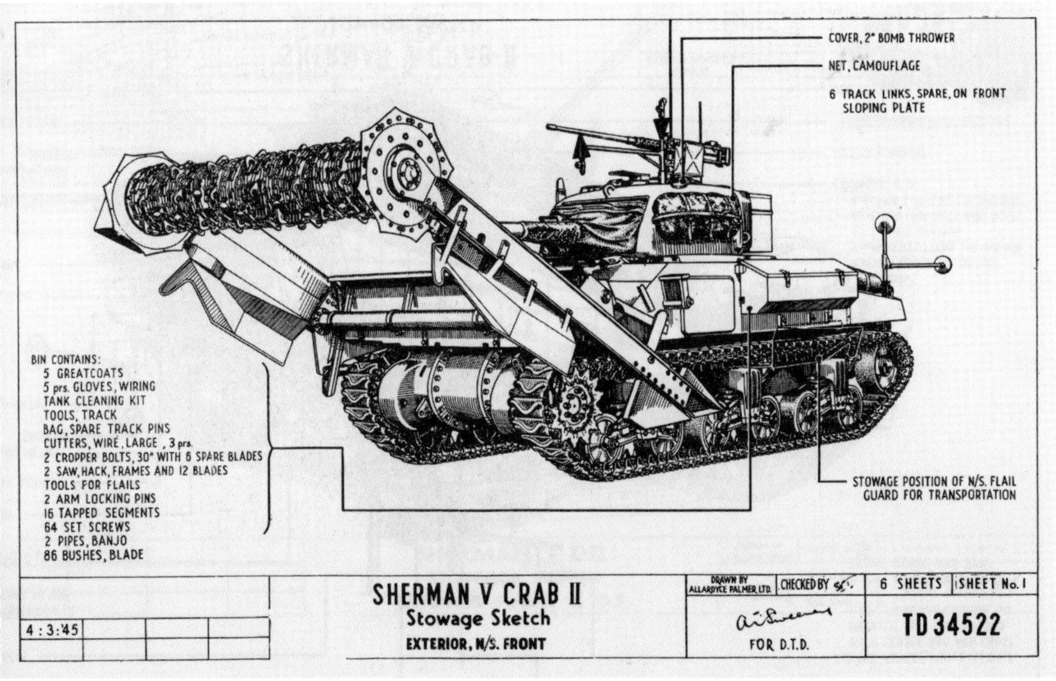

A picture taken by the above-mentioned cameraman of Lieutenant Hammerton (rear) flailing through the minefield and ahead of him the Scottish infantry behind his troop corporal's Crab.

several mine casualties. The other two platoons and company headquarters, however, wheeled south and headed for Hammerton's flailed path through the minefield and relative safety. The infantry was eventually followed through the gap by the leading squadrons of the Coldstream Guards' Churchills and together they resumed their advance without meeting serious opposition. The divisional historian described the second phase of the battalion's attack, which took them a further 1,000 yards into the enemy's forward defences, where they encountered some resistance in houses between Boersteeg and Haus Kreutzfurth:

> At Boersteeg at 11.50 A.M. the barrage paused for twenty-five minutes: here the Glasgow Highlanders leap-frogged companies. By 1.15 P.M. they had crossed the Dutch-German frontier to reach Haus Kreuzfuhrt and Hettsteeg, their final objectives, having taken 230 prisoners at the cost of very few casualties. The supporting Coldstream had had several of their tanks bogged by the way, but they had knocked out three 75mm A/Tk guns. For the next forty-eight hours of continuous rain the Glasgow Highlanders were to be kept extremely busy in the neighbourhood, digging out countless vehicles of all sorts along the 46th Brigade's axis [Route AYR].[5]

227th (Highland) Brigade

Brigadier Villiers' brigade was also to attack the German forward defences on a single battalion frontage. The 2nd Argyll & Sutherland Highlanders, along with

227 Brigade's Grouping for the Initial Attack

2 A&SH

Two sqns 3rd Tank Battalion Scots Guards (3 Tk SG) (including two bridge layers)
Two tps 22 DGNS (Flails)
One tp 141 RAC (Crocodiles)
One tp 198 SP A/Tk Bty (17-pdr)
One-half tp AVRE
One tp 289 A/Tk Bty (6-pdr)
One pl 20 Fd Coy RE
One Pl 1st Battalion, The Middlesex Regiment (1 MX) (machine guns)
One OP from Hy Mortar Coy 1 MX
Three Wasps

10 HLI

One sqn 3 Tk SG
One tp 22 DGNS
One tp 141 RAC
One-half tp AVRE
One tp 289 A/Tk Bty (6-pdr)
One tp 289 A/Tk Bty (17-pdr)
Half pl 20 Fd Coy RE
One pl 1 MX (MG)

2 Gordons – Brigade Reserve

The Wasp flame-throwing carrier was introduced into British and Canadian service during the Normandy campaign and proved to be a potent addition.

Churchills of 3rd Scots Guards and infantry of 10 HLI moving into their FUPs.

two squadrons of 3rd Tank Battalion Scots Guards and another two troops of B Squadron's flails. As their area of responsibility opened out beyond Hochstrasse at the limit of the 2nd Canadian Division's attack, 10th Highland Light Infantry (10 HLI) would move up and join the brigade's advance eastwards. The village of Kranenburg on the Nijmegen–Kleve road was the objective of 10 HLI, while the Argylls' task was to secure positions on the Kleve road 1,000 yards beyond the village. The 2nd Battalion Gordon Highlanders were the brigade reserve, moving up behind the forward battalions to the Hettsteeg area.

A combination of resistance and ground conditions initially delayed the advance of 2 Argylls. The commander of A Company was wounded and one of the platoon commanders was killed, while the flails were all bogged in short of the minefield and the advance of tanks of S Squadron on the battalion's left flank along with the infantry came to a halt:

> One of the troop leaders, however, spotted a small track which seemed to indicate a gap. He led his troop through it exploding *Schü-mines* as they went. The initiative of this officer enabled the infantry and tanks to close up to the barrage and continue the advance.

The tanks drove over a mixture of first US anti-personnel and then German *Schü-mines*, thus allowing the infantry to follow in their wake, keeping to the tank tracks. Company Sergeant Major Green of A Company had also 'very coolly and

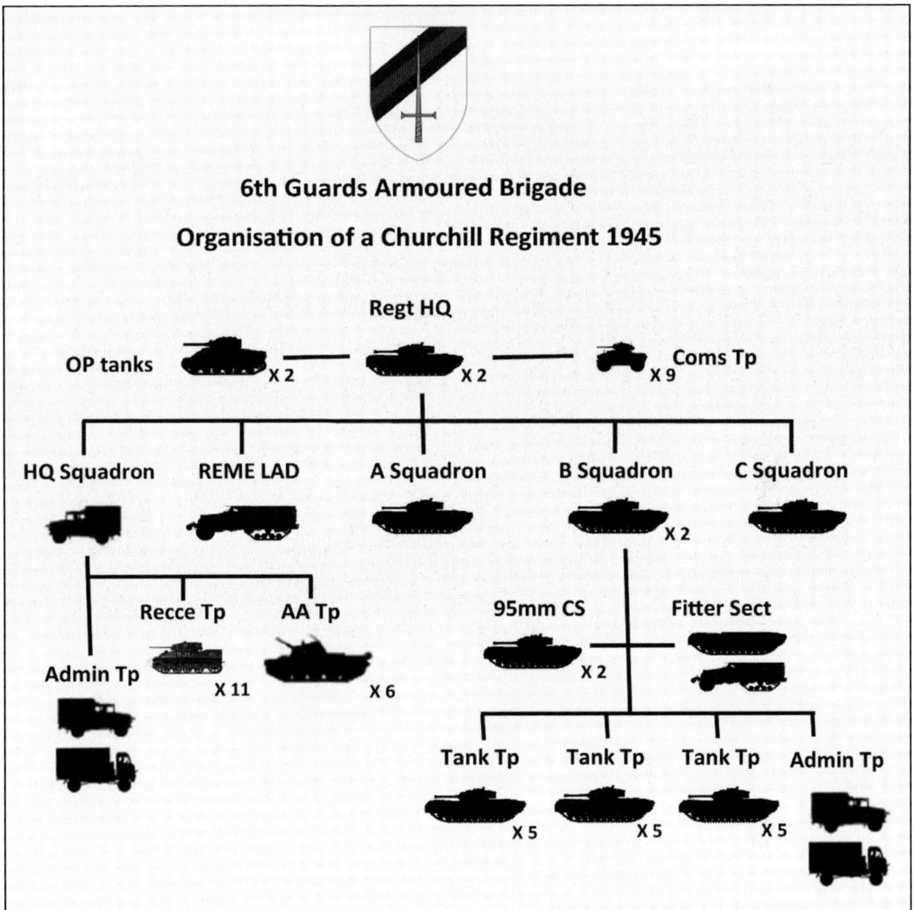

The earlier five troop squadron organisation was abandoned in favour of three troops during the autumn of 1944.

In most cases a 6-pounder per troop was retained to fire APDS ammunition.

gallantly rallied the coy, and brought them through to the first objective, for which he was awarded an immediate DCM':[6]

> On the right B Coy was held up for a time by a thickly-sown AP minefield and for a short time fell behind the barrage. It was here that Sjt Page[7] lost a foot in a gallant attempt to lead his platoon through and the coy lost in all one killed and six wounded before a gap was found.

The Argylls and their supporting tanks, despite the delay on the minefield thanks to the realistic speed of the barrage, continued the advance with its full benefit. The battalion's war diary records that: 'Until the barrage halted for half-an-hour

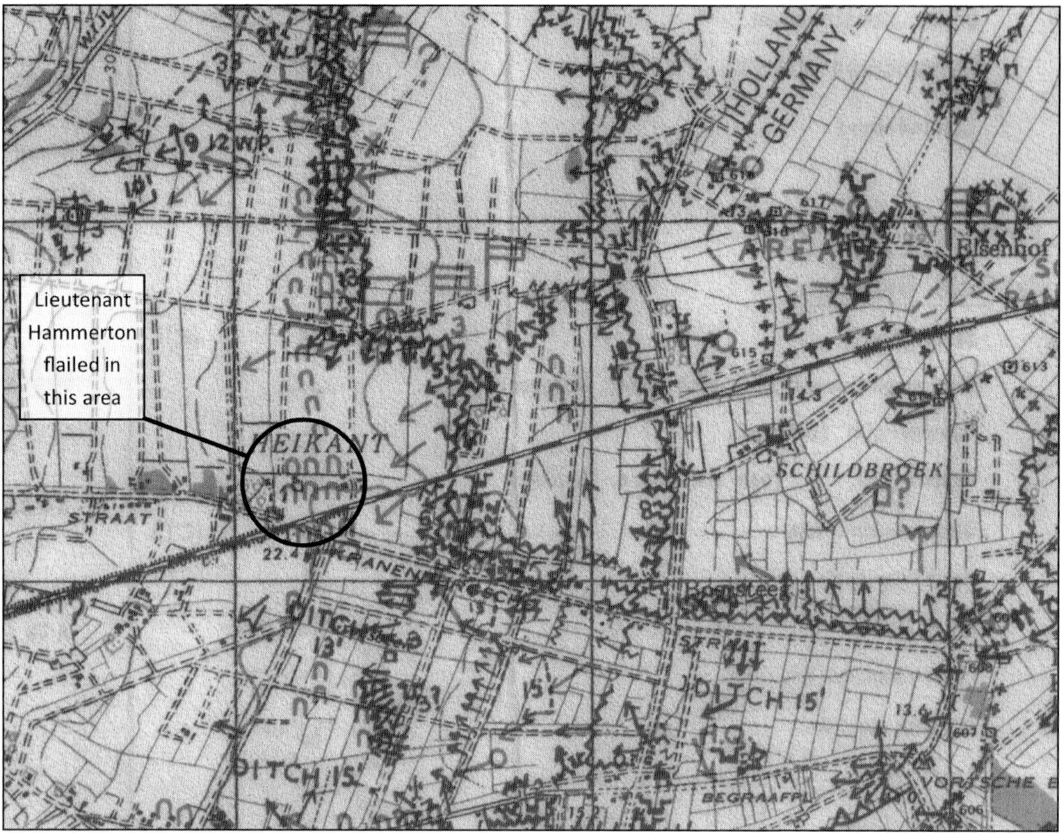

An extract of the 1:25,000 tactical overprint showing the 84th Division's forward defences.

on the German frontier, all went more or less according to plan.' Here according to 10 HLI's war Diary '1115 Bn moved fwd to pass through gaps made in minefields by 2 A&SH. Going very bad which held up RE Specialist Equipment.'

Thus far, the attack on VERITABLE's left flank had gone remarkably well. The 15th Scottish were through the forward German defences and while the Canadians had arrived at their objectives, they were still overcoming determined resistance in Wyler. For the Scots it was now a question of another stern test to close up to the Siegfried Line defences, which necessitated fighting through enemy positions on the Galgensteeg Ridge and in Kranenburg.

Chapter Six

Closing up to the Siegfried Line

> Probably no assault in this has been conducted in more appalling conditions than this one. [*General Eisenhower*]

During the course of the morning, General Blaskowitz turned down Schlemm's request for reinforcement of the Reichswald area and countermanded the 7th *Fallschirmjäger* Division's orders to reinforce LXXXVI Corps. By 1300 hours, however, with the Allies entering the Reichswald and 15th Scottish Division renewing its advance north of the forest, the situation was visibly deteriorating. General Fiebig ordered the remnants of his forward battalions to withdrawal in favour of manning the main Siegfried Line defences. With most battalions locked in battle and unable to disengage from the fighting, or the message failing to get through, this order proved to be almost impossible to execute, while other commanders under heavy artillery fire decided that withdrawing would be impossible without suffering heavy casualties. Consequently, most remained in position and the Siegfried Line defences were less heavily manned than they otherwise would have been.

To place 44 Lowland Brigade in a position to deliver their planned assault on the main Siegfried Line, several objectives had to be secured by the forward brigades. Firstly, 227 Highland Brigade had to capture the substantial village of Kranenburg, standing on the vital Nijmegen–Kleve road, and secondly, both 227 and 46 Highland Brigade had objectives on the road running north–south through Frasselt.

The barrage paused at the frontier between 1140 and 1215 hours, as this was the point where the 227 Brigade's boundaries opened out, 10 HLI passed through A Company 2 A&SH and prepared to attack Kranenburg. Having reorganised, B Company 2 A&SH resumed their battalion's advance in the centre of the 2,000-yard wide divisional sector. To their right, 9 Cameronians had taken over the advance to the Gangensteeg Ridge and Frasselt itself. In this village the Argylls and the Cameronians were to secure the start line for the breaching teams of 44 Brigade, which was within 500–600 yards of the Siegfried Line defences.

When the advance was resumed it was, however, made without much of their assault armour and the three battalions' carriers. The problem was that the flails and leading squadrons of Churchills had so badly cut up the ground that the armour following bogged down. The initial task of C Squadron 141 (The Buffs) Regiment, RAC, was for '13 and 14 Tps to advance in support 'on call' with 2 A&SH. No definite role was given to them and they were in fact not required.

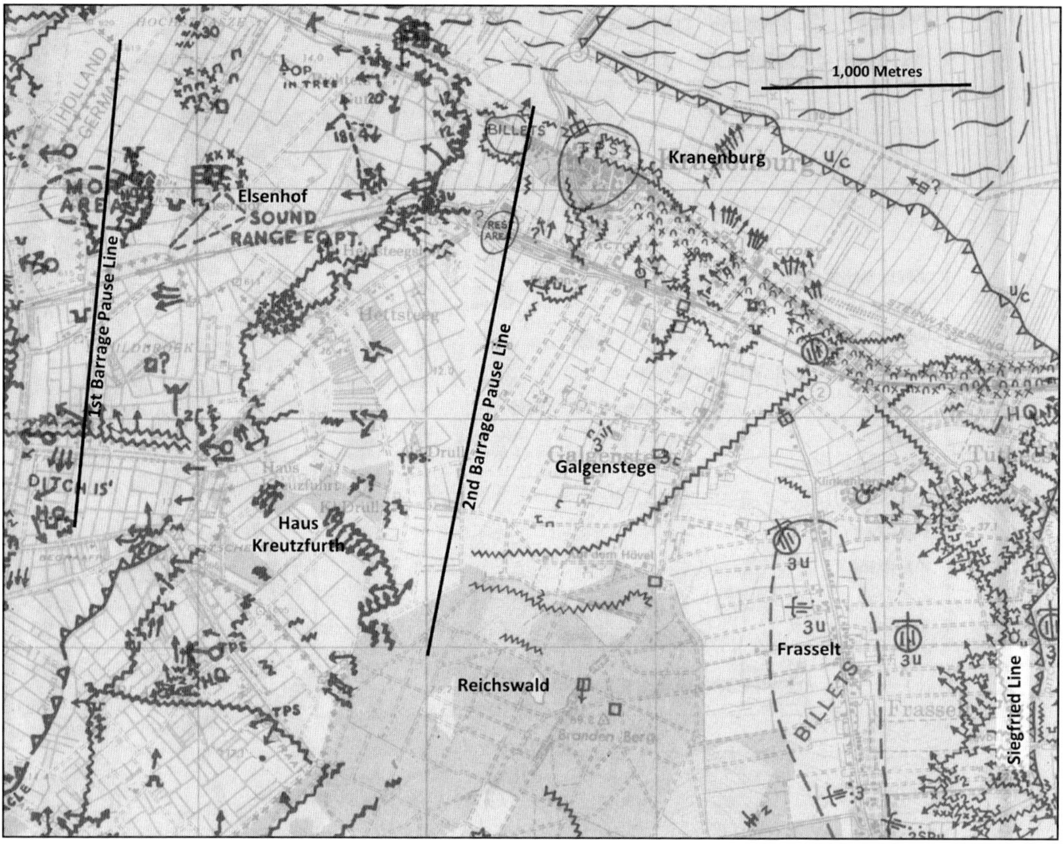

An extract of the tactical overprint map showing German defences north of the Reichswald.

Their next task was to support the HLI into Kranenburg.'[1] Trooper Smith describes their difficulties:

> We now received the order to move against this place [Kranenburg] but the going was becoming increasingly difficult. Incessant rain and, no doubt, the nearby flooding, had turned the ploughed ground into slush and we were down to the air louvres in places.
>
> In fact, there were bogged tanks all the way from Nijmegen to the Siegfried. There were not nearly enough ARVs to serve them all and those that there were had to work in couples. So it looked as if we were in for a long wait. On the positive side, it seemed as if our area was now out of range of German guns because for some time it had been quiet.

Bogged down and left manning the radio while other members of the crew investigated the remains of gliders abandoned in no-man's-land after MARKET GARDEN, Trooper Smith had a surprise:

> Then a piece of cloth fluttered from a crater on my left. I pulled out my pistol and ran to where four dishevelled and woebegone figures trudged with a handkerchief tied to a shovel. I was so excited at having four prisoners all to myself that my hands were shaking and I doubt if the pistol would have

> been much use had I needed it. As it was, there was no need. Their leader, a corporal, spoke in English. 'Please put that thing away,' he said. 'We shall not hurt you. We are surrendered.'
>
> Although we had four prisoners, we had no means of dealing with them so we told them to walk towards Groesbeek and report to the first infantry they saw. The last we saw of them they were heading in the right direction with the white flag still much in evidence.[2]

After waiting for several hours, the armoured recovery vehicles arrived to extricate Trooper Smith's Crocodile from the mud:

> By the time the ARVs – ours and that of B Squadron – had got up to us it was growing dark. To make the task of extricating bogged tanks the harder, we discovered that the airborne troops had wired up a lot of hand grenades as booby traps and, obviously, my friends had been lucky not to encounter these during the afternoon. The ARVs, shunting about among the gliders, frequently exploded these unpleasant contraptions.
>
> Our tank was dragged forward, we unhitched, moved about 20 yards and bogged again. Then the whole process was repeated and it was only at the third attempt that we reached ground that seemed to be able to take our weight. By this time it was completely dark and with darkness came rain.

C Squadron's war diary concluded that 'All three tks of 13 Tp plus 1 comd tk bogged and 14 Tp found the going so heavy that they were unable to keep pace, The infantry gained their objective without loss [*sic*].'[3]

A troop of 141 RAC's Crocodiles pass a Churchill and a carrier that have bogged in.

British and Canadian Infantry Battalions

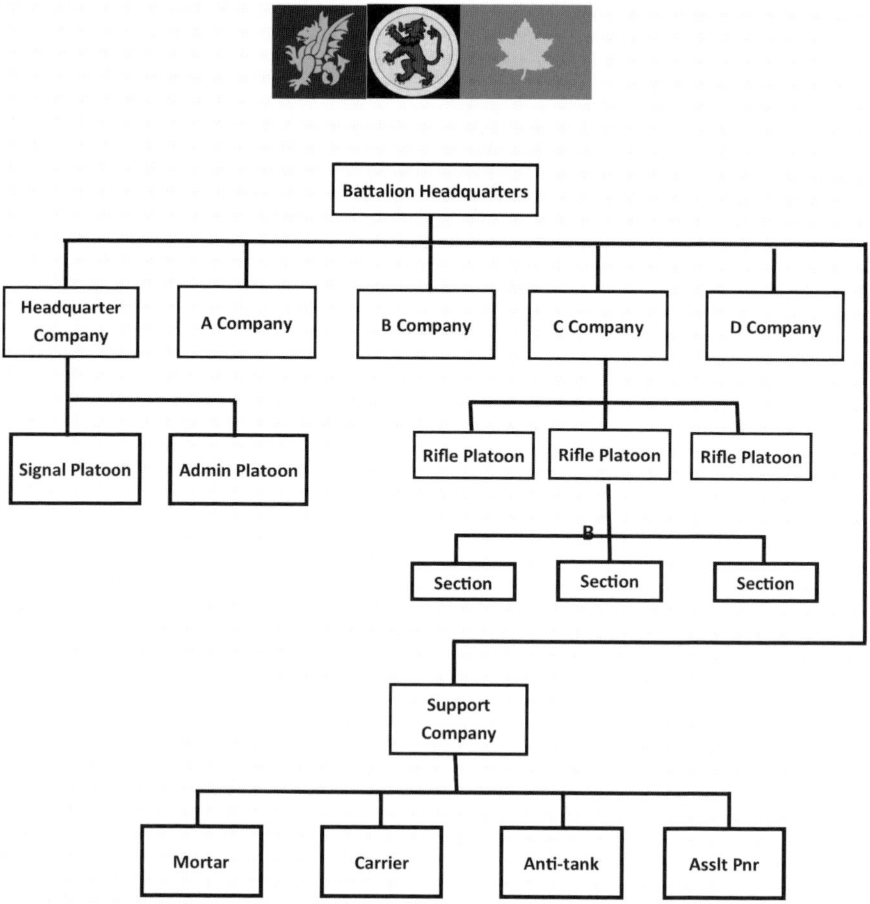

By February 1945 the British manpower crisis was such that battalions were authorised, if necessary, to reduce to a three rifle company ORBAT.

The Carrier Platoon of infantry battalions had a wide range of roles including recce, patrolling, for instance, open flanks and on occasions logistic resupply of forward companies.

The platoon consisted of a headquarters of one Universal Carrier and two utility vehicles commanded by a captain and for sections of three carriers normally led by sergeants.

The Crabs fared no better than the Churchills and Crocodiles, as Lieutenant Hammerton, of B Squadron, 22 Dragoons, recalled:

> Progress was painfully slow as the fields were waterlogged: in fact every Crab in the Squadron was bogged in deep mud. I jumped down and sank almost up to my knees in it. We were useless in these conditions and had to wait until the Guards' heavy recovery was available to help us.[4]

As the barrage resumed its progress forward at 1215 hours, the infantry followed with little supporting armour and as 10 HLI advanced through 2 A&SH's left flank, they ran into a minefield that intelligence had not identified. The regimental history provides more detail. 'Almost immediately, "A" Company ran into an anti-personnel belt and lost several men.' Sergeant Stansbury, commander of the battalion's stretcher bearer section, received the Military Medal in rescuing the wounded. His citation describes his action:

> Two men were quickly blown up and while endeavouring to evacuate these, five S.B.s were wounded in the minefield. Sjt Stansbury led his party and successfully evacuated all seven casualties from the mined area. All seven were badly wounded and by his own disregard for safety their early evacuation probably saved their lives.

The regimental historian continued: 'Once clear of the minefield, the battalion swung left and despite the appalling ground conditions managed to regain and retain their positions close behind the barrage. It was a notable achievement.' To the right of the HLI the Argylls were now advancing east against slight opposition. Their war diarist wrote:

> Moving on to German soil, B Coy took the lead and captured some eighty PWs in what was intended to be the strong point of ELSENHOF suffering one casualty – a chance splinter from our own barrage. C Coy mopping up behind then took as many PWs but had a rougher time from the enemy's DF.
>
> The Argylls had 'leant on the barrage' so closely that when it lifted the Germans did not have time to man their defences around Elsenhof. The battalion was in fact so quick that the haul of prisoners and equipment included a battery of 88mm guns, with breach and muzzle covers still on, along with the crews. Risking a few casualties from their own artillery was better than suffering the inevitable cost of breaking into and fighting through an enemy position.

In 46 Brigade's area on the right of the division's advance, where 2 Glasgow Highlanders had earlier broken through the German forward defences, the brigade's first phase was to be completed by the 9 Cameronians (Scottish Rifles). Their mission was to capture the Galgensteeg Ridge and the bulk of the linear village of Frasselt. As the barrage lifted, they began their advance with A and B Companies leading, concerned about flanking positions along the northern edge of the Reichswald that could enfilade their advance.

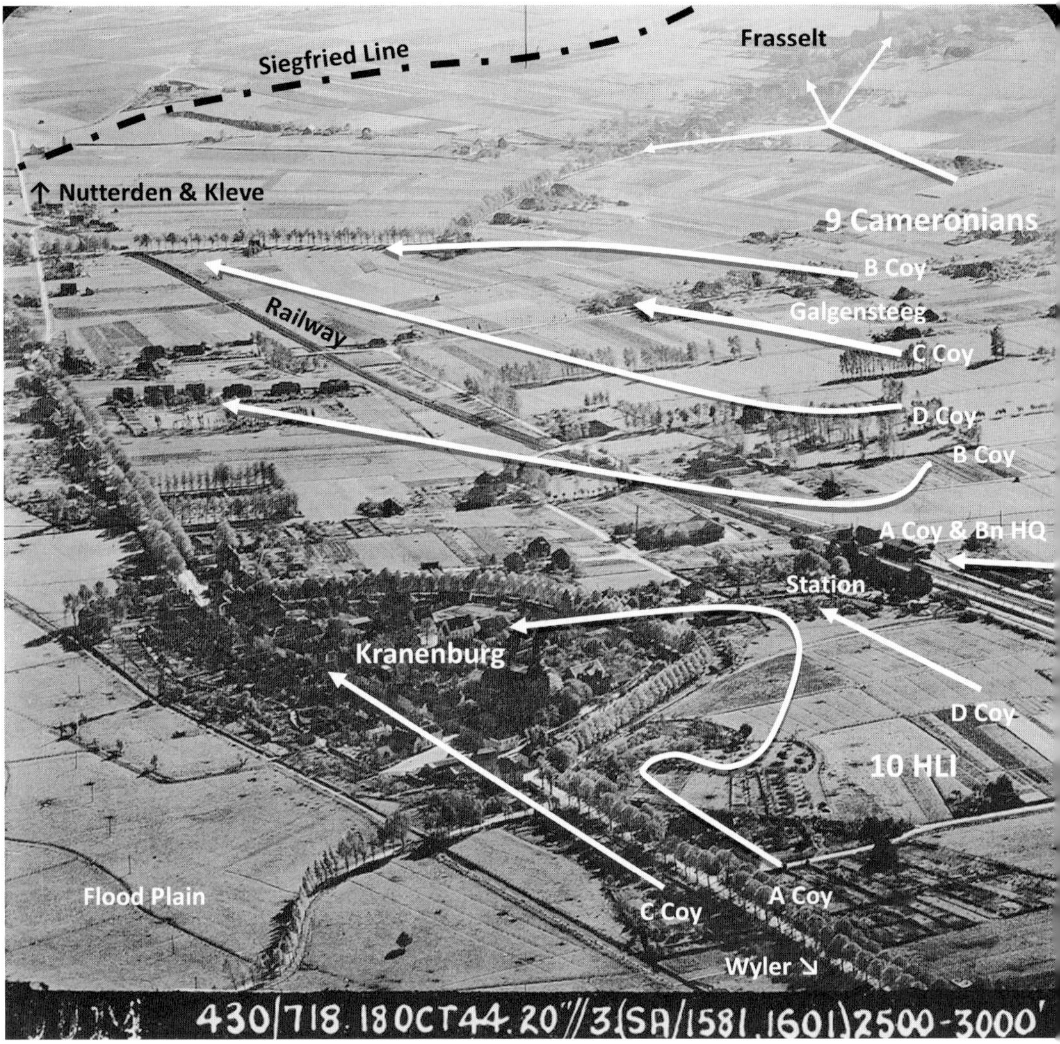

An oblique air photograph of the Kranenburg area and the attack of 227 and 46 brigades. See the tactical overprint map.

Kranenburg

The HLI's A and C companies reached the anti-tank ditch within an hour and the barrage paused for a second time. The regimental historian noted:

> During their advance so far, 'C' Company had successfully cleared RICHTERS GUT, a roadside farm, and another group of houses in front of the ditch [13 Platoon]. Meanwhile, 'B' Company, with the Carrier Platoon attached in infantry role, had been working up the railway and had reached a point just short of the station.

As they approached, C Company could see that the bridge that carried the main road over the anti-tank ditch was still standing and, having waited for the barrage to lift beyond the village, 15 Platoon promptly rushed it with the support of the

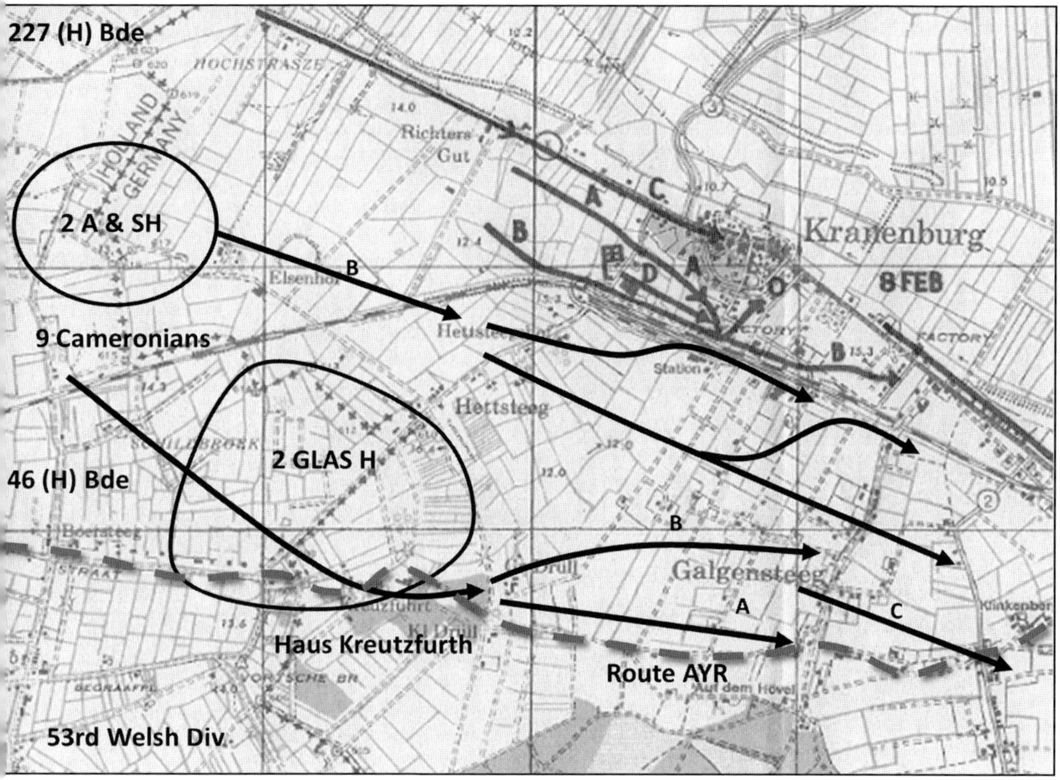

Operations of 15th Scottish Division, afternoon of 8 February 1945.

Scots Guards' tanks. In deploying, eight of the Churchills became bogged down or had suffered mine strikes and only one tank got forward to support the HLI. This tank was directed across the bridge, which had been prepared for demolition, by Lieutenant Scott Barret, who had earlier lost his own tank to a mine. His Military Cross citation reads:

> Seeing that one tank was still going, he led it forward on foot over the bridge which he knew was prepared for blowing and then acted as Liaison Officer between it and the infantry, an action at a very critical moment, since the tank was able to give great assistance to the infantry in dealing with machine gun nests and snipers, and it is doubtful whether without it KRANENBURG could have been captured before dark.

Sergeant Aitken, commanding the Churchill, received an MM for this action as well. His citation concludes:

> The Inf Coy Comd reported that the effect of his supporting fire undoubtedly did much to force the enemy to surrender, that the way in which he fought his tk was quite magnificent and that his action undoubtedly saved the inf many cas.

C Company, with 13 Platoon right, 14 centre, and 15 left, having crossed the bridge, with the help of the Churchill, forged ahead into Kranenburg and cleared the badly battered houses and shops on the main street as far as the 'lateral road'.

The regimental history concluded that: 'C Company task had been completed. For his great part in this action, Major I.H. Murray was awarded the Military Cross.'

To their right, A Company, with no lucky bridge, found the ditch filled with water and covered by machine gun fire. Their plan was for 7 Platoon to secure the south-west corner of the village as a firm base; 8 and 9 Platoons would then start the house clearing when the guns [barrage] lifted. No. 7 Platoon moved over very exposed ground to the flooded anti-tank ditch but could not get across it as it was covered by accurate machine gun fire.

At this point Company Sergeant Major Green was prominent:

> ... undaunted, [he] quickly reorganised and continued the advance. He was here there and everywhere encouraging men of the company and through his complete calmness, disregard for his own safety and fine example of leadership his men were inspired to such a degree that they quickly overcame the opposition and cleared the objective.[5]

Most of 7 Platoon were either killed or wounded in their attempt to get across the ditch and to break into the village. As a result, with his frontal attack proving all too costly and slow, Major Merrifield led his company to the right, where B Company was making good progress having fought their way to the north of the railway line towards the station and beyond. Major Merrifield was killed by machine gun fire and with the station under *Nebelwerfer* fire coming directly down a street 'for some considerable time was a most unhealthy place'.

Captain Foulds came forward from A Company's main HQ to take command and followed 8 Platoon, which was making good progress into Kranenburg and joined C Company in clearing the village. B and D companies, meanwhile, made their way round farther south along the railway. Having thus bypassed Kranenburg itself, these companies first cleared the factory area to the south-east and then came onto the main road east of the town.

Here B Company, with the aid of the Carrier Platoon, cleared a sparsely housed part of the village, while D Company, which had followed closely behind, took over the station area. A single C Squadron crocodile having been freed from the mud is recorded as being in action at Kranenburg but there are no details of where it flamed. C Company's action in the village is recorded in some detail and makes no mention of Crocodiles. It is therefore probable that it was in action supporting B Company along the railway line and in the eastern extension of the village.

Having consolidated the main part of Kranenburg and the rounding up of prisoners, Major Murray was surprised when 'some stray Canadians arrived to announce that they had captured it!!!' By 1800 hours 10 HLI were firmly in control of their objectives and the battalion was rightly proud of its achievements:

> And so, by early evening of Thursday, 8th February, Kranenburg was ours – casualties had been fairly heavy, but the enemy had suffered much more, and

> into the bargain we had secured positions vital to the success of the Corps plan. That it was achieved with a bare minimum of close support, and under the most appalling conditions of mud and bog and in such a short time, is a remarkable feat of arms. No praise can be too high for the men of the Infantry Companies – it was a superb action.

The HLI's commanding officer, Lieutenant Colonel Bramwell-Davies, was awarded a well-deserved DSO for 'his outstanding leadership' and the significant progress of the battalion under his command.

The Galgensteeg Ridge

The Argylls' advance from Hettsteeghof to the south of the railway line was to take them beyond Kranenburg, over the low northern extremity of the Galgensteeg Ridge to the Frasselt road, an advance of some 3,000 yards. The battalion deployed on a two-company frontage and soon met growing resistance and increasing amounts of mortar fire, 'evidently directed on them from the high ground in front of 9 Cameronians'. B Company on the left was under fire from the station and put in a successful quick attack supported by the last three un-bogged tanks of 3 Tank Scots Guards and benefitting from the fire of D Company 10 HLI.

Despite enemy fire, D Company pressed on 'through smoke and mud, [and] had to go all out to close on the barrage before it lifted'. As a result, the company

A Bren gunner of 10 HLI during street fighting in Kranenburg.

had to leave a platoon to deal with enemy dug in along the southern side of the railway line and with the aid of B Company 10 HLI, together they cleared the enemy. Meanwhile, the other platoons were locked in close-quarter, house-to-house fighting in the northern half of Galgensteeg, where two platoons of D Company were fighting well ahead of 9 Cameronians, who were to their right rear.

As the barrage made its final lift at 1600 hours, the Argylls 'found themselves rather precariously positioned on their final objectives, painfully vulnerable to the counter-attack'. With the two companies thinly spread and lacking armoured or anti-tank support, it is fortunate that the enemy did not launch its habitual response. 'There was no sign of a counter-attack. Instead, a steady trickle of Germans with white flags came into our forward platoons.'

At 1700 hours D Company watched with relief as the Cameronians and their un-bogged half squadron of Churchills 'swept over the Galgensteeg spur and into Frasselt'. Thereupon the enemy's mortar fire slackened greatly. By evening the Argylls had consolidated on their objectives, and the Scots Guards had recovered five of their Churchills:[6]

> Towards last light four [Scots Guards'] gun tanks got up to D Coy's forward position. The CO, who had followed the battalion throughout the attack on foot, had already come up to the station and taken over from Major Goodwyn, and by darkness the battalion was securely dug-in for its first night on German soil.[7]

A map from the Argylls' regimental history showing their 4-mile fight from the Nederrijksche Wood to the Galgensteeg Ridge and the Frasselt road.

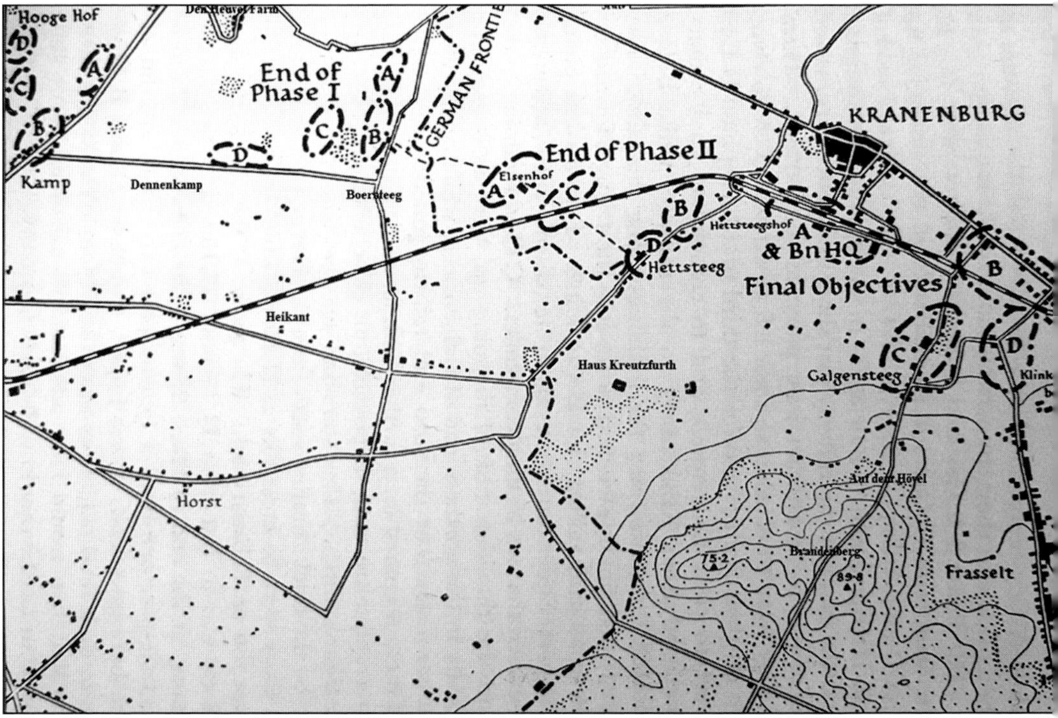

Between 1800 and 1900 hours, 227 Brigade was secure in its objectives and digging in, but the handful of Churchills that had been not too badly bogged had only arrived at the front in time to be ordered to pull back to leaguer! Cynical though the infantry may have been about the departure of the tanks to the rear, there was, however, little option as the engineers were still working to establish Routes AYR and SKYE and wheeled transport could not get through to replenish the tanks.

9 Cameronians' Attack on the Galgensteeg Ridge

The 9 Cameronians had spent the morning following the Glasgow Highlanders to the woods around Haus Kreuzfuhrt, where they formed up and rendezvoused with their squadron of tanks of the 4 Coldstream Guards. As the barrage moved on at 1415 hours following its second pause, the two forward companies crossed the start line on time. The Churchills, however, were delayed in finding a way out of the wood and the infantry initially advanced on their own. 'The Cameronians could see troops of the 53rd Division abreast of them [in the Reichswald] on their right, while reports from the left told that the 227 Brigade was also up in line.'

Having covered a mile in less than an hour, the Cameronians' forward companies were approaching the Galgensteeg Ridge, which juts northward from the Reichswald to the south-west of Kranenburg:

> Here the left company, B, ran into an anti-personnel minefield and suffered many casualties. Most of these wounded men had legs blown off: their evacuation was a most painful process, which they bore with the utmost courage.

The company fought alongside the Argylls to clear the buildings, during which the Cameronians were to have been supported by two troops of Crocodiles from C Squadron, 141 Regiment RAC. Their war diary reads:

> 12 Tp was supporting B Coy 9 Cams in securing Galgensteeg. The going was very bad and close to the objective two tanks bogged and one blew up on a mine. The infantry proceeded without Croc support and found the objective, opposition being nil.

On the battalion's right flank, A Company faced a well-developed system of field defences around Auf den Hövel at the north-westerly tip of the Reichswald with barbed wire and trenches sited to be mutually supporting. The battalion made the point that:

> If the enemy had manned these defences, the attack would have been a very different story. Instead, it seems that what enemy there had sought shelter from the bombardment in the cellars of Frasselt.

The final stage of the battalion's attack was to clear Frasselt itself, which was due to be launched by C Company at 1600 hours but neither the Churchills nor Crocodiles had reached the Galgensteeg Ridge. Consequently, the attack was

Crocodiles of 141 Regiment RAC in action flaming buildings and scrubland earlier in the campaign.

postponed until 1715 hours. Eventually, having been pulled out of the mud, enough armour arrived for the company to advance the 800 yards from the ridge down to Frasselt, where several more Crocodiles of C Squadron, now free of the mud, in one of the few such actions, flamed the houses. Their war diary noted:

> 11 Tp went through and attacked Frasselt with C Coy 9 Cams. This was successful. The Tp flamed the west end of the village and the infantry followed in. Flame was continued for about 800 yards down the village but was discontinued as there was no further opposition. Some POWs were taken. 11 Tp rallied at Auf den Hövel and spent the night in their tanks. Sups [supplies] organised by the 4 Coldm Gds did not reach them that night.

Many Germans were killed, and forty-eight prisoners and a battery of 88mm guns taken. By 1830 hours the Cameronians had consolidated on a two-company front beyond Frasselt, securing the start line for the divisions' second phase, the breaking of the Siegfried Line.

The 15th Scottish Division was behind schedule but not by as much as the Welsh and Highland divisions, which had also broken through the forward defences and were now fighting in the Reichswald to their right. Difficulties behind the 15th were, however, piling up as tracks broke up under the weight of armour and the breaches in the minefields and approaches to bridges across ditches became morasses.

The two leading brigades had reached their objectives, but the question was would the division's advance be sustained and could the Wessex Division be brought forward? The 44 Lowland Brigade battled its way through mud to reach its start lines. General Martin explained the problem:

> The 46th Brigade's axis [AYR] became that afternoon the 15th Scottish Division's only axis. It was a narrow, unmetalled track with deep ditches on either side. Along it had passed already 'F' [Fighting] Echelon unit transport of the 46th Brigade, together with the tanks and lorries of the Coldstream and the 'Funnies' – and they had done it no good. On to it was now thrown the extra load, not only of the 227th Brigade's transport but also of five field regiments, which, about 4 P.M., began their forward move into new positions from which they could cover the advance to Cleve. And there was still the 44th Brigade Group to follow. It was to be a nightmare night, throughout which every officer and man in the 46th Brigade was to be at work without a let-up on traffic control and vehicle recovery in an effort to produce some sort of order out of chaos – and this despite the fact that Division had made the most careful provision for traffic control. After that night the 46th Brigade axis, too, was finally finished: traffic had to go by the main road or not at all.[8]

PEARL BLACK, the main Nijmegen–Kleve road, was only opened by the Canadian engineers later that evening after the fighting in Wyler was over and it was via this road that 10 HLI were almost unique in getting their battalion transport forward complete with a hot meal!

Conditions on the axis after the passage of the tanks delayed the move up of 44 Lowland Brigade.

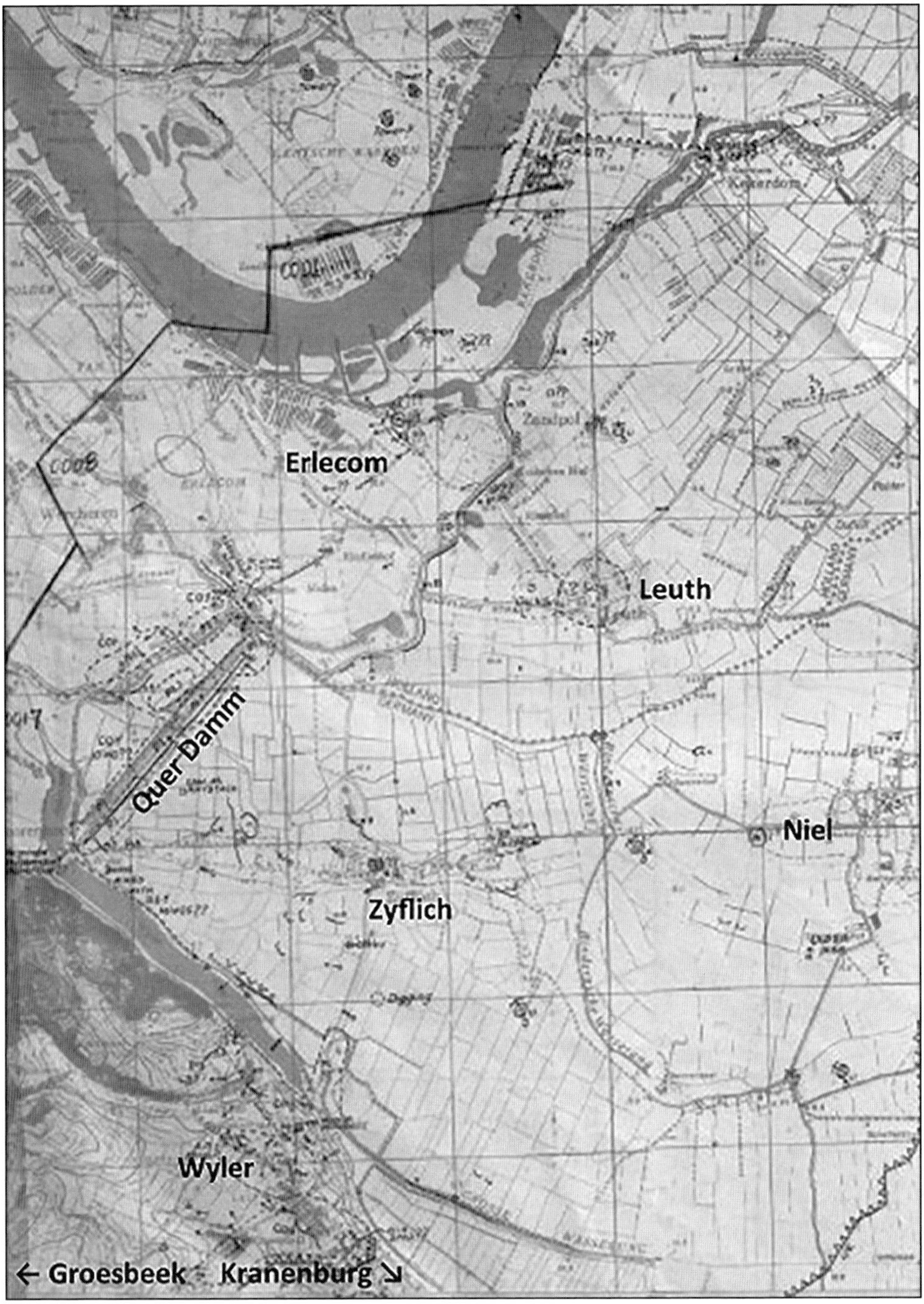

The Rhine flood plain the area of operations for 3rd Canadian Division.

Chapter Seven

Enter the 'Water Rats'

At 1600 hours the artillery barrage lifted, having marched through the German positions so effectively in front of the four divisions that had been in action since 1030 hours that morning. The guns now concentrated further north to prepare the final divisional operation of the day by the 3rd Canadian Division out on the Rhine floodplain. The 12 Canadian Field Regiment RCA recorded in their war diary that hitherto they had been firing 'a smokescreen on the left of 30 Corps since 1015 and continued same till 1600. Reverted to normal role in support of the 7 CIB [7 Canadian Infantry Brigade] and was ready to engage targets on call.'

The area to be attacked by 3rd Canadian Division had also seen the attention of Second Tactical Airforce during the 7th, before both rain and artillery fire put the airspace above polder land out of bounds to aircraft. Headquarters XXX Corps reported in their Air Notes for 8 February that:

> KRANENBURG was attacked by 2 Group RAF but again it was through cloud and no results were observed. NIEL and MEHR and MILLINOEN in the front of 3 Cdn Div were all given fighter-bomber treatment and strafing was carried out on a line of dyke foxholes near ZANDPOL and on the road between KESSEL and HEKKENS.

With the thaw and the rise in the level of the Rhine, by 6 February water was pouring through the breaches the Germans had blown in the winter dykes and the floodplain was worryingly being steadily inundated:

> 3 Cdn Inf Div's role was somewhat different from that of the other divisions. Its H-Hour was not until the evening, six and a half hours later than the others, its front between the Nijmegen–Cleve highway and the river was considerably wider, and the ground over which it had to advance was practically covered with water.[1]

As the river continued to rise, water was threatening to cover the lower sections of Route PEARL BLACK through Wyler and Kranenburg. Securing this increasingly flooded area in order to protect the flanks of 2nd Canadian and 15th Scottish divisions was the task of Major General Spry's 3rd Canadian Division. 'As the flooding came only a few days before the battle opened, it was necessary to make many extensive last-minute changes to the plans which had been made for operating with tanks on a hard surface.'

The Canadian objectives were now lengths of dyke where the enemy, 2nd Battalion 1052 Infantry Regiment and two police battalions along with sundry

Volkssturm platoons, were dug in above water level and a series of positions in villages on slightly higher ground that were now in effect islands. To reach them, in addition to the AVREs of two Assault Regiments RE from 79th Armoured Division, the Canadians had hastily attached to them 114 amphibious Landing Vehicles Tracked, otherwise known in British service as Buffaloes or Alligators. The LVTs were provided by A and B squadrons, 11 RTR, and two squadrons of 5th Assault Regiment, RE, both of 79th Armoured Division. Fortunately, the Canadians were familiar with the Buffaloes, having used them during the autumn in the Scheldt Estuary. They also had a divisional pool of fifty of the lighter Weasel amphibious carriers and a dozen Royal Army Service Corps amphibious DUKW trucks for logistic resupply.

The detailed task given to Major General Spry's 3rd Canadian Division in the opening stages of Operation VERITABLE was to clear the enemy from the low-lying polder land as far the railway running north-east from Kleve to Griethausen. The attack was to be made on a two-brigade front with 7 Canadian Infantry Brigade on the right and the 8th on the left. Two squadrons of the 13th/18th Hussars Shermans provided support in the initial phase of the battle from 'dry' land.

During the day of waiting, the 'dry land' shrunk considerably when a section of the dyke known as the Quer Damm collapsed due to the Germans' digging of defences on the embankment that weakened the structure and the amount of

An aerial photograph taken of one of the gaps blown in the dyke prior to the rise in the level of the Rhine and consequent inundation.

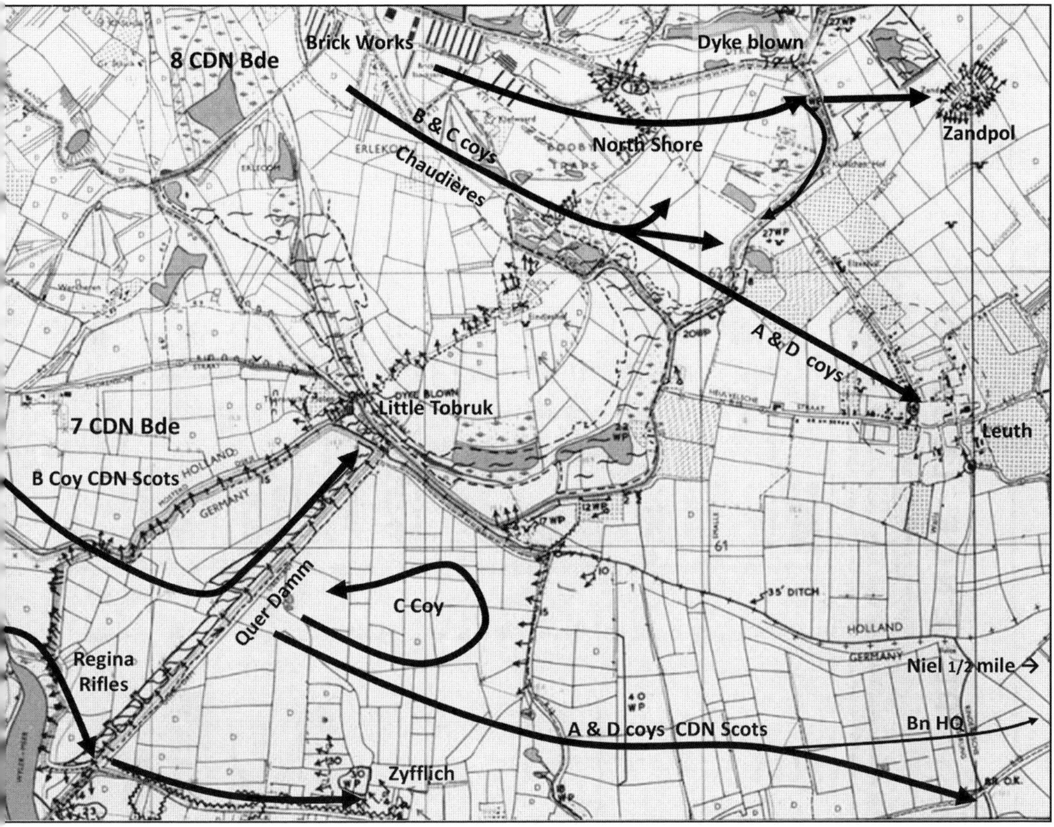

The final 'Stop Press edition' of the 1:25,000 tactical overprint of the 3rd Canadian Division's area, with their operations during the night of 8–9 February 1945 added.

water it was containing to the north. Breaches in the dykes east of the Erlecom brickworks had allowed water onto the floodplain.[2] This necessitated a precipitate withdrawal by the North Shore Regiment from parts of the brickworks and surrounding area through rapidly rising water to starting positions further back on higher ground.[3] Of the floods, ignoring the fact that initially some Canadian infantry had to wade through the rising water to their objectives, the BAOR historian concluded:

> Thus, the efficacy of the enemy anti-tank ditches, wire and mines were largely lost, the Canadians being able to float over them in their amphibians; of which 114 Buffaloes and 50 Weasels from 79 Armd Div were on hand.

Flooding the polder land, of course, made offensive operations by 3rd Canadian Division more difficult, but it also isolated the German defenders on stretches of dyke and prevented them mounting all but small-scale local counter-attacks.

Attack of 7th Canadian Brigade

Under the cover of darkness and artillery fire, at 1800 hours in the first phase of the 3rd Canadian Division's operation, the brigades started to move forward. For 7 Brigade their first objective was the substantial but now breached Quer Damm

Landing Vehicle Tracked 4 – Water Buffalo

Developed by American industry from a civilian vehicle used in swampy areas, the Landing Vehicle Tracked was used extensively during the island-hopping Pacific campaign. The LVT-2s and -4s came into British service at the end of 1943 and by early 1945 they had been used by 79th Armoured Division during the fighting in the Scheldt in support of operations by the First Canadian Army.

The LVT-2 could carry sixteen fully equipped troops, but they had to embark and disembark over the side of the vehicle. Based on reports of casualties being suffered disembarking, the more capacious LVT-4 was developed with a rear-loading ramp that provided greater flexibility, including the carriage of vehicles. The troop-carrying capacity was increased to thirty.

Canadian infantry embarking on a LVT-2.

Known as the Water Buffalo, the LVT-4 weighed 13½ tons plus armour that was added in British service. It was armed with a 20mm Polsten gun and usually a pair of .5 cal Browning machine guns. Its speed on land was 14mph and afloat 7mph.

The rear ramp of the LVT-4 in use.

One of the problems encountered in shallow water such as that encountered in the inundated parts of the Rhine floodplain during Operation VERITABLE was that if one track grounded or hit an obstacle such as a fence post, the vehicle was spun off course and at night this led to disorientation of both driver and commander. Therefore, maintaining the correct direction particularly at night was difficult, as indicated by the DUKWs on occasion needing to turn on their lights. This in turn attracted enemy fire when in forward areas.

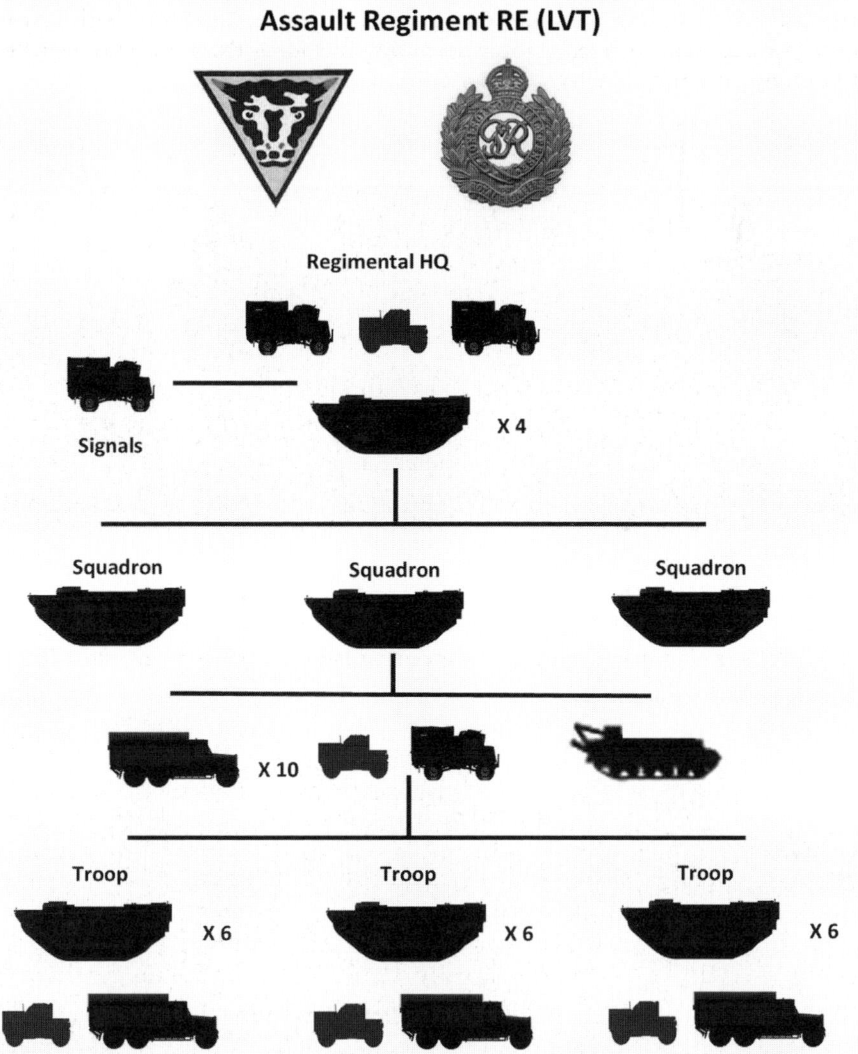

The organisation of an Assault Regiment RE equipped with LVTs. Squadrons with their own communications, recovery and logistics were organised to operate away from the regiment.

The LVT demonstrating its amphibious credential climbing out of the water on its tracks.

approximately 300 yards to the east of their start line. Their original operation order read:

> Intention
> 5. 7 Cdn Inf Bde and atts will attack and destroy enemy, between RIGHT, bdy with 2 Cdn Inf Div and 15 (S) Div and LEFT, 8 Cdn inf Bde up to gen line of a tk ditch 8657 – 8661 and R RHINE.

Following the prospect of the flooding of the polders, the tasks were adjusted in an amendment issued on 30 January:

> Phase I: 'WALKING'
> (a) Attack with one bn to clear of enemy from houses at 7981631 SOUTH to incl rd junc 794623 and capture Zandpol 7962.
> (b) On orders this HQ pass through the second bn clearing dyke xxxxxxx from excl rd junc 794623 to 786612 incl and to capture LEUTH 7961.
> Phase II: 'RUNNING'
> To pass through fresh coys and Capture rd junc 827633 – KEKERDOM 8164.
> Phase III: 'SWIMMING'
> (a) To pass res bn thorough RIGHT fwd bn and capture MILLINGEN.
> (b) On orders this HQ LEFT fwd bn will mop-up the area between the rds – rd junc 794628 – dyke junc and the R RHINE.[4]

The Regina Rifles' B and C companies advanced but soon found themselves wading through increasingly deep water as they moved out onto the floodplain, towards the southern portion of the Quer Damm. They were supported by the Lothians' flail tanks and three troops of Shermans from 13th/18th Hussars but the armour was confined to the mostly submerged road that followed the Wyler Meer from its northern point and then headed directly to Zyfflich. Consequently, throughout the operation none of these tanks bogged in. The first objective on the Quer Damm was quickly secured but thanks to the breach they were unable to work their way further north along the dyke, which left Major English's B Company of the Canadian Scottish with a significantly larger objective than originally planned.

Two platoons of the Scots' B Company mounted in Buffaloes reached the Quer Damm north of the cut with little difficulty, from where 10 Platoon fought their way towards the Little Tobruk strongpoint, taking twenty-three prisoners in the process. However, they were advancing along the dyke on a very narrow front. As the leading section made its way along the damm they were brought to a halt by enemy fire from Little Tobruk, and 11 Platoon, which was to attack directly from the west aboard Buffaloes, had not arrived. This required Major English to make a fresh plan for a better-supported attack. After finding 11 Platoon with some difficulty and a protracted bombardment:

> Sgt Cummings and five of his platoon including L/Cpl. Gehl boarded a Buffalo with Brens and a PIAT while Cpl Thomas in the meantime cleared the house on the right. They netted five prisoners, a machine-gun and a good position to cover the pillbox from the right flank. Sgt Cummings then made a wide circle with the craft and approached from the left flank.

During the attacks, having dropped their loads, the Buffaloes manoeuvred into positions from where they could provide fire support with their 20mm Polsten light anti-aircraft guns and .30 or .50 Browning machine guns. Fire support by the artillery and Buffaloes was a significant factor in the success of 10 Platoon in assaulting and capturing a pillbox at the heart of Little Tobruk. With this success 12 Platoon advanced through 10 Platoon and drove on through the enemy strongpoint on to the dyke beyond, rounding up a total of three officers and sixty-one other ranks, i.e. a German company of the period, in a protracted fight. It was only at 0520 hours that Major English sent a report back to his battalion's headquarters that B Company had cleared and secured Little Tobruk.

During the reorganisation on the objective after the attack, Major English realised that the German company commander was a particularly nervous prisoner and:

> ... he immediately ordered his men out of the strong point and a short distance down the embankment. Minutes later 'Little Tobruk' was blasted with enemy shellfire. Knowing capture was imminent, the *Hauptman* had ordered artillery fire on his own position.[56]

Having quickly secured the southern part of the Quer Damm during early evening, the leading companies of the Regina Rifles pressed on with the second phase

A photograph taken during Operation VERITABLE showing the Buffalo and its armaments.

(nickname RUNNING), the attack on Zyfflich (nickname DAVENTRY), which was a further mile to the east. C Squadron of the 1st Lothian and Border Horse (flails) recorded in their war diary:

> Thursday, 8th Feb
>
> D Day for Op VERITABLE 3rd Tp moved to assembly area in BEEK 7650, in sp of 7 Bde, 3 Div. Only 1 Tk, Cpl Koonan required to clear the dyke road into ZYFFLICH, the first objective of Regina Rifles Regt.
>
> This task was carried out perfectly by Cpl. Koonan's tk. He led the attack into the objective at 1800 hrs, blowing 4 teller mines and several schumines. 150 Germans came out of the cellars as he entered the village and surrendered. He was supported by 1st and 2nd Tps, B Sqn 13/18 H. Tanks could not proceed further than the first objective and the tank was withdrawn. 4th Tp were not called upon by 5 Bde and were released.

Zyfflich was reached at 2000 hours and during its clearance, the Reginas reported taking approximately 100 prisoners, most of whom put up little fight, and again had to be winkled out of the cellars in which they had been sheltering from the bombardment.

While B Company was fighting to take Little Tobruk, A and D companies of the Canadian Scottish crossed the Wyler Meer and bypassed Zyfflich heading for Niel (nickname LAXTON), according to the war dairy 'sailing time "30 minutes"'. The Canadian official history describes the action:

> The battalion's remaining rifle companies, embarking in Buffaloes from the Wyler Meer [at about 2000 hours], set course by compass through the darkness for Niel, 2 miles east of Zyfflich [held by 2nd Battalion 1052 Infantry Regiment].

The company's navigation was aided by an occasional bombardment of Niel, but other villages, farms and houses were attacked with only the dubious help of compasses in an armoured vehicle, and the attackers became disorientated. Matters, however, got worse:

> Communications failed, and shortly after midnight the CO, Lt-Col D.G. Crofton, headed towards the objective with his command group in two amphibians. But Niel was still in German hands, for the Scottish 'A' and 'D' Companies through faulty navigation had become engaged with a group of houses 1500 yards to the south-west. Crofton's party ran into point-blank fire from houses on the western outskirts. Two officers and two men were killed, and the CO and his Intelligence Officer were among the wounded. Day was breaking when 'A' and 'D' Companies arrived to clear the village.

Lieutenant Colonel Crofton, commander of the Canadian Scottish, and the regiment's cap badge.

The battalion's war diary provides some more detail:

> 04:30 A and D Coy arrived in NIEL and cleared from opposite ends of the village.
>
> 05:20 B Coy reported ALL CLEAR and they also returned back to Goring House.
>
> 07:00 All Coy-C [Commanders] met each other in the centre of NIEL, discussing the plans for the final steps and to consolidate their position. As a barrage of the enemy arrived on the scene, this turned out to be the last shelling on NIEL but killed Lt Ferguson and his batman.

A and D companies realised their error and having cleared the hamlet of GERMENSEE, they re-embarked on their Buffaloes and sailed north to Niel. This explains the delayed arrival of the two companies. It only remains to record the activities of C Company, who had a frustrating night:

> In the meantime, C Coy was sailing in and around the polder lake looking for someone to help. In the early morning C Coy returned back at the starting point, they reported that they had nothing but trouble all night. C Coy stayed at the control point as reserve the rest of the day.

Phase III of the 3rd Canadian Division's attack, which would see the Royal Winnipeg Rifles advancing across the flooded polder land during 9 February to Keeken, will be covered in Chapter Six.

Attack of 8th Canadian Brigade

Brigadier Roberts established his tactical headquarters in one of the substantial brick kilns at Erlkom as the best place to command the attack by 8 Canadian Brigade on the division's left flank. The brigade's objectives were a defended dyke that both battalions were to attack first and then the villages of Zandpol and Leuth (nickname BARTON).

The attack was begun on time with A and B companies of the North Shore Regiment aboard Buffaloes. They had boarded the LVTs behind a dyke that protected them from enemy view but it was, however, steep and according to Brigadier Roberts 'the tracks of the Buffaloes dug into the wet earth … and proceeded to dig themselves, deeper and deeper, into the slope'. The Buffaloes' commander 'was doing everything possible to disengage his machines from the soft mud, but nothing happened'. Meanwhile, as the minutes ticked by the PEPPERPOT shoot on Zandpol was due to end, so Roberts requested that the fire plan 'dwelled' for a ten-minute extension while the amphibians took an oblique approach to the dyke. Roberts wrote that he '… was deeply relieved when the gouging tracks cut into the earth on the diagonal and, one by one, the machines crested our [dyke] and plunged into the flooding waters on the other side'.

The two North Shore companies, A and B, aboard a dozen LVTs waded or swam according to the depth of the water to their first objective, the embanked road that ran south from the area of the gap that the Germans had blown. Le Régiment de Chaudière's attack on the brigade's right flank was to be coordinated with the North Shores. Coordination, however, failed when a Buffalo carrying A Company's commander with a signal lamp broke down short of the first objective at 1835 hours. Consequently, without the signal to move, the Chaudière waited in a wood for the signal that never came.

This was not the only misfortune as B Company became disorientated and lost cohesion, while A Company, minus its headquarters, eventually sailed on to the dyke, which they cleared of shocked *Volkssturm* defenders, complete with grey hair and First World War-vintage weapons. B Company landed further down the dyke a quarter of an hour later but did so at a time and place that enabled them to disrupt one of the few German counter-attacks. Between them the companies took about 120 prisoners.

Eventually, after a considerable delay while communication was established across the brigade, realising that his plan had miscarried as a result of the simple failure of the lamp signal, Brigadier Roberts himself ordered the rest of the Chaudières forward. To reach the dyke a French Canadian company had to wade half a mile through water that was in places waist deep and, arriving at the objective, they found that the North Shore companies had already cleared most of it.

The brigade's main objectives were the two villages and as planned the North Shore's second pair of companies had pressed on for another mile and attacked

An aerial photograph taken of one of the gaps blown in the winter dyke prior to the rise in the level of the Rhine and consequent inundation.

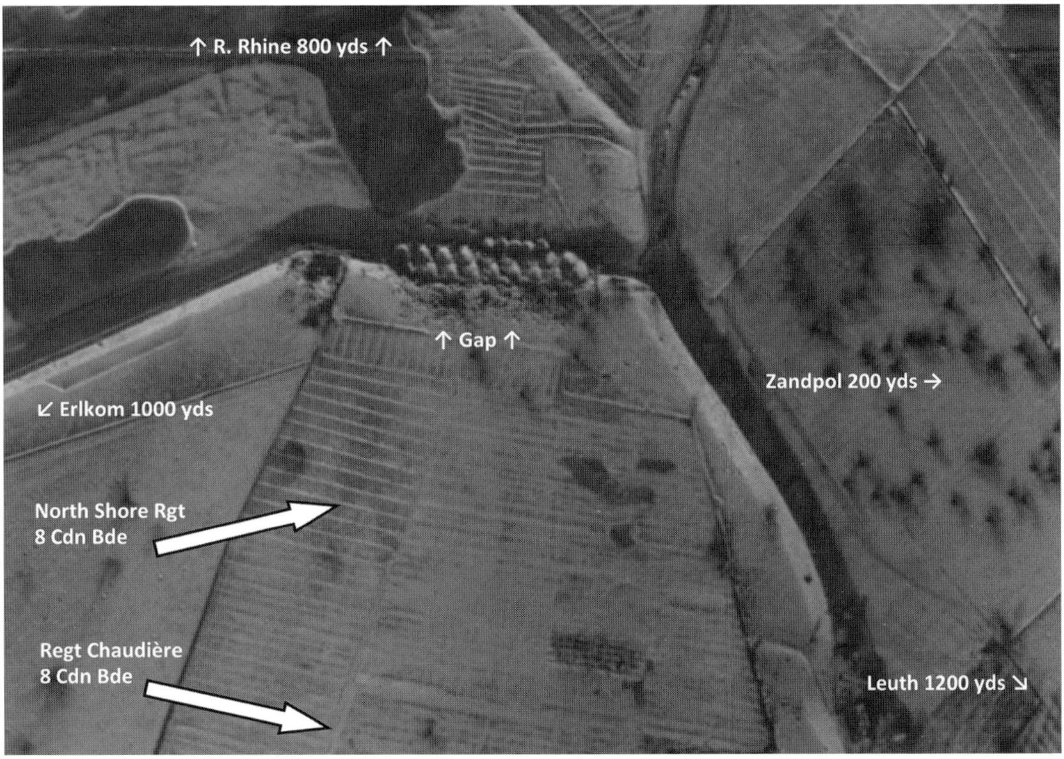

A marked oblique aerial photograph from the North Shore's report taken before the floods showing the route taken by the rifle companies.

their objective, the village of Zandpol, which was held by the Munster Police Battalion. Two companies mounted in Buffaloes had little difficulty in clearing and crossing an intermediate dyke east of the village and by 2100 hours were reporting that the village was secure, with the enemy having largely abandoned their positions.

Meanwhile, the remainder of the Chaudières left the area of the Erlecom brickyard in canvas and plywood assault boats that they referred to as 'skiffs' for their advance on Leuth. The battalion's history records the operation to cross 1½ miles of flooded country:

> The skiff-like craft sufficient to transport two companies at a time, arrived at the makeshift quays. Companies A and D were the first to embark, their

The villages and dykes the Germans defended could increasingly only be reached by Buffaloes.

> objectives were to seize the village of Leuth and a dike leading to a fortification christened 'Little Tobruk'. The soldiers of the Support Company became boatmen and under the skilful direction of Lt E. Carrier, the flotilla manoeuvred through bushes, houses, fences and enemy 20mm fire, which was fortunately above the boats. There was, however, an annoying exception: one of the boats was hit by shrapnel, in which were Capt L. Larose, second in command of A Company, Sargent Major G. Nadeau, and soldiers L. Provencal, J. Roy, M. Boucher and V. Blondin. They went hurriedly towards a half-submerged house, but at the moment the men caught hold of the second floor, the boat sank … The operation was conducted in torrential rain and faced by a strong easterly wind. The darkness was total, so we needed to resort to powerful projectors [search lights] the light from which reflected on the clouds creating 'artificial moonlight', which dimly lit the ground.

Running well behind schedule, it took three hours for the Chaudières' A and D companies to reach their objectives. Consequently, 'they decided to ignore for the moment' 'Little Tobruk', believing that once they had outflanked it by capturing Leuth, the garrison there would withdraw. As already described, the strongpoint was under attack by the Canadian Scots and fell to them early on 9 February. Leuth was quickly cleared and by dawn the Chaudières' assault boats had returned with B and C companies to join the rest of the battalion in Leuth

LVTs bearing Canadian infantry take to the water.

but, as we will see, with the water still rising the Chaudières' difficulties were far from over.

As a result of the operations conducted amidst the flood waters of the Rhine in the opening phase of Operation VERITABLE, Major General Spry announced on 9 February that the 3rd Canadian Infantry Division was being referred to as the 'Water Rats' and that this henceforth would be the division's nickname.

Of the opening day of Operation VERITABLE General Horrocks concluded that: 'After the first hour almost every tank was bogged down, and the infantry had to struggle forward on their own. The chief enemy resistance came from the cellars in the villages.' It may have been the infantry boots that secured the ground, but full credit must be also given to the British and Canadian artillery for clearing the way for them. It has been calculated that the psychological impact of the bombardment greatly helped XXX Corps break through the German forward defences and into the Reichswald and Kranenburg. Almost twenty PoWs were taken for every German casualty, of which the latter were only 5 per cent of those manning the defences.[7]

Chapter Eight

The Siegfried Line

The opening phase of Operation VERITABLE had developed as well as could have been expected, bearing in mind the dramatic deterioration of ground conditions after the thaw. As midnight approached on 8 February, a staff officer of XXX Corps writing up the intelligence summary concluded with some exaggeration that: 'By the end of the day the whole of 1051 GR, one battalion 1052 GR and 84 Fus Bn had been captured or killed and all except three battalions of 84 Inf Div had been in action.'

From headquarters LXXXVI Corps upwards German reaction to the attack had been slow and confused, with the certainty in their minds that the Allies would take the Venlo option slowing decision-making. Consequently, the story of the attack on the Siegfried Line north of the Reichswald during the night of 8–9 February 1945 could have been very different, especially if General Fiebig had made his decision to pull back and properly occupy the defences. Schlemm's counter-attack by 7th *Fallschirmjäger* Division had been planned to be launched south of the Reichswald and would have fallen squarely on 51st Highland Division. Even though 15th Scottish would not have been attacked, the loss of the guns to defeat the *Fallschirmjäger* would have made closing up to and breaking the Siegfried Line much harder.

During 9 February, the challenge for General Horrocks was to break through the Siegfried Line, which stretched from overlooking the Maas floodplain through the Reichswald, across the Kranenburg–Kleve road and out onto the Rhine floodplain. The forest was regarded by the Germans as impractical for a major offensive and was in their minds a key feature of the Reichswald defences. Consequently, although work on the Line had been under way since Operation MARKET GARDEN, it was a lower priority than stretches of border defences further south. There were some concrete shelters in the Reichswald but most of the positions were revetted field defences.

In essence, the operations conducted by XXX Corps on 9 February would be the continuation of the previous day's fighting on a frontage of four divisions. These were, 3rd Canadian Division resuming its increasingly amphibious advances on the Rhine floodplain, 15th Scottish forcing its way through the narrow strip of land between the forest and the floods towards Kleve and the 53rd Welsh and 51st Highland fighting through the Reichswald itself.

15th Scottish Division at Frasselt and Schottheide

With the 15th Scottish Division holding the corps' main effort, the first priority was for its battalions to break through the Siegfried Line where it lay just beyond

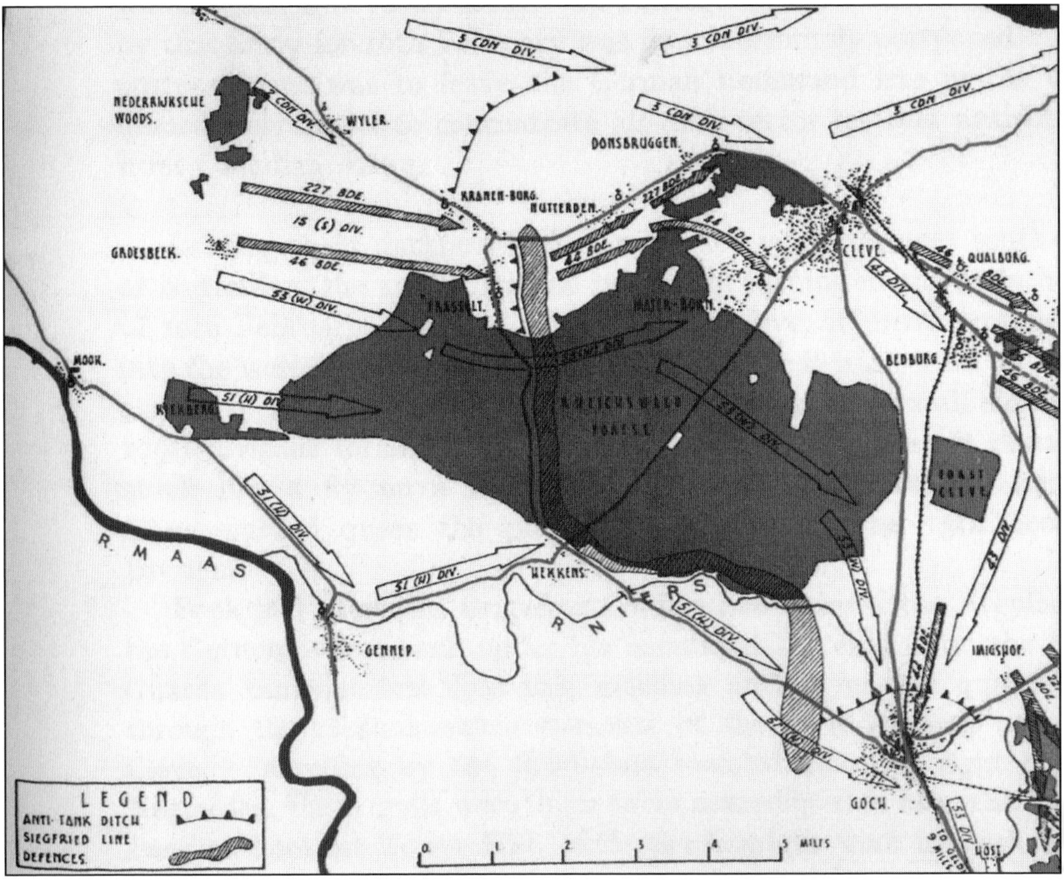

The Siegfried Line in the VERITABLE area.

their forward positions in the village of Frasselt, which 46 and 227 Highland brigades had reached at last light. From aerial photographs and maps, in a meticulously pre-planned operation, 44 (Lowland) Brigade, reinforced by 2nd Gordons, was to assault the Siegfried defences, amply supported by the specialist vehicles of the 79th Armoured Division. Supported by the Churchills of 4 Tank Grenadier Guards and the infantry mounted in Kangaroo APCs, they were then to dash to the vital high ground overlooking Nütterden and the Materborn feature along with their Forward Observation Officers. The latter high ground had to be reached before German reserves arrived in significant number if rates of progress further south into the Rhineland were to be maintained. H Hour for the attack was planned for 2100 hours with the aid of movement light.

The Siegfried Line beyond the northern edge of the Reichswald stretched north for just over 2,000 yards before petering out on the floodplain beyond the line of the road and railway. Compared to all the stretches of the Line attacked by XXX Corps this was potentially the most well defended, covering the obvious approach around the north of the forest to Kleve. In addition, it extended in depth 3 miles back to pre-prepared positions on the high ground around Materborn. It was, however, appreciated by Brigadier Cumming-Bruce

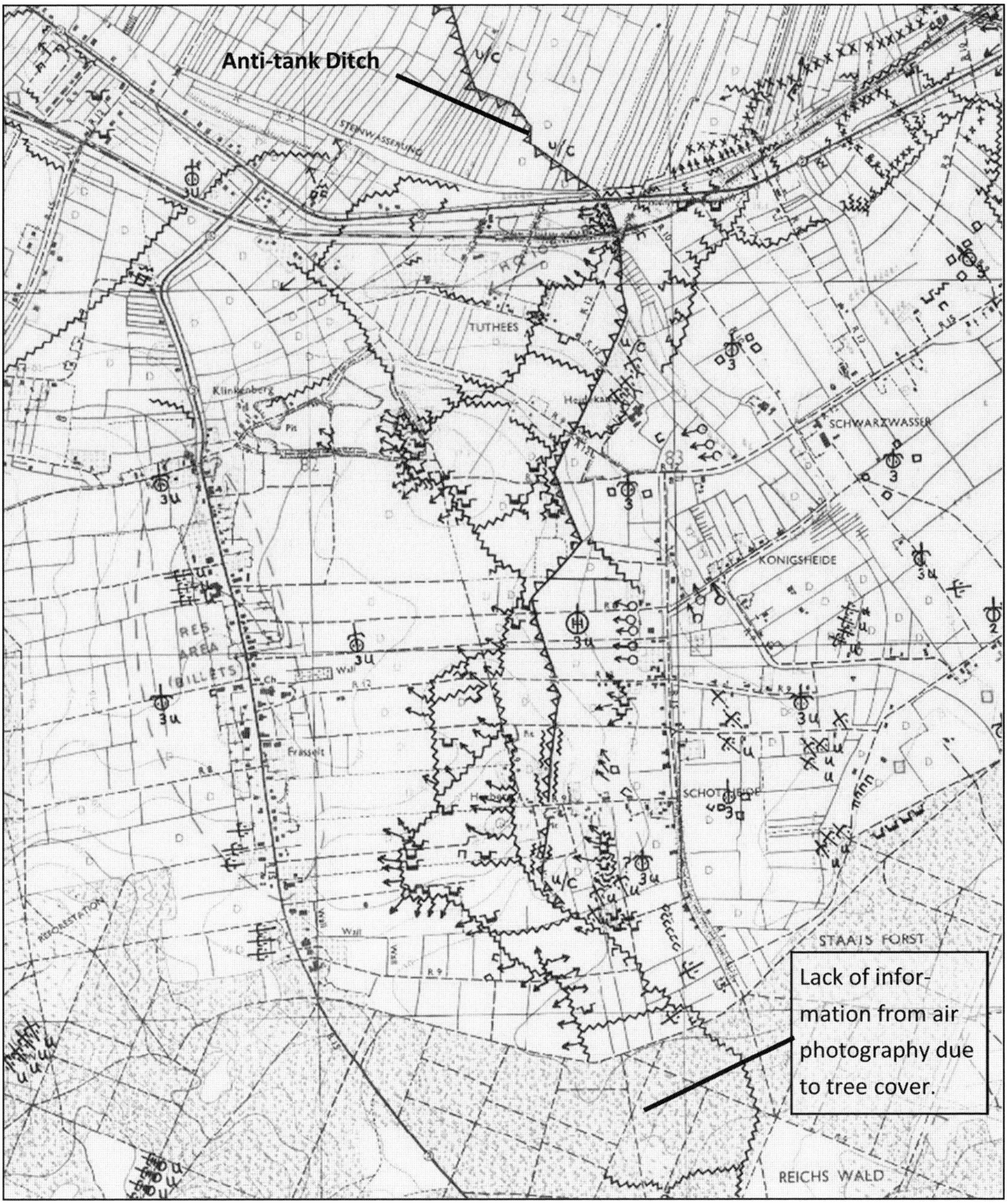

The Siegfried Line defences between the Reichswald and the Rhine floodplain.

that the enemy was unlikely to have sufficient troops to man the defences of such depth in detail.

The brigade commander's original plan was to form a breaching force, consisting of vehicles from 79th Armoured Division and two companies of infantry from the assault battalions (6 RSF and 6 King's Own Scottish Borderers (6 KOSB)), all under the second in command of the 22nd Dragoons (Flails).

They were to flail routes through the minefields and force five crossings of the anti-tank ditch, which was to be bridged, by AVREs, with the infantry providing close protection and establishing bridgeheads on the enemy side of the obstacle. Meanwhile, 2 Gordons, advancing on foot, were to fight their way up the Kleve road across the anti-tank ditch and secure the rail crossing several hundred yards beyond (see map on page 140). The BAOR battlefield historian wrote:

> Two battalions [mounted in Kangaroos] were then to cross the ditch and capture the village [of Schottheide] with the following objectives:
> Right – 6 KOSB – HEVBERG ridge and the Right half of SCHOTT-HEIDE to inclusive the road junction 829541.
> Left – 8 RS – Left half of SCHOTTHEIDE to inclusive buildings at 828547.

In the next phase, the Wolfsberg and Hingstberg features overlooking Nütterden were to be secured as a stepping stone in the dash to Materborn, which 6 Royal Scots Fusiliers (6 RSF) moving up from brigade reserve was to help secure.

In the military adage that 'No plan survives contact with the enemy', 'the enemy' should in this case be replaced by 'mud'. Some armour had got forward with the leading brigades during 8 February, but the HQ BAOR historian describes the problem facing the Royal Engineers:

> The engineer story here is almost entirely one of very bad going and a search for alternative routes. The GUARDS managed to get their tanks through by throwing rubble and brushwood into the rapidly deteriorating route. This method would have been more effective if working parties had been made available all along the route. You will realize that engineer resources for such tasks are very limited within the division. The maximum working strength of the divisional engineers was about 360 without any other commitments.

Consequently, following in the muddy wake of the rest of the division, 44 Brigade had found it almost impossible to keep to time. Lieutenant Colonel Lord Tyrone, commanding officer of 4th Grenadier Guards, recalled that:

> 4 Tk GREN GDS was under command 44 (L) Bde for this operation. I went on ahead of the battalion in my scout car to keep in touch with Commander 44 (L) Bde, who was moving with 46 (H) Bde HQ. The route up was blocked by a mass of vehicles all trying to get forward, and progress was very slow, and the going indescribable ... From about 1800 hours onwards I spent my time ... hopefully looking to see if anyone was coming. But I had to keep on reporting no one in sight, and the Brigade Commander had continually to put off H Hour.

Major Pike, commanding 2 Squadron, was one of those that Lord Tyrone was waiting for. His Churchills were moving forward or Route AYR:

> As soon as the column left the metalled roads and took to the tank tracks our real difficulties began. It was very dark, and at each bend in the track both

the Flails and the AVRE bridges dug such deep grooves that it became very difficult for the heavy vehicles following behind. Eventually the whole column was diverted from its original approach and moved along a track from KREUZFUHRT to KRANENBURG. It reached the road junction 819553 about 0300 hours.

The divisional CRE, Lieutenant Colonel Wood, recalled that:

When it became apparent that the Breaching Force would have to be diverted on to the main road in order to reach FRASSELT, I decided that the only thing to do was to reconnoitre a route myself. I had gone forward on a motorcycle to HQ 44 (L) Bde. Still on a motorcycle with rain making matters more uncomfortable I found a route across to the main road at

AVREs negotiating deep muddy furrows left by those ahead of them.

KRANENBURG . . . and [found] 20 Fd Coy's bulldozer was clearing a route through the village. After the dozer had completed a twelve foot wide passage, I led it along the main road to the East. By artificial moonlight, the wet road glistened through a thick covering of branches and twigs, shot off the trees during the heavy bombardment. An R mine crate gave warning of mines. I had to lift some of this type of mine to make way for the dozer, which followed behind, sweeping away the branches and turning them to the side when the pile mounted too high. In the uncanny stillness the work went on until we reached the North end of the FRASSELT road. I then returned

The R Mine

The German Riegel mine 43 (*Sprengriegel*/R.Mi.43) was an anti-tank bar mine first encountered by the Allies in Normandy. Rather than the round Teller anti-tank mine, the R Mine's longer bar shape meant that fewer had to be laid to form an effective anti-tank barrier.

The mine was just under 3ft long and weighed 20lb, including an 8lb explosive content. It consisted of three main elements: the steel case, the explosive charge and the cover, which was linked to the various ways to the usual range of fuses. The R.Mi.43 was very sensitive and components corroded quickly, making it difficult to disarm. In addition, it had three anti-handling device options. The recommended method of clearance was to blow the mine in situ.*

The three main component parts of the R.Mi.43.

**Jane's Mines and Mine Clearance, 2005–2006* (Jane's Information Services, 2005).

A 95-mm Mark V Churchill support tank of 33 Armoured Brigade in the Overloon Museum that suffered an R Mine strike. The damage to the running gear is obvious, less so is the penetration of the hull that killed two of the crewmen.

> post haste to report that the armour could safely reach the start line by a good road.

To the rear of 44 Brigade's column, 8 Royal Scots' (8 RS) Kangaroos struggled to make headway on Route SKYE and cut across to the Kranenburg road. They were reported by the military police as being particularly badly delayed by the mud.

Even with a 'good road', Lord Tyrone described the difficulties of moving heavy armour at night:

> Finally in the small hours the columns started to rumble by; even then our troubles were by no means over, for one of the AVRE bridge-layers decided that it had carried its bridge far enough, the wire holding the bridge snapped and down it fell into the road. All vehicles then had to get over this entirely superfluous bridge. Needless to say, after a few had passed over, an RE contrivance pulling a sledge arrived, and got well and truly stuck. Having sorted this out, a further delay occurred. One of the AVRE bridge layers in going round a corner, on our one and only road, overbalanced and toppled over sideways. However, everything has to come to an end sometime and finally, at 0400 hour, the attack on the SIEGFRIED LINE duly went in.

The Ram Kangaroo was used by both the 49 APC Regiment RASC and 1st Canadian APC Regiment during VERITABLE.

The brigade's start line in Frasselt was held by 9 Cameronians and 2 A&SH, which had been in position since early evening, and by 0330 hours most of the breaching force had arrived in the village. However, they were incomplete and missing a number of commanders. Major Pike, who had earlier made his way forward with the sub-unit recce groups, performed miracles in reorganising essential equipment into the five assault teams. Of the armoured infantry, only 6 KOSB had reached Frasselt, but on foot 2nd Gordons had reached their FUP in Kranenburg. Brigadier Cumming-Bruce could see that there was little chance of other elements of the brigade including 8 RS and his reserve 6 RSF arriving for some time; he knew he could not delay any longer. Consequently, he ordered the breaching force into action and to attempt all five planned crossings of the anti-tank ditch, after which 6 KOSB was to cross the obstacle as soon as gaps had been made and capture Schottheide. At the same time the 2nd Gordons were to carry out their original task of clearing the vital main road from Kranenburg, via Nütterden to Kleve.

Finally at 0500 hours, as recorded in the 15th Division's history 'without the formality of assembly area or forming-up place, the armoured breaching force struggled into action somehow under the direction of Major Pike of the Grenadiers'.

Major Pike (2 Squadron) was detailed to support the right sector of the attack and force gaps with the armoured breaching force, and subsequently to enlarge the small initial bridgehead using infantry in Kangaroos supported by his tanks. He recorded that 'My Squadron task was therefore twofold':

> (i) To support the Flails across the obstacle and get established on the far side in a small bridgehead, i.e. The Breaching Operation.
> (ii) Subsequently to support 6 KOSB, the infantry battalion which was to enlarge the bridgehead.
>
> A similar task was set to 3 Sqn on my Left, which was [planned to be] supporting the ROYAL SCOTS and which was to make two crossings over the ditch.

Major Pike's half of the breaching force consisted of the following:

> Sqn HQ and three tps 22 DGNS
> *2 Sqn 4 Tk GREN GDS, less two troops
> One Sherdozer (borrowed from 4 Tank GREN GDS)
> Three AVRE bridges, with attendant fascines
> Three RE gapping parties in Kangaroos

The pre-planned target areas for the attack on the Siegfried Line and the advance to the Wolfsberg and Nütterden.

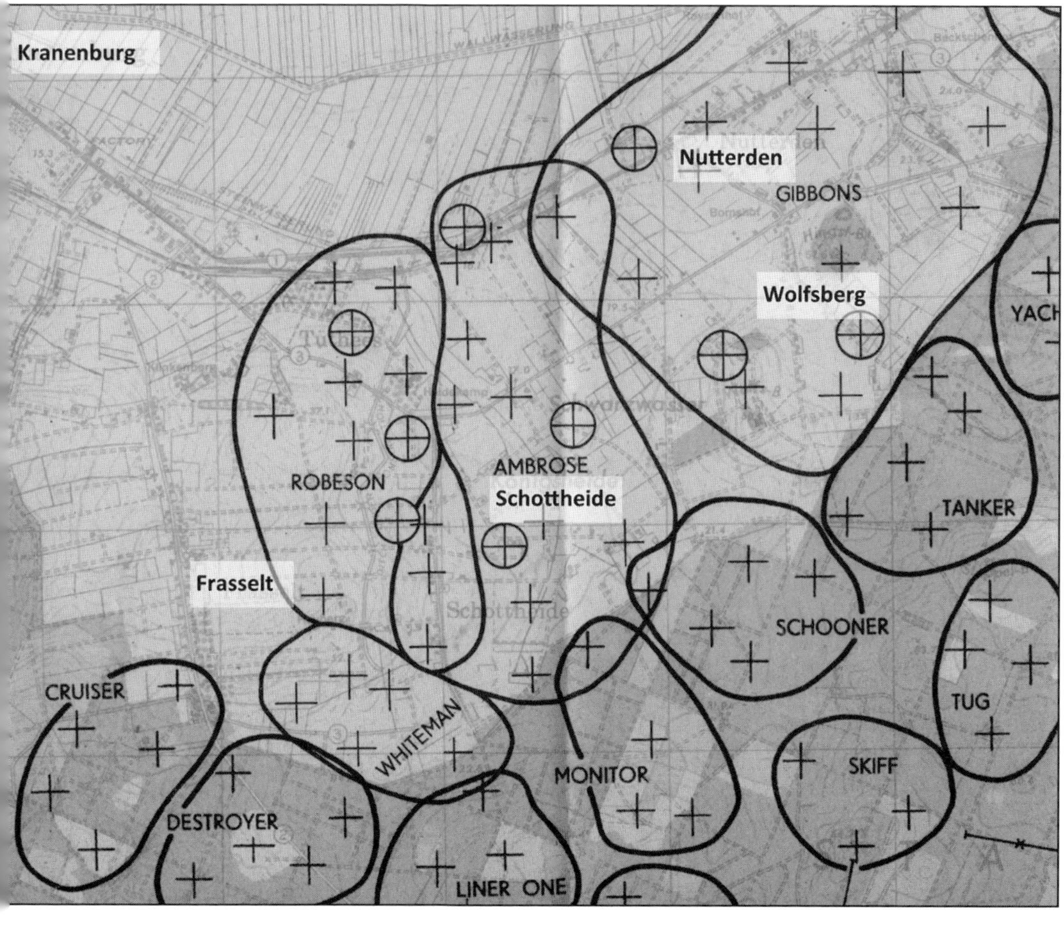

*One Coy, 6 KOSB in Kangaroos
*A Gunner FOO in a Churchill tank
(The units marked * were to be used to gain the initial bridgehead and support 6 KOSB thereafter).

The flails followed by an AVRE bridge layer with a small box girder bridge advanced to the anti-tank ditch via three of the more or less parallel tracks that led to it from the Frasselt road. If they had to approach across fields rather than tracks, it was the considered opinion of 44 Brigade that they would 'never have made it'. Major Pike explained the breaching procedure:

> The drill for the breaching operation on each lane was for the Flails to flail in echelon from the start line to the anti-tank ditch. They then were to flail to the flanks and allow the bridge-carrying assault vehicle [AVRE] to pass through and lay the bridge over the ditch. Once the bridge had been laid the Flails were to across and continue flailing until SCHOTTHEIDE had been reached.

With a heavy supporting bombardment falling on the Siegfried defences, the armoured breaching force started preparing the lanes to the anti-tank ditch. Few if any mines were found by the flails on the selected approaches and the anti-tank ditch in 2 Squadron's area was reached about 0415 hours. The obstacle that in principal should have been covered by German fire was approached with only one anti-tank engagement being recorded.

From the assault engineers' perspective, however, the approach to and the bridging of the anti-tank ditch was far from straightforward. Bridging was impeded by the fact that the sides of the anti-tank ditch collapsed thanks to the rain. Captain Du Vivier, of 279 Field Company, RE, recalled:

> On arriving opposite the entrance to Lane 2, there was no halt and the gun tank commander gave the order to move forward. We turned left along the track on the south side of the FRASSELT church. When the gun tanks got past the cemetery, they opened out to both sides and started shooting. The Flails went on along the track and we followed in the Kangaroo with a Sergeant and four sappers marking the track on the right-hand side as we went. The artificial moonlight provided by searchlights made things easily distinguishable 50 to 100 yards away and we could easily see the track. All went well up to the ditch. We got out of the Kangaroo 20 yards short of it and marked the last bit on foot.

Major Pike continued his account:

> Meanwhile, the sapper parties in Kangaroos had marked the lanes, and the AVRE bridges were called up to the ditch. It was still dark, and raining, and conditions were thoroughly unpleasant. However there did not appear to be any serious opposition, though there was a little shelling of the FRASSELT area. Our own artillery was still firing very heavily on SCHOTTHEIDE.

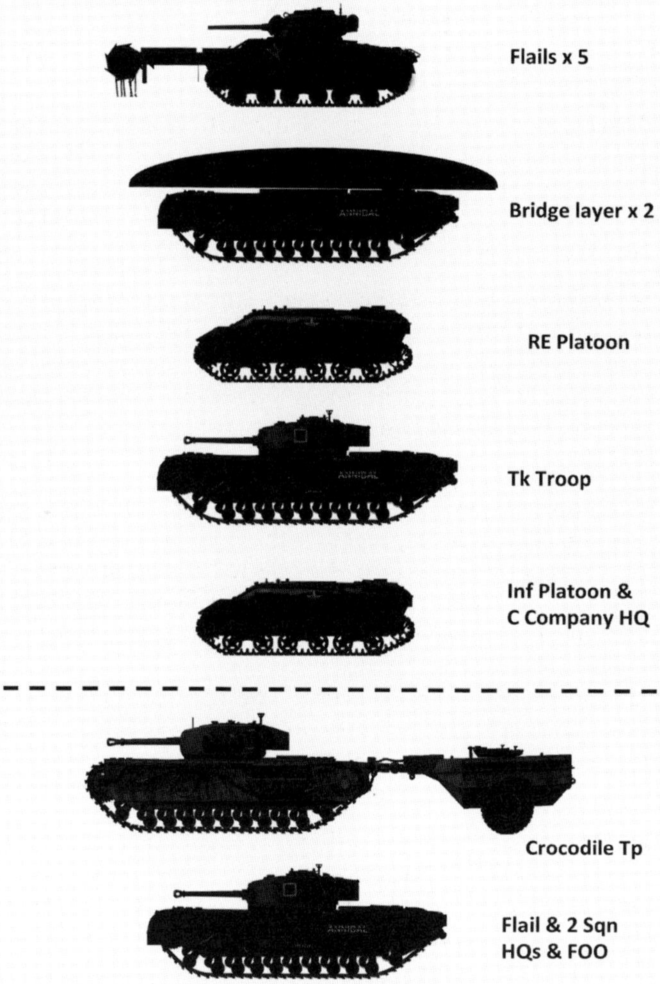

The planned composition of the Breaching Force for Lane 2, plus the right-flank headquarters. The deployment for the other lanes was similar.

44 (Lowland) Brigade's History: For the operation the brigade had in support the 4th Tank Grenadier Guards, one squadron of the 141st Regiment RAC (with Crocodile flamethrowers), one and a half squadrons of the 22nd Dragoons (with Flails), the 81st Assault Squadron Royal Engineers (with tanks carrying bridges and fascines), the 49th APC Regiment and one squadron of the 1st Canadian APC (equipped with Kangaroos), and the 2nd Gordons of the 227th Brigade (after completion of the first phase). The brigade was thus once again completely mounted in Kangaroos with a full team of armoured 'Funnies' – Churchill tanks, Flails, Crocodiles, and AVRE bridging tanks. There were also vast quantities of artillery, mortars, [land] mattresses and other pieces of ordnance in support. The real danger was that the ground would be so wet that this huge collection of armoured vehicles would get bogged going across country, and that the roads and tracks would not last for long.

An AVRE with a Small Box Gurder (SBG) bridge in its travelling position, which made it difficult and slow to get along the tree-lined roads and through villages.

> The AVRE bridge came up, was dropped, and dropped short [of the far bank]. The AVRE commander found that Lane 3 SBG AVRE had not crossed the start line yet, so he ordered it up Lane 2. It very soon arrived and dropped its bridge correctly in position immediately on the Left of the first one. Flails then crossed and flailed a short distance forward on to the track, setting off a mine. They then flailed forward to within a short distance of SCHOTTHEIDE, stopped, and proceeded to shoot at the village.

In the case of one of the lanes:

> Two flails got bogged almost immediately, and half an hour later three of the proposed lanes were useless. The Lane 2 crossing of the anti-tank ditch was established fairly quickly, and the first vehicles moved forward at about 0600 hours. Major Pike's squadron HQ crossed after the flails, followed by C Coy 6 KOSB in its Kangaroos, then the remaining two troops of tanks.

Captain Baggaley, of 6 KOSB, explained how C Company crossed into the bridgehead and the rest of the battalion followed:

> A few minutes after six o'clock the bridge on Lane 2 was working, and soon after C Company was ordered across the ditch. The other Companies, unable to move across country to Frasselt, soon followed, using the road through Kranenburg which was held by the 2nd Argyll and Sutherland Highlanders [*sic* Cameronians]. D Company went straight over Lane 2, swung right in Schotteheide and sent a Platoon on to the Hevberg feature which dominated the southern part of the village. A Company, under Major Malone, took the northern part of the village, and B Company, under Major Tinniswood, pushed some distance beyond them and seized some out-lying farms. A prisoner of the Fusilier Battalion of the 84th Division, captured by 46 Brigade, had said that his battalion had one company up in Frasselt with three behind, while the supporting artillery was in the area of Cleve. This proved fairly accurate, but the enemy had no fight left, and Schottheide was occupied with little difficulty.[1]

Lane 2 was, however, later blocked as 'an anti-tank gun fouled one of the bridges and brought movement forward to a halt until cleared'. Meanwhile, a new track used by the Germans through the defences had been located that ran south-east from the northern end of the road from Frasselt to Schottheide (marked X on the map on page 140). Fortunately, this track still had a bridge across the anti-tank ditch in place, which kept 44 Brigade moving forward.

Due to the sundry mishaps, as described earlier, initially only two gaps were created and of these only Lane 2 was opened in a timely manner using an SBG bridge, while another was made shortly afterwards using a fascine dropped by an AVRE. Other crossings of the anti-tank ditch were later established using bulldozers and further fascines. The main delay to operations was, however, not breaching the Siegfried Line but the continuing difficulties the battalions and squadrons were having in getting forward to maintain the attack's momentum. If the opposition had been in greater numbers and had greater resolve to fight, the breaching of the Siegfried Line could have been a difficult and protracted operation.

Meanwhile, 2nd Gordons and their supporting Churchills of the Left Flank Squadron of 3rd Tank Scots Guards were in action:

> The route allotted to them they had found obstructed by all manner of obstacles – mines, road-blocks, trenches – so it was almost dawn before they passed through the HLI in the ruins of Kranenburg to force the Siegfried Line where it crossed the main Kranenburg–Kleve road. An hour later A Company reported that they had captured intact the road-bridge over the main anti-tank ditch. The large trees, which lined the road, had not been felled, though they had all been prepared with charges ready for felling. Quite clearly the bombardment had completely disorganised the defence.[2]

In less than an hour the Gordons and their supporting Churchills had broken through the Siegfried Line, finding that not only had the Germans failed to blow the roadside trees they had prepared for demolition but the road where it crossed the anti-tank ditch had not been cratered either. The bridge layers that had caused the battalion so much trouble on the route forward during the night march were not needed after all. Now was the time to dash to Materborn.

The AVRE Fascine

The use of fascines in warfare, usually bundles of sticks, is as old as the necessity to fill ditches or moats and has been used by military engineers since ancient times. With the advent of anti-tank ditches, in the case of VERITABLE the presence of numerous drainage ditches, they were used extensively in the Rhineland by British and Canadian engineers.

The vehicles in the photograph opposite are standard Armoured Vehicle Royal Engineer, which was either based on the obsolescent Mk III or IV Churchill tank. When needed AVREs were fitted with locally produced wooden racks to carry the fascines, often as can be seen here varying in construction. The turret would be traversed left at the nine o'clock position and the fascine would be freed by releasing the securing cable, allowing it to fall in front of the tank. When fascines were not required, the T-shaped wooden framework was simply removed and the AVRE would revert to its usual role. Occasionally, the fascines were carried on the engine decks, but this could result in them catching fire from the hot exhausts!

An example of the type of fascine used to fill anti-tank ditches photographed during 79th Armoured Division's trials at Orford Ness prior to the invasion.

An AVRE carrying a fascine. While the driver could see where he was going from his normal position, it was a different matter for the commander!

One type of cradle for carrying a fascine.

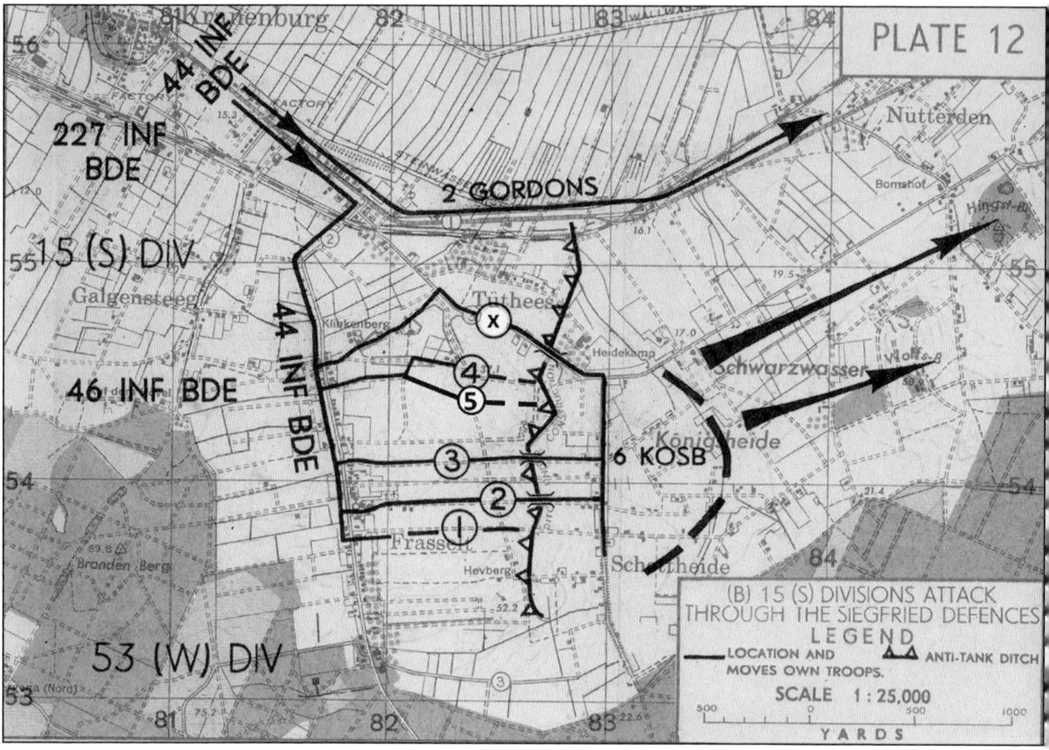

15 Scottish Division's attack on the Siegfried Line early on 9 February 1945.

The infantry of 44 Lowland Brigade and the tanks of 6 Guards Armoured Brigade were through the vaunted Siegfried Line with comparative ease, but at 0800 hours there was still no sign of the brigade reserve 6 RSF, which was due to take over the advance east. Consequently, '6 KOSB were ordered to push straight on to the Wolfsberg feature without waiting for the Fusiliers [6 RSF] who were making slow progress owing to the mud.' Meanwhile, on the adjacent Kleve road axis, 'Meeting little to stop them other than mud and a few R type mines, the Gordons reached Nütterden, which they cleared by 10 A.M., taking two hundred or so very "bomb-happy" prisoners in the large concrete bunkers.' Such was the power of the bombardment in Target Area GIBBONS (see map on page 133).

The Gordons in Nütterden advanced to secure the Hingestberg at 0830 hours, while the KOSB's A and B companies, having cleared their respective parts of Schottheide, had re-mounted their Kangaroos and motored another mile to seize the Wolfberg. Both of these features overlooked Nütterden and the vital road axis to Kleve. Captain Bagley wrote:

> At H Hour A Coy went straight for the WOLFSBERG feature, fanning out across country on a broad front. Unfortunately, the leading APC and another were hit by bazooka fire as they moved on to the hill. One driver was killed while a platoon commander and several others were seriously wounded. The platoon serjeant quickly reorganised the platoon and led it on to its objective. In the meantime, a troop of 88 mm self-propelled guns had been captured by the remainder of the company.

The 2 Gordons and the tanks of the 4 Scots Guards at the western end of Kranenburg preparing for the attack.

> B Coy moved in its APCs up the road to the Hingstberg feature and there joined the troop of tanks of the Grenadier Guards. While clearing this feature B Coy seized a large dugout, which, judging from the wireless and telephone equipment inside, must have been a headquarters. On this feature B Coy also captured eight officers, including the Commander of 184 Arty Regt and a battalion commander. Although the distance between these two features and SCHOTTHEIDE is short there was no communication between these two companies and the rest of the battalion, except the tank net.

Of this exploitation the BAOR historian commented that: 'From the armoured point of view it is for consideration how costly the operations of these two companies might have been had the enemy had a well laid out tank defence.' It is, however, worth noting again the role of artillery fire power: 84th Medium Regiment RA engaged targets on the two features for five minutes prior to the assault and 1 Middlesex supplemented this with 200 4.2in mortar bombs.

The advance of the KOSB had, however, been pre-empted by the second-in-command of 2 Squadron. Having supported the KOSB in their attack on Schottheide, enveloping the village as normal, they had encountered no opposition. Consequently, while Schottheide was still being secured by the KOSB, the two troops of Churchills had pressed on to the Hingstberg. Major Pike 'finding the tanks securely in possession of the hill', returned to the rest of his squadron,

The Kangaroo APC

The first tracked armoured personnel carriers had been used in the First World War, when Mark V tanks were adapted to carrying troops, normally specialists such as machine gunners and engineers. Between the war the British Experimental Mechanised Force identified the need for APCs for the infantry be able to keep up with the tanks, but the proposal was shelved due to cost and a reluctance to embrace wholesale mechanisation and armour.

In the Second World War the gap was filled in British armoured divisions by the adoption of American half-tracks, but these were open topped and with the armour only being proof against small arms fire and light shell splinters. Following a series of costly assaults in Normandy, where progress was only made by battering away at the enemy and accepting far higher than ever anticipated infantry casualties, Lieutenant General Simonds came up with a solution. In order to provide his infantry sufficient mobility and protection to penetrate 5 miles into the enemy defences, he converted seventy-two American M7 Priest self-propelled guns into armoured personnel carriers, nicknamed kangaroos, by removing the gun and ancillary equipment and thus making space for ten to fourteen infantrymen. Their debut in the opening phase of Operation TOTALIZE was little short of spectacular.

As originally agreed, the Priests had to be returned to the Americans, but across 21st Army Group the idea of the Kangaroo had taken root and the first hundred

A 'Defrocked' Priest Kangaroo photographed with 51st Highland Division during Operation TOTALIZE. Most of the later Kangaroos had a .30 Browning in a ball mount in the hull, which dispensed with the small auxiliary turret for the machine gun.

A convoy of Ram Kangaroos on the move. It can be clearly seen that it had a much lower profile but could carry fewer passengers.

obsolescent Ram Mark II Cruiser tanks were converted in August 1944 for the Canadians. However, at a meeting at Headquarters Twenty First Army Group, on 9 October 1944 it was agreed that both First Canadian and Second British armies would raise an Armoured Personnel Carrier Regiment of two squadrons using Ram Shermans. Each regiment was established to be able to carry two infantry battalions, with its squadrons a battalion each, a troop of Kangaroos an infantry company and a section of three Kangaroos a platoon. A fleet of 650 Ram gun tanks and previously converted Ram armoured gun towers became Kangaroos.

The Ram Mk II was used exclusively in north-west Europe, providing up to 75mm of protection to the ten infantry passengers and two crew rather than the 12mm of the half-track. The Kangaroo, however, weighed 23.5 tons.* It retained its hull machine gun, but provision was also made for a second, pintle-mounted, 30 calibre Browning. Communication for the crew and passengers was via a No. 19 radio set.

In the opening stages of Operation VERITABLE, the two units, 49th APC and 1st Canadian APC regiments, were sufficient to mount four infantry battalions and elements of the Royal Engineers breaching force.

Both APC regiments served with 79th Armoured Division, with 1st CDN APC Regiment being the only Canadians in that formation.

A variety of armoured vehicles, mainly Mark III Shermans and the M7 Priest self-propelled guns, were also converted to Kangaroos in Italy during the winter of 1944/45. They were used in the Po Valley offensive, Operation GRAPESHOT, to provide protection to increasingly scarce infantry and to provide mobility to those troops accompanying armoured formations. Production and organisation of Kangaroo APCs was altogether more ad hoc in Italy than it was in North West Europe.

*The Sherman Mk III and the Priest were used for conversion to Kangaroos in northern Italy towards the end of the war.

A Ram Kangaroo in Germany.

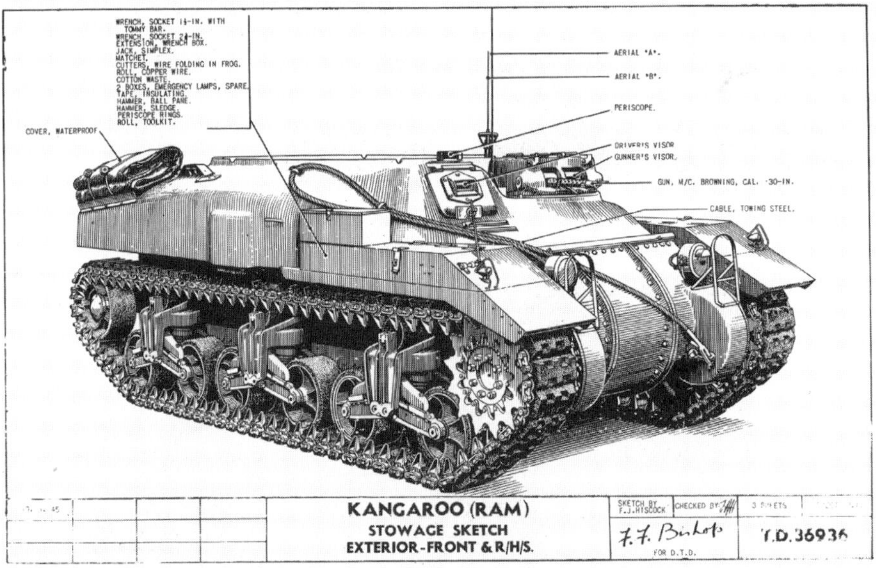

A technical drawing of the Ram Kangaroo.

The organisation of an APC regiment

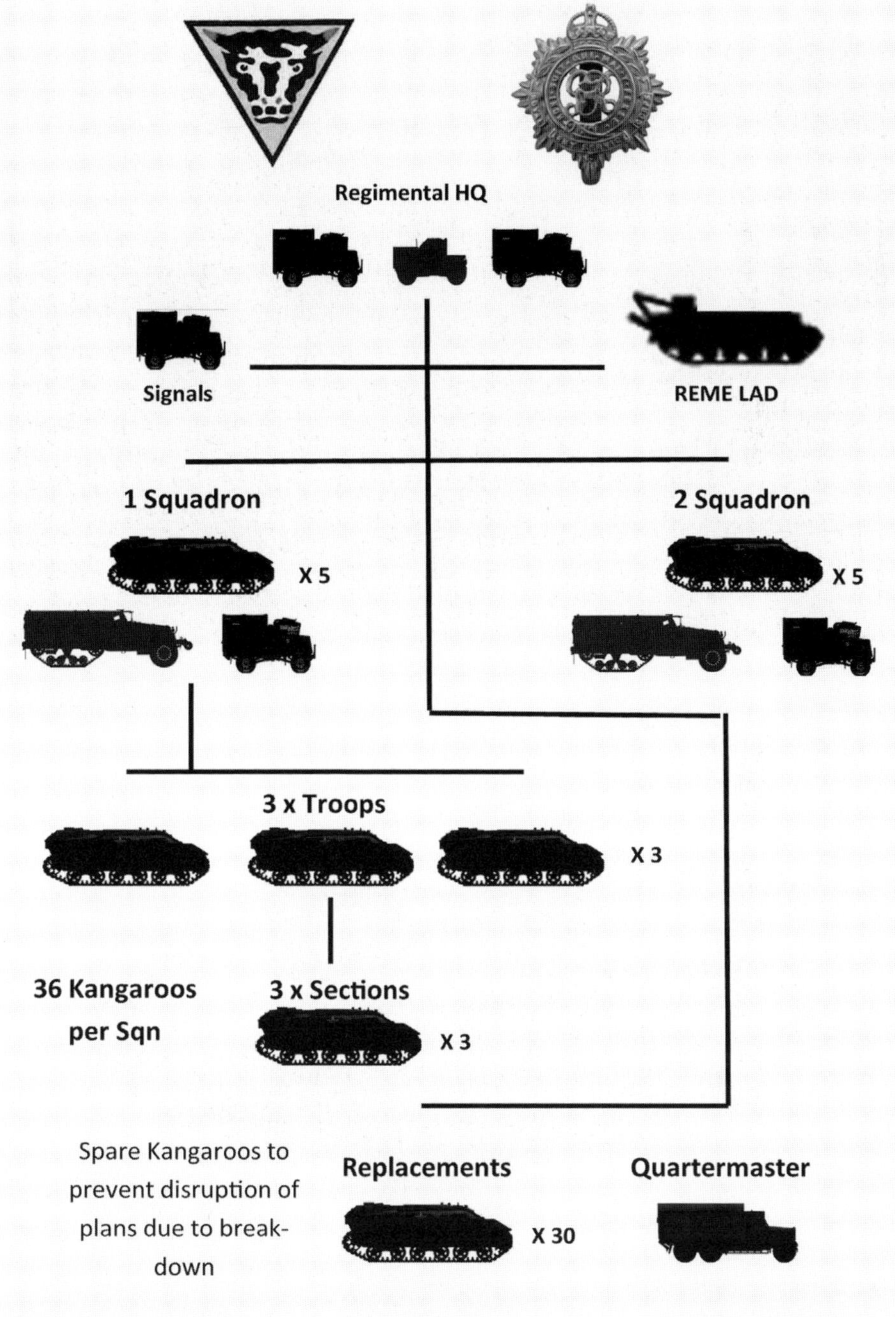

Infantry sections boarding Kangaroos. The only way in and out of the vehicle was over its sides.

leaving the second-in-command, and the two troops had to weather the friendly artillery concentrations fired in support of A and B companies' attack. When B Company arrived in its Kangaroos at 0930 hours, they were rather surprised to be greeted by the Guardsmen.

53rd Welsh Division in the Reichswald

Advancing alongside the 15th Scottish Division in the northern half of the Reichswald, the 53rd Welsh Division was fighting its way east through the forest. The initial attack on 8 February was delivered by 71 Brigade, which faced very similar problems to the Scots in fighting through the forward defences, plus breaking into the Reichswald. The Welsh historian recorded that:

> After we had crossed the initial belt of organised defences, which included anti-tank ditches, *schumines* and fortified farms and villages, we now faced our biggest obstacle – the natural fortress of the Reichswald.

Inside the forest immediately to the right of 44 Lowland Brigade, 160 Brigade was tasked to push on to the key terrain of the Stoppelberg, which lay at the north-easterly tip of the forest between Nütterden and the Materborn feature.

It had been planned for 160 Brigade's leading battalions to follow on straight through positions secured by 71 Brigade and secure the line of the Frasselt–Hekkens road by 1600 hours, but the brigade had spent most of the previous day waiting and, as in the case of 44 Lowland Brigade, timings had slipped badly.

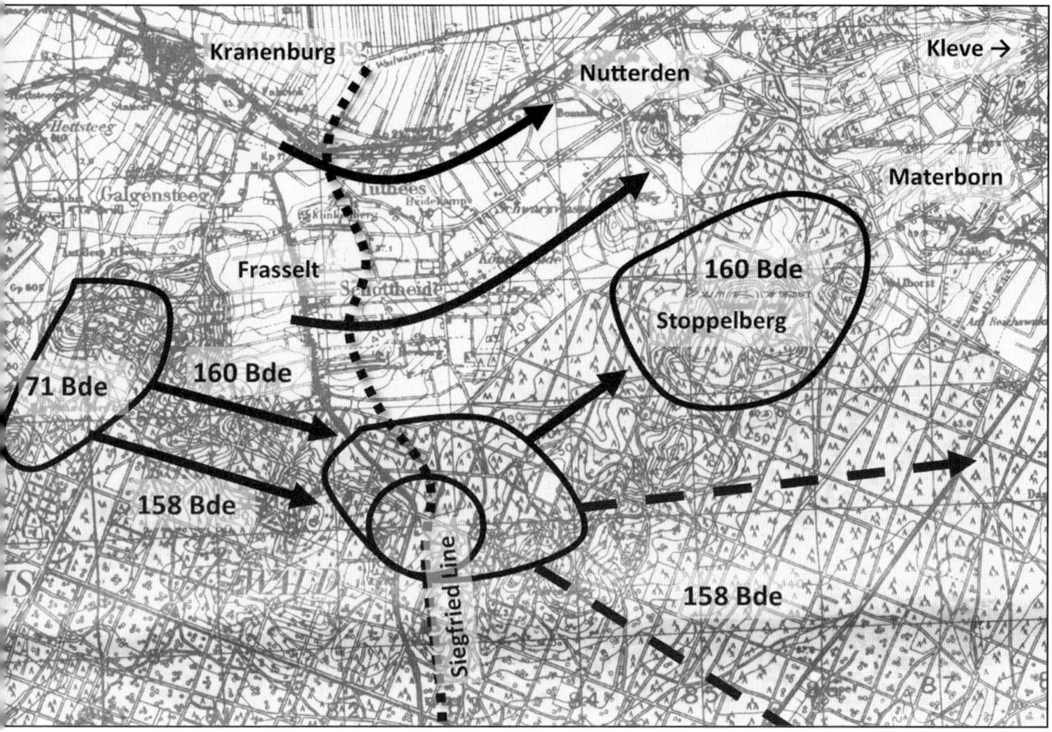

53rd Welsh Division's plan for the clearance of the northern part of the Reichswald.

The Welsh diarists all tell familiar stories of their difficulties, and it was not until after 1815 hours that 160 Brigade's move from the western edge of the forest to their start line secured in the forest by 71 Brigade began.

As was the case with 44 Brigade, the Welsh battalions' armoured support had difficulty in getting forward through the mud and when the infantry finally crossed their start line at 2300 hours only 6 RWF had Churchills with them. Inevitably, 160 Brigade's 2,000-yard advance through the forest, along the tracks and rides, in darkness was slow. Due to the threat of mines the tanks of 9 RTR avoided the tracks, with the Churchills bulldozing their way through the trees following one behind the other. The squadron reported that the Welsh infantry appreciated 'their noisy movement that had been comforting and helpful in traversing dense woodland full of disorganised enemy troops'.

The surviving Germans, in accordance with General Fiebig's order, were mostly withdrawing to the Siegfried Line, so opposition on the 2,000-yard advance to the Frasselt–Hekkens road was light.

The 1 East Lancs and 6 Royal Welsh Fusiliers and their tanks continued their advance beyond the road to attack the Siegfried Line defences, which they reached at 0005 hours, some six hours behind schedule, and found them to be thinly manned and the resistance patchy. In several instances, however, the East Lancs had a stiff fight involving hand-to-hand combat with bayonet and grenade to clear trenches and bunkers, taking some fifty prisoners. On the left of 6 RWF's advance, the tanks of C Squadron reported resistance that 'needed dealing with'. The battalions reported themselves firm and digging in at 0200 hours.

COMPOSITE RATION PACK

TYPE A

(14 men for one day)

Contents and Suggested Use

BREAKFAST	Tea	*	3 tins (2 tall, 1 flat—Tea, Sugar & Milk Mixture)
	†Sausage (1 hr.)		2 tins
	Biscuit	*	1 tin
	Margarine	*	1 tin

(* Items marked thus are also to provide for other meals)

DINNER	†Steak & Kidney Pudding (½ hr.)	11 tins	
	†Vegetables (¾ hr.)	4 tins	(2 large, 2 small)
	Tinned Fruits	2 tins	
TEA	Tea	—	(* see above)
	Biscuit	—	(* see above)
	Margarine	—	(* see above)
	Jam	1 tin	
SUPPER	†Baked Beans (¾ hr.)	3 tins	
	Biscuit	—	(* see above)
EXTRAS	Cigarettes	2 tins	(1 round, 1 flat—7 cigarettes per man)
	Sweets	1 tin	
	Salt	—	packed with sweets above
	Matches	—	packed with sweets above
	Chocolate	—	(1 slab per man—packed with biscuit)
	Latrine Paper		

DIRECTIONS

Tea, Sugar and Milk Powder.—Use a dry spoon and sprinkle powder on heated water and bring to the boil, stirring well. 3 heaped teaspoonfuls to 1 pint of water.

† May be eaten hot or cold. To heat, place unopened tins in boiling water for minimum period as indicated. Sausage may be fried (using margarine) if preferred.

Wt. /G.2618 1,568M in 7 Sorts 6/42 KJL/652 **Gp. 698/3**
Wt. 41076/5747 200,625/5 Sorts 12/42 KJL/3222 **Gp. 698/3** **J.6393**

COMPOSITE RATION PACK

TYPE B

(14 men for one day)

Contents and Suggested Use

BREAKFAST	Tea	*	3 tins (2 tall, 1 flat—Tea, Sugar & Milk Mixture)
	†Bacon (1 hr.)		3 tins
	Biscuit	*	1 tin
	Margarine	*	1 tin

(* Items marked thus are also to provide for other meals)

DINNER	†Steak and Kidney (½ hr.)	10 tins	
	†Vegetables (¾ hr.)	4 tins	(2 large, 2 small)
	†Pudding (1 hr.)	3 tins	(2 large, 1 small)
TEA	Tea	—	(* see above)
	Biscuit	—	(* see above)
	Margarine	—	(* see above)
	Jam		1 tin
SUPPER	†Soup, Scotch Broth (1 hr.)	2 tins	(mix with equal quantity of water)
—	Biscuit	—	(* see above)
EXTRAS	Cigarettes	2 tins	(1 round, 1 flat—7 cigarettes per man)
	Sweets	1 tin	
	Salt	—	packed with sweets above
	Matches	—	packed with sweets above
	Chocolate		1 slab per man packed with biscuit
	Latrine Paper		

DIRECTIONS

Tea, Sugar and Milk Powder.—Use a dry spoon and sprinkle powder on heated water and bring to the boil, stirring well. 3 heaped teaspoonfuls to 1 pint of water.

†May be eaten hot or cold. To heat, place unopened tins in boiling water for minimum period as indicated. Bacon, and pudding cut into ½-inch slices, may be fried (using margarine) if preferred.

Wt. /G.2618 1,568M in 7 Sorts 6/42 KJL/652 Gp. 698/3
Wt. /G.2341 1001M in 7 Sorts 9/42 KJL/1987 Gp. 698/3

A day's menu for one of the types of Composite (Compo).

A fourteen-man Compo ration box of tinned and packeted food.

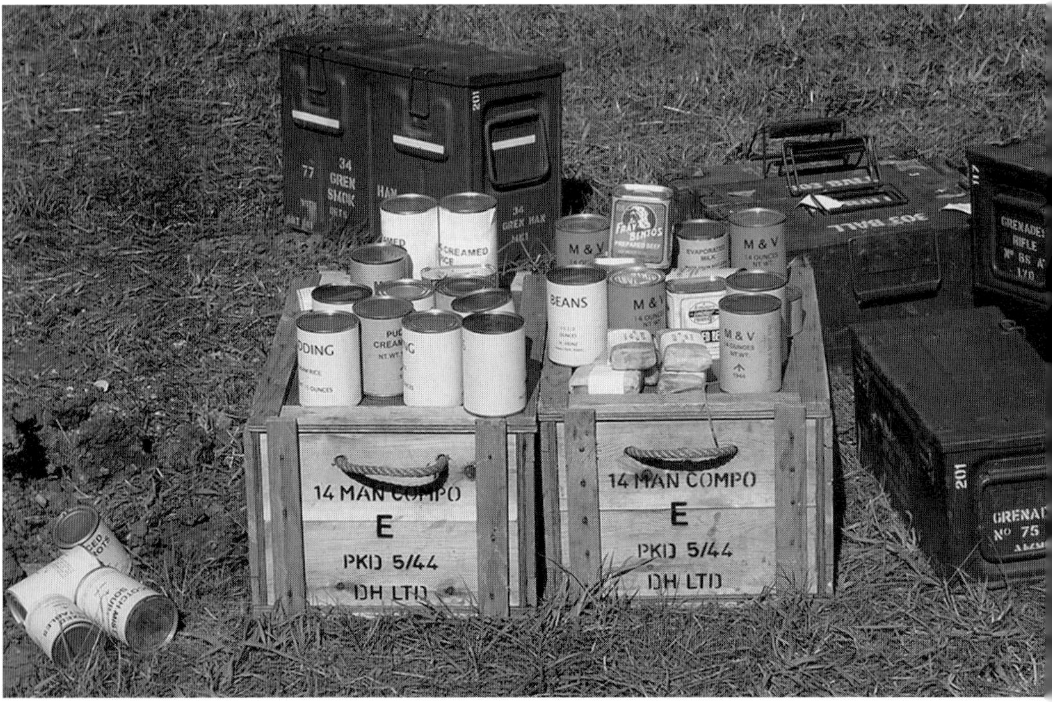

The Siegfried Line defences in the forest had proved to be far less formidable than the glimpses through gaps in the canopy of pine trees in aerial photographs had led the planners to believe. It was later discovered that the Germans had considered that the Reichswald was itself sufficient to deter attack. One German officer taken prisoner confessed that: 'Our appreciation of the forest was that it was impassable to tanks.'

At 0730 hours the 4 Welch and 2 Monmouthshires took over the advance east to the Stoppelberg alongside 44 Brigade on their left, who secured the Wolfberg and Hingestberg features.

15th Scottish Division Seize the Materborn Feature

By 1000 hours 44 (Lowland) Brigade had broken through the Siegfried Line and were preparing, in the next phase of the divisional plan, to secure the high ground of Bresserberg and Esperance, collectively referred to as the Materborn feature. General Barber's intent had been to commit 46 and 227 brigades to the renewed advance, but their transport and supplies were still well to the rear, stuck in traffic and mired in mud. Due to the critical nature of the Materborn feature and as the operation was 'already considerably behind schedule timings', 44 Brigade had to continue the advance. Fortunately, casualties to men and equipment had been nothing like as serious at the Siegfried Line as anticipated and 6 KOSB and 8 RS, which had now reached the front, could continue eastwards in place of the two brigades. Brigadier Cumming-Bruce, realising the urgency, ordered the KOSB to once again mount their Kangaroos and with the Royal Scots also aboard, advance to secure the Materborn feature. To release the KOSB, the Brigade's dismounted battalion, 6 Royal Scots Fusiliers, replaced them on the Hingstberg and Wolfsberg features. Colonel Richardson, the commanding officer of 6 KOSB, recalled that:

> It was with no enthusiasm that I received instructions to push on yet again and capture BRESSERBERG. It was obvious that C and D coys [now in reserve] would have to be brought up to carry out this attack supported by 2 Sqn 4 Tk GREN GDS, whilst A and B coys, having handed over to 6 RSF, would have purely consolidation roles. The battalion group was to move by the most direct route, through the gap in the woods at 857557 along the road as far as 869558.

Still located back at Schottheide, 6 KOSB's battalion headquarters was not in radio communication with A and B companies forward on the Wolfsberg. Consequently, as the attack was laid on at short notice, C and D companies, now in reserve, remounted the Kangaroos and motored forward. Meanwhile, the Royal Scots had a straightforward passage of lines through 2nd Gordons via the Kleve road, as recorded by the BAOR historian:

> At 1100 hours 8 RS moved through NUTTERDEN capturing twenty prisoners on the [south-western] outskirts of the village. There was fifteen

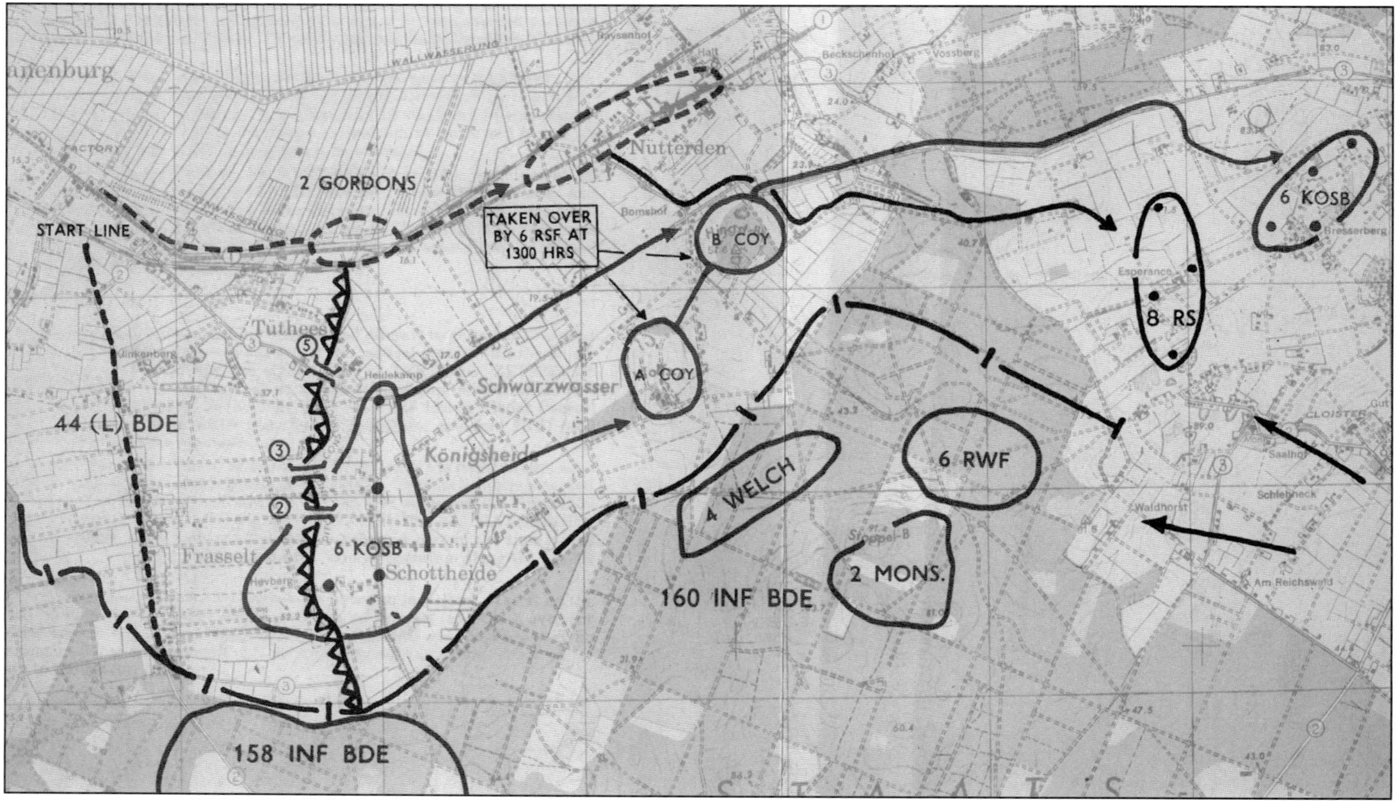

The Advance of 44 (Lowland) Brigade to the Materborn feature during 9 February 1945.

> minutes delay when the battalion moved across 6 KOSB, but no great hindrance was caused to either battalion. The leading company 8 RS reached ESPERANCE at 1500 hours. There was little fighting, and the battalion was established in that area some two hours later and made contact with troops of 53 (W) Div [in the forest] on the Right.

Captain Baggaley recalled how 6 KOSB was:

> ordered to push right forward, round the tip of the Reichswald, and seize Bresserberg, a feature commanding the approaches to Kleve itself. Here the track ran between two woods, and on either side the widening fields were found to be mined. D Company led, picking up A and B Companies and the tanks [2 Squadron of 4 Tk GREN GDS] on the way, and all speed was made to this vital hill. We arrived only just in time. As it was, there were some sharp engagements on the hill, but had we delayed, the enemy would certainly have had time to occupy it in strength.

During this speedy advance made under pressure from the chain of command, battalion signal logs are full of protests that they were outstripping the artillery support of their 25-pounder guns. The gunners were having considerable difficulty in getting out of their gun position, making their way through the traffic on appalling routes and deploying on saturated ground. Consequently, they were rarely available to engage opposition the infantry encountered during the advance, but fortunately the battalion's mortar platoons were able to deal with the limited enemy resistance. The Bresserberg and Esperance were however, subjected to pre-planned shoots by the guns of the AGRAs' medium regiments (target areas

Ram Kangaroos during the Rhineland campaign.

KUNZ and ROY) and the two features were occupied almost according to plan. Colonel Richardson recalled: 'The troops from 84 Inf Div did not offer much resistance except in C Coy area, where there was some stiff fighting, but, with the assistance of Crocodiles, the defences were overcome. Twelve officers and two hundred and fifty other rank prisoners were captured.'

About 1700 hours, however, while the reserve companies were still organising their defensive positions, 6 KSOB was attacked by units of the 7th *Fallschirmjäger* Division, which had just arrived too late to reinforce the enemy's defences on the vital ground. Captain Baggaley noted:

> The parachutists proved to be very aggressive, and our occupation of the position was disturbed by a strong patrol which worked along the trenches near Battalion Headquarters and attacked the Platoon of medium machine gunners as they were arriving. The position was, however, secured and the enemy forestalled in his attempt to occupy the feature, which was the key to Cleve.

This extract of the defences overprint map shows that the Materborn feature area was well prepared for defence, but at this stage, with 84th Division having failed to fall back, they were not occupied in strength.

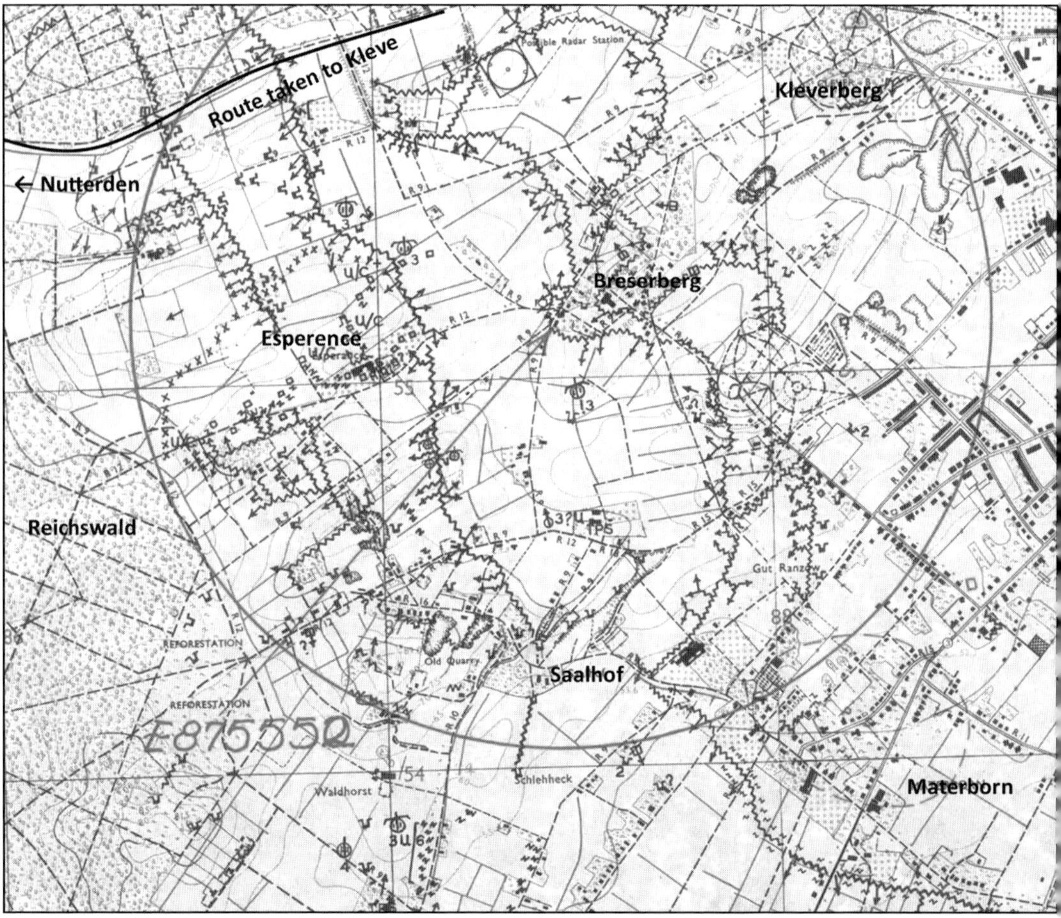

15th (Scottish) Recce Regiment had the usual mix of armoured cars and carriers.

After what were several sharp encounters in the area of the Materborn cemetery the enemy withdrew, but a patrol returned after dark and infiltrated into part of 6 KOSB's area and inflicted casualties: 'Three machine guns were knocked out before the patrol was driven off.'

Meanwhile, the Scots' divisional Recce Regiment mounted armoured car patrols beyond Esperance and Bresserberg, in an endeavour to secure routes for the advance of the 43rd (Wessex) Division. During the night, contact was made between 44 Brigade and patrols from 2nd Monmouthshire (53rd Welsh Division).

53rd Welsh Division's Advance to the Stoppelberg

After a torturous night march, at 0730 hours it was light enough among the trees for 160 Brigade's advance north to the Stoppelberg to begin, now supported by the Churchills of A and B squadron of 9 RTR. Leading the way, 4 Welch advanced some 2,000 yards following the northern edge of the Reichswald to secure two features just inside the forest, while 2nd Monmouthshires – starting out an hour and a half later at 0900 hours – was to secure the wooded high ground of the Stoppelberg. Major Lewis recorded:

> So bad were conditions 2 Mons and B Squadron encountered in the wood early in their advance they attempted to come out of the forest into 15th Scottish Division's area near Schottheide but this move was thwarted by German anti-tank guns that were later dealt with by the Scots. The Churchills of B Squadron, despite the earlier passage of A Squadron along the edge of the Reichswald, also came under fire from a couple of artillery

pieces sited in the open ground north of the forest. They were promptly engaged and knocked out by 95mm high explosive at a range of 2,200 yards.[3]

By 0903 hours, 4 Welch had 'assaulted and captured their objectives against slight opposition', taking three officers and 101 German other ranks prisoner. An hour later, 2 Mons passed through their rear and had occupied the Stoppelberg by midday, much to their surprise, without a fight. Also against scant opposition, 6 RWF, now mounted on the tanks of C Squadron, had secured positions near the edge of the forest east of the Stoppelberg, except one small tongue of wood held by the newly arrived II Battalion, 16 *Fallschirmjäger* Regiment. This too was cleared after a sharp fight and another fifty prisoners were taken.

From this position 6 RWF were able to see German reinforcements heading north-east on the Herkkens–Materborn road and were able to harass enemy infantry, motor vehicles, tanks and staff car with artillery fire. This included helping 8 RS by engaging a German infantry position centred on four machine guns that was holding up their advance.

During 9 February the soldiers of 15th Scottish and 53rd Welsh Division had done very well to break the Siegfried Line and reach the Materborn and Stoppelberg features, and to get there before the bulk of the *Fallschirmjäger* arrived. If the Scots had been any later the German defences once again could have been bolstered and the story of the battle for the Reichswald and Kleve could have been very different.

3rd Canadian Division on the Floodplain

On 9 February, in common with the other three Allied divisions in action in Operation VERITABLE, 3rd Canadian Division, thanks to delays the previous evening, began the day completing its Phase 1 tasks out on the Rhine flats. Overnight, the river levels had continued to rise rapidly, some 18 inches in twelve hours, thanks to the combination of melt water and heavy rain. On top of that, during the day matters got worse, with the inundation of the floodplain and flanking roads continuing to increase in both depth and extent. It is, therefore, not surprising that operations out on the floodplain were 'becoming increasingly difficult'. This was, of course, not just a problem for the Canadians and the Scots but also for the Germans. For the Scots, the use of the road through Kranenburg was vital, and the Germans, who had not expected such high water levels, were both fixed and isolated in their positions out on the floodplain.

With the villages of Zyfflich, Niel, Leuth and Zandpol in Canadian hands, 8 and 9 brigades were to continue the advance east across the flooded country to complete the capture of the day one objectives. The problem, however, of mustering the limited number of Buffaloes amidst competing demands for their services, which included evacuation of the wounded and prisoners, resupply and the time spent loading the infantry companies, all reduced the tempo of operations.

The attack overnight had reached a point where, as the Rhine meandered, the floodplain widened significantly, and on this increased frontage 9 Canadian

Brigade was deployed to resume the advance on the right, with an advance from the area of Niel to take Keeken and the village of Mehr. On the left, 8 Canadian Brigade was to continue its advance to Millingen, which stood on a relatively large 'island' amidst the flood waters. Meanwhile, 7 Canadian Brigade remained in reserve, ready to take over the advance to the division's second set of objectives, the extension of the Siegfried Line out to the Rhine flats.

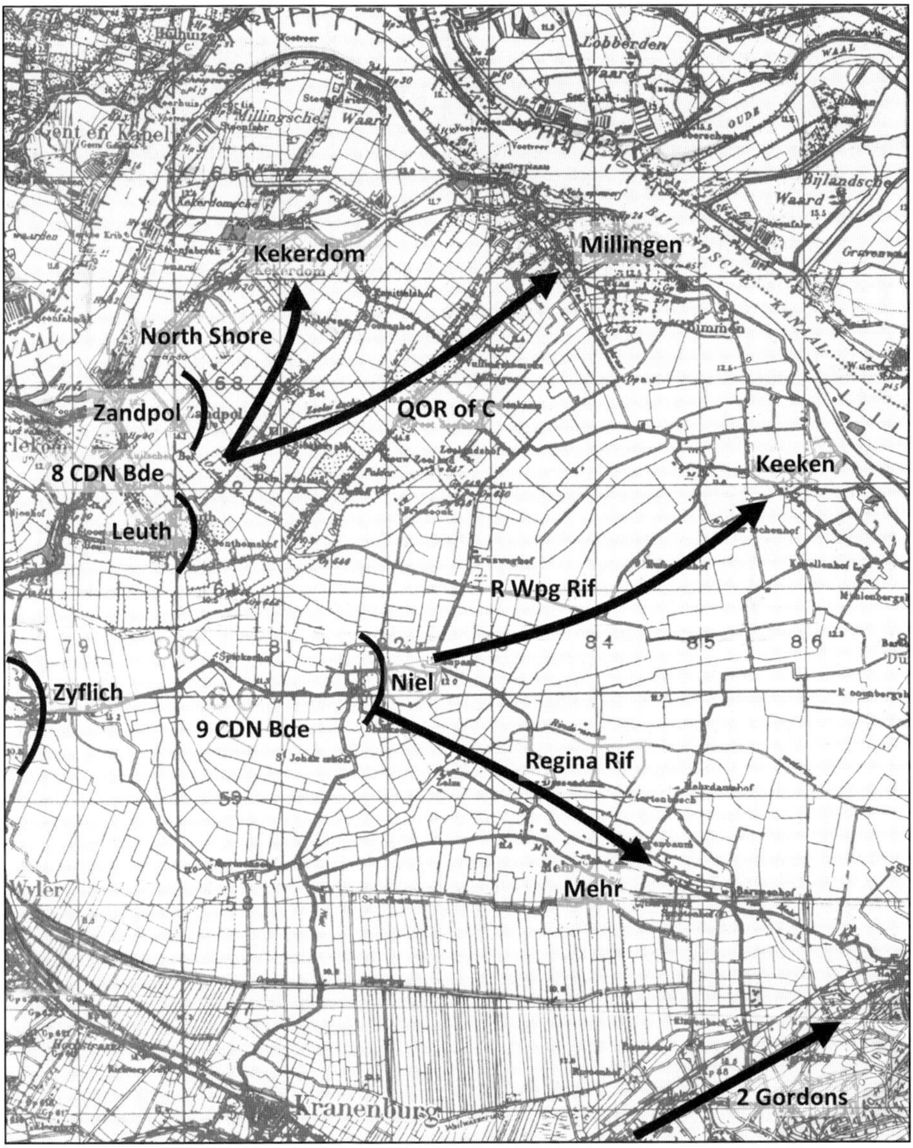

Canadian operations from villages seized by dawn by 9 February to complete Phase 1.

Smoke Operations

First Canadian Army's Report on Smoke Screens:

> A notable feature of the division's advance was the tremendous smokescreen laid by four smoke companies under Army command. Since the sector was dominated by high ground on the other side of the Rhine, a continuous smoke screen was laid along the south bank. By the end of the operation a continuous line of smoke belched from some 8,500 generators which had been laid for a distance of 30,000 yards. 400,500 gallons of fog oil and 40,000 gallons of derv were used to produce the screen which was considered 'a contributing factor in the success of the operation. Formations were more than satisfied.'

The smoke was designed to screen the west bank from observation from the other side of the river. It was started by First Canadian in the Beek area and as the Canadians advanced it eventually extended by the time of the Rhine crossing south-east for 66 miles past Wesel to the Ruhr. The screen was maintained by four Pioneer Corps smoke companies made up of 1,350 men, who one old soldier described as 'ineligible for any other arm of the service, with a sprinkling of intellectuals considered to be of no military value elsewhere'.

Zinc chloride smoke generators lined the Rhine dykes.

As the advance progressed, smoke generation equipment replaced the generators, burning vast amounts of fog oil.

Now, in fighting their way forward in daylight, an important new factor came into play; the Canadians out on the floodplain were overlooked by dominating higher ground on the opposite bank of the Rhine from where German artillery observers and machine gunners were able to see over the dykes. The threat they posed, which was greater the further east the Canadians advanced, was negated by extension of the prodigious use of smoke.

On the left flank, Brigadier Roberts ordered the North Shore Regiment to press on and capture Kekerdom. This they did with C and D companies aboard Buffaloes, and under cover of a short bombardment they occupied the village around mid-morning, with the handful of Germans surrendering promptly. A further attack planned on some factory buildings nearby proved to be unnecessary as they were already under water. With Kekerdom secured, the Queen's Own Regiment of Canada took over the advance on Millingen, which was reached at about 1430 hours. Again, there was negligible opposition and a handful of prisoners taken. At the same time the Royal Winnipeg Rifles was directing its efforts on Keeken. This small village was occupied by 1600 hours and a company pushed on across what was a substantial island to secure the Customs House on the banks of the course of the Old Rhine. Meanwhile, the Regina Rifles also advanced in Buffaloes on Mehr, which, despite expectations, was not held by the enemy.

The capture of these Phase 1 objectives had taken all day thanks to the 'ground' conditions and as the Canadian official historian commented '... the rising water

The Chaudières being rescued from the houses of Leuth by Buffaloes during the afternoon of 10 February 1945.

virtually cut off the battalions on their objectives, where they had to exist as best they might, until Buffaloes became available to evacuate them'. For example, the village of Leuth, which had been secured by the Régiment de Chaudière, was being progressively flooded and the French Canadian soldiers along with their German prisoners were forced into the buildings as the waters continued to rise. The Chaudières' war diary records that at 2100 hours, with the water still rising, the battalion headquarters staff were forced to move to the upper storey of the house they were occupying. The Chaudières were evacuated to Nijmegen the following morning. For the North Shore battalion, upper floors and higher ground within the villages was not enough and they were forced to abandon Zandpol and Kekerdom and take refuge on the nearby dykes as the waters continued to rise.

The majority of air support operations were cancelled on 9 February due to the low cloud and rain that persisted throughout the morning and early afternoon. Use was, however, made of the SCR 584 radar equipment[4] to bomb Goch, Kalkar, Moyland and Till. One important raid did, however, take place; General Schlemm's headquarters of the First *Fallschirmjäger* Army had been located at Dinxperlo on the Dutch–German border due east of Emmerich and was attacked in the late afternoon by eight Typhoons of 146 Wing with 1,000lb bombs. 'This success' it was reported 'was a most valuable contribution to the tactical battle'. The weather, however, precluded planned attacks on other targets, including on the enemy command and control facilities, such as the telephone exchange at Arnhem and the headquarters of LXXXVI Corps.

Chapter Nine

The Advance to Kleve

10 February 1945

The attack by the First Canadian Army on 8 February 1945 had taken the Germans by surprise and had benefitted from the enemy's conviction that the blow would fall further south but, as a staff officer recorded, 'This could not last'. As expected, on the morning of 9 February, German troops from across the Rhineland, including, as already mentioned, elements of the 7th *Fallschirmjäger* Division, were marching towards Kleve and Goch. Despite poor flying weather, the Allied air forces did their best to interdict and slow enemy movement.

For General Schlemm, who had predicted that the Allies would attempt to force the Reichswald Plug, this reinforcement was too late as XXX Corps had broken through the forward defences and the Siegfried Line, and by nightfall on 9 February were on the Materborn feature. Of the deployment of reserves, he explained to his interrogator in post-war questioning, how little influence he had as a German army commander over the conduct of the battle in the Rhineland:

> Once the battle was joined, it became obvious that the control of First Para Army no longer rested solely with Schlemm. Berlin had taken an interest in the matter, and Schlemm merely became a receptacle for the passing of orders. The Reichswald battle from that time on was to become for Schlemm a nightmare of excuses, entreaties and explanations. His first indication that he did not have a free hand came with the order that under no circumstances was any land between the Maas and the Rhine to be given up without the permission of Rundstedt, who would first ask Hitler. This prohibition on his freedom of movement considerably restricted Schlemm's options. He realized that if the Allies once captured the west bank of the Rhine, his complete army would be trapped. His own plan was to build a series of lines facing north, between the Maas and the Rhine, and retire slowly from position to position exacting as heavy a price as possible for every loss of ground. These tactics were not permitted, however, and 86 Corps was ordered to stand where it was and not yield an inch. As a result, the British troops broke through vital positions time after time, forcing Schlemm to make a hasty adjustment to the new situation. In addition, a detailed explanation for each withdrawal had to be sent back.[1]

Schlemm later added that Hitler threatened to execute any commander who lost a Rhine bridge intact and that 'as I had a dozen bridges in my area, prospects of me living a long life seemed slim'.

Only once the level of the River Roer fell and the speed of the current reduced could the Ninth US Army begin to build bridges for Operation GRENADE.

There was, however, a fundamental problem facing the Allies, namely with VERITABLE's US counterpart, Operation GRENADE. With XXX Corps' attack under way, the Germans, anticipating the American attack, had during the course of 9 February badly damaged the dams, releasing the flood waters; Bradley's prevarication in January had come to haunt the Allies. General Horrocks wrote:

> It was now that I heard a really bad piece of news – namely, that ... the Germans had blown the dam over the Roer, which meant that the Ninth US Army was faced by a wide strip of surging water which was quite unbridgeable. So their attack from the south had to be postponed. It was estimated that the floods would continue for at least two weeks. In fact, it was not until 23 February that Simpson's leading troops were able to start crossing the Roer.

As a result, German reserves were able to be concentrated against the First Canadian Army, condemning them to a hard, protracted and costly battle.

The Wessex Division's Advance to Kleve

With the battle to break into the Reichswald complete and the fight through well under way, plus parts of the vital Materborn feature overlooking Kleve in 15th Scottish Division's hands, VERITABLE was moving into another stage.

General Horrocks explained that during the early evening of 9 February, after thirty-six tense hours:

> I received a message that they [15th Scottish Division] had captured the Nutterden [*sic* Materborn] feature and were moving into the outskirts of Kleve. This was the information for which I had been eagerly waiting, because speed in capturing Kleve before the German reserves got established there was essential. So, I unleashed my first reserve, the 43rd Wessex Division, which was to pass through the 15th Scottish, to burst out into the plain beyond and advance towards Goch.

The orders given to Major General Ivor Thomas' 43rd Wessex Division were simple:

> (i) Be prepared to pass through 15 (S) Div on capture of the MATERBORN feature by that fmn.
> (ii) Capture Goch without delay.[2]

As the assault divisions moved forward, the Wessex had taken their place in the crowded Nijmegen suburbs during 8 February and the morning of the 9th. Their role in the battle, with 8 Armoured Brigade under command, was a swift drive through the suburbs of Kleve before heading south to capture Goch. When 51st Highland Division had broken through south of the Reichswald, the Guards Armoured Division committed to what was hoped would be a rapid drive into the Rhineland. On the northern axis General Horrocks received optimistic reports, as recorded in the history of 44 Brigade:

> After dark the 15th Reconnaissance Regiment pushed forward patrols into Cleve; they drove right through the town and reported that there were some Germans still there but that they did not appear to be organised. The enemy at this stage was bringing up reinforcements as fast as he could, but they were being committed into battle piecemeal to plug holes.

The corps' plan was to send 8 Armoured and 129 Infantry Brigade, followed by 214 Brigade, on the road from Nijmegen to Kleve via Kranenburg and swing south towards Goch. The tanks of the Sherwood Rangers were to support 129 Brigade; the 4th/7th Dragoon Guards, 214 Brigade; and the 13th/18th Hussars, 130 Brigade, which was the divisional reserve.

It was assumed by corps HQ that 15th Scottish Division's units would by then be, if not in Kleve, very nearly there and that the road would be clear for the Wessex. This, however, was not the case and the early committal of the Wessex Division proved to be an error. Horrocks continued:

> This turned out to be one of the worst mistakes I made in the war. The 15th Scottish had not reached as far as had been reported and one of their brigades had not yet been employed at all [*sic*]. The chief enemy at this time was not the Germans but the congestion caused by the flooding which almost

precluded cross-country movement. The arrival of this fresh Division, bursting for the fray, caused one of the worst traffic jams in the war – equalled only, I believe, by the scenes in the Liri Valley in Italy after the Battle of Cassino. My only excuse is that all too often during the war I had witnessed a pause in the battle when one division was ordered to pass through another, which allowed the enemy time to recover. In this case, speed was absolutely vital, and I was determined that our attack should flow on.

Major General Thomas, commander of 43rd Wessex Division, dressed for campaign. He is seen here with General Sosabwoski during MARKET GARDEN.

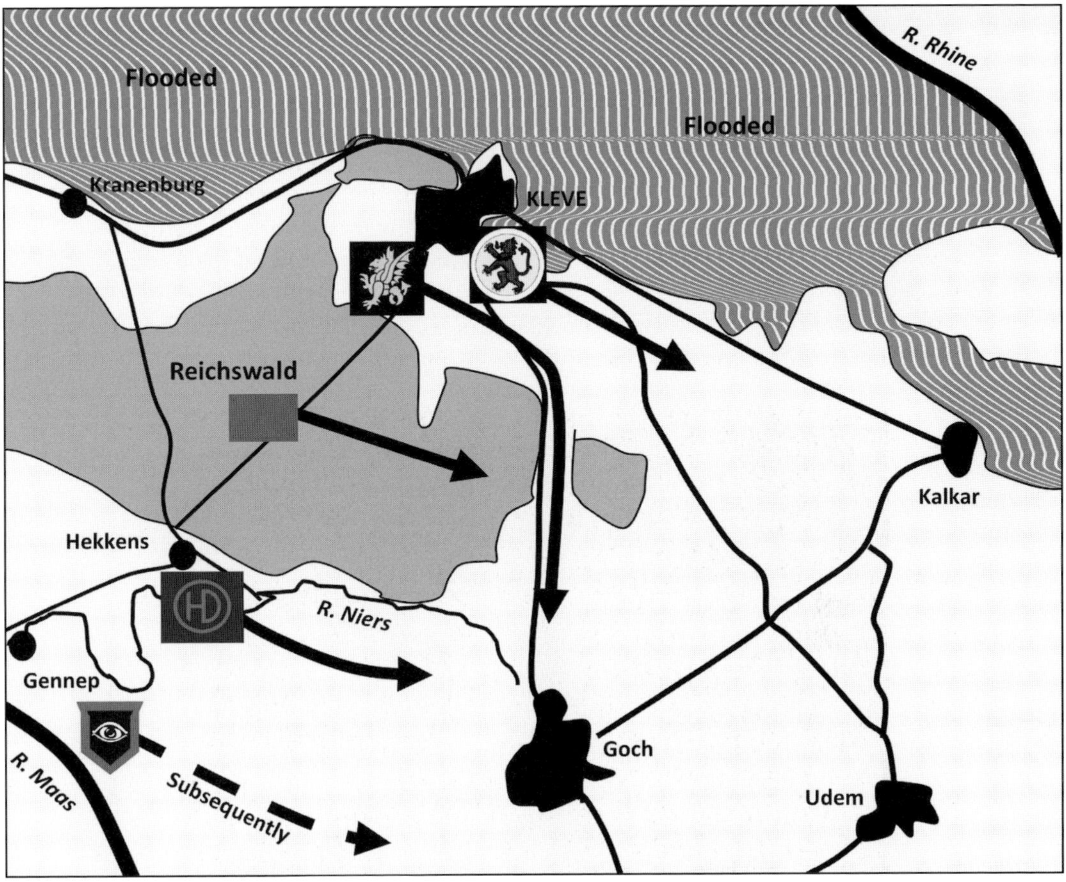

XXX Corps Concept of Operations for the breakout into the Rhineland.

The original plan for 15th Scottish Division, on the capture of the Materborn feature, was to bring 227 Brigade forward to clear and hold Kleve and if possible, to dispatch mobile columns to capture Uedem and Kalkar and secure the Emmerich road. However, 227 Brigade, with both armoured and wheeled vehicles bogged in, was strung out back beyond Kranenburg, and with too few troops forward and German reinforcements arriving, occupying Kleve was not possible.

A passage of lines by one formation through another always requires considerable coordination by the staff and route discipline among units executing it. In the conditions prevailing on the evening of 9 February, it proved to be an all but impossible task for the Wessex Division to maintain cohesion and develop momentum. Brigadier Essame of 214 Brigade recorded that the decision to launch the 43rd 'produced in the next forty-eight hours a situation unrivalled in its exasperating complexity throughout the campaign'.

The intelligence brief given to the division as they left was that the city had been flattened and that there was only scattered opposition. That may have been the case during the evening of 9 February, but overnight the recce regiments reported that German reinforcements were rushing to man the preprepared

The Armoured Regiment

In contrast with the more heavily armoured Churchills of the tank regiments, the lighter and faster cruiser tanks (Shermans and Cromwells) of the armoured brigade's regiments were designed to be unleashed once a breakthrough of the enemy defences had been achieved. In VERITABLE, the three British infantry divisions fighting through the Reichswald and the Siegfried Line required tank support. This was provided by the Churchills of 6 Guards Armoured and 34 Armoured Brigades, while 43rd Wessex, which was planned to be released into the Rhineland, had two of the Sherman regiments of 8 Armoured Brigade under command.

4th/7th Dragoon Guards
13th/18th Hussars (3rd Canadian Division minus one squadron detached to 2nd Canadian Division for the initial attack)
Sherwood Rangers Yeomanry
147 (Essex Yeomanry) Field Regiment RA

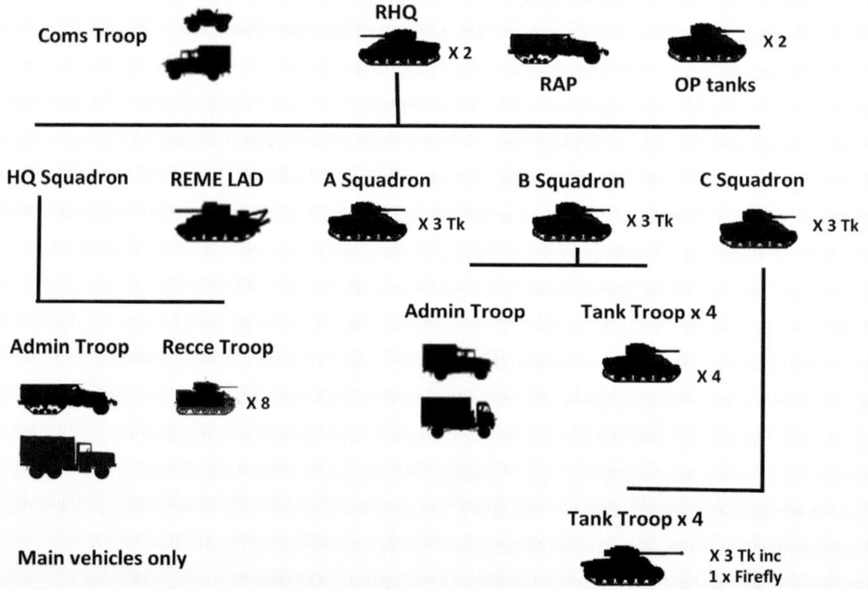

Due to the lack of air threat, the anti-aircraft troops had been disbanded during the Battle of Normandy.

defences out on the western flank of the Materborn feature. By dawn on 10 February there were, as 129 Brigade was to find out, a considerable quantity of German infantry and armour deployed to contain the offensive.

129 Brigade Leads the Wessex Division

> None of us will ever forget Kleve. It was our only consistently unpleasant battle, and it had no redeeming features, except that it resulted in ultimate victory. [*4th Somerset LI*][3]

With the Scots having broken through the German lines, 129 Brigade's objectives were the Kleve *Staatsforst* to the west of the city and the Goch escarpment, which was a further 5 miles to the south. It was expected that with its infantry battalions mounted on the Shermans of 8 Armoured Brigade, the battle would be mobile and conducted at speed in order to gain ground before the enemy could respond. The mud, floods and now traffic jams bought time for Schlemm to reinforce and 'speed' was simply not possible with the single road blocked by the Guards' tanks and the Scots' transport during the evening and night of 9 February. There was also no viable alternative route through the Reichswald, as in the 53rd Welsh Division's area the tracks across the Groesbeek Heights through the forest were already untenable. Consequently, the only option for General Horrocks was to send the Wessex on the Kranenburg road, which was not only the 15th Scottish Division's axis and main (and only) supply route but stretches of it were now under rising water.

At 1800 hours on the evening of 9 February, divisional headquarters put 129 Brigade and its attached regiment from 8 Armoured Brigade, the Sherwood Rangers Yeomanry, and motor company of 12 King's Royal Rifle Corps (12 KRRC) on one hour's notice to move. At 2115 hours they finally received the code word to set out on what would be a torturous journey. The leading battalion group was 4 Wiltshire. Their history records that:

> Under command of the battalion were B Squadron of the Notts Yeomanry [Sherwood Rangers], a platoon of machineguns and a platoon of 4.2in mortars from 8th Middlesex and one troop of 17-pounder anti-tank guns. One troop of tanks without infantry on them led, followed by the rest of the squadron carrying C Company, then D, B and A companies in that order riding on tanks or other vehicles in the column. It was a tight fit with thirteen men riding on each Sherman.[4]

Brigadier Essame described the first stage of the road move east towards Kleve:

> Night had closed in when 4 Wiltshire Regiment, the leading battalion of 129 Brigade Group, passed the traffic post on the eastern outskirts of Nijmegen and took the road to Kranenburg and Kleve. For the first time since Normandy most of the wheeled vehicles had been left behind and the troops were riding 'quick lift' on the tanks of the Sherwood Rangers and

A pre-war photograph of Lieutenant Colonel Christopherson, the Commanding officer of the Sherwood Rangers Yeomanry.

> the other tracked vehicles. It was bitterly cold, with spasms of icy rain. An air raid on Nijmegen enlivened the departure of the long column. To the north an occasional gun flash lit up the great expanse of water north of the road. Spasmodic shelling from long-range guns caused splashes in the surrounding bog. Now and then a few German aircraft bombed the road by the light of flares. Here and there, a few searchlights cast a vague, intermittent light over the desolation. At last, about midnight, the ruins of Kranenburg were reached. Here the roads were awash. The floods were obviously rising fast.[5]

Having struggled past Kranenburg, the commanding officer of 4 Wiltshire, Lieutenant Colonel Corbyn, found the headquarters of one of the Scottish brigades and gathered some up to date information on the situation ahead. 'He was told that their forward troops were 2 miles short of Kleve and that the defences were thought to be disorganised by the heavy [air] raid on the night of the 7th.' All the while the infantry, chilled to the bone, were hanging onto the tanks 'there was an awful feeling of nakedness as we sat perched on top of tanks driving down this single road'.

It soon, however, transpired that the main road to Kleve was blocked by the enemy and numerous felled trees before the Wiltshires reached Donnsbrüggen. Colonel Corbyn was, however, informed that 15 Scottish Reconnaissance

Regiment had located an alternative route south of Nütterden through a narrow neck of woods in the northerly extension of the Reichswald. Corbyn therefore:

> decided to take this route, and with a troop of 15th Scottish Reconnaissance Regiment and one of his own platoons [No. 15] personally led the head of the column forward into the darkness ahead. After passing Nutterden, the head of the column eventually reached the woods. A *Spandau* suddenly came to life. The leading troops were off their vehicles in a flash. Lieut.-Colonel Corbyn found that the road ahead was blocked by a fallen tree. A fierce battle now developed in the darkness.

The Scottish recce patrols had warned the Wiltshires that enemy outposts were likely to be encountered on the outskirts of Nütterden and, expecting trouble, C Company in the lead was soon clearing opposition around a blown-down tree that blocked the track. The enemy were cleared 'in a spirited action in the dark, supported by tanks' of B Squadron. The battalion's history records that:

> While 15 Platoon held both sides of the road, Lieutenant Smith led 13 Platoon up to and beyond the roadblock to cover mine detection and clearance by the Pioneer Platoon. 13 Platoon had been much reduced owing to a tank having broken down soon after leaving Nijmegen and now consisted of platoon headquarters and one section commanded by Lance-Corporal Miller. Lieutenant Smith himself had been forced to release his grip on his Sten, when it became entangled in some telephone wires, rather than be swept off the turret of his tank.

Private Pinner, a clerk, was with battalion tactical headquarters travelling behind the leading platoon and recalled the departure from Nijmegen:

> So off we set, the roads being in an appalling condition, as the thaw, coupled with heavy rain created great havoc. Flood water lapped the sides of the road, the surrounding field being saturated. The water rose higher and higher, until it seemed that our column must be halted, but somehow, we pressed

The intended and actual advance of 4th Wiltshire battlegroup on the night of 9–10 February 1945.

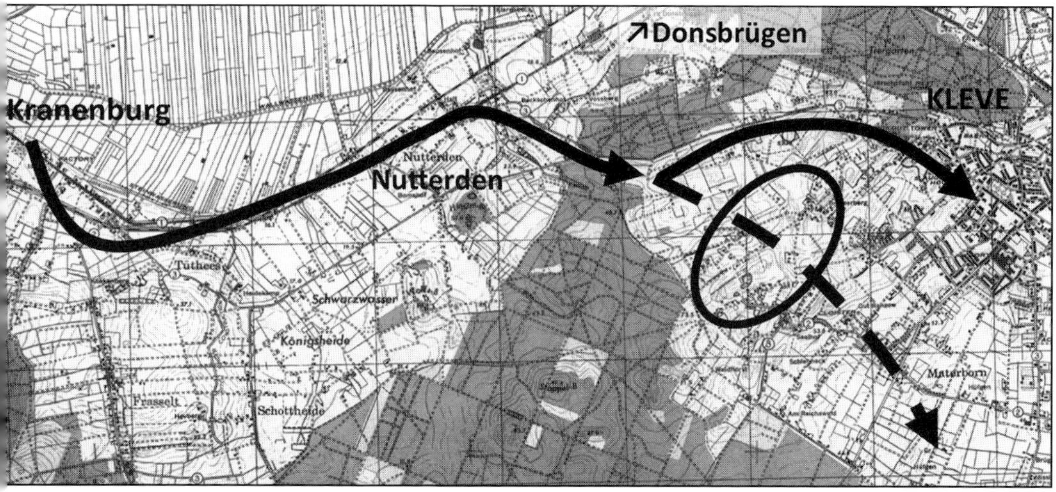

Private Pinner (right) and a fellow member of the 5th Wiltshires' tactical headquarters.

> on … The water was still rising, and somebody remarked, with feeling 'if they want me to swim to the buggers, I'm not – I'm pissing off home to my mum …' We soon came under sporadic small arms fire and the column was halted …
>
> Off we set along a small track through the trees with our vehicle axle deep in mud, every tree, in the imagination, hiding a sniper. We were soon halted by a roadblock constructed of branches from trees. 'Smithy' said 'come on lads – grenades – these sods are only second grade'. So, there we were throwing grenades into the roadblock until all resistance was overcome. Second grade troops or not, we lost two men killed, one of them being the lad who had threatened to 'go home to his Mum'.[6]

During the fight the battalion's historian recalled that Lieutenant Smith, while clearing the roadblock:

> was armed with a pistol in addition but had no ammunition for it. This did not prevent him doing a true 'Wild West' draw on a young German parachutist manning a *Spandau* at the roadblock, frightening him into surrender before he fired a shot.

The platoon were unable to move the tree, so while they waited for the assault pioneers, Lieutenant Smith took four men forward to prod for mines while the remainder of the platoon provided covering fire. 'Heavy fire was returned, whereupon the tanks opened up with Besa machine guns and 17-pounders at the houses on either side of the street.' The tanks:

> were completely blind in the darkness and, though their fire proved most demoralising to the enemy, it was often difficult also for our own men to keep out of the way of it. Sergeant Jenkins shot a young German who had been crawling with a bazooka to within a few yards of the leading tank. House clearing then proceeded beyond the block, with 13 Platoon dealing with the left of the road and 15 Platoon the right.

With the opposition cleared, the advance resumed with D Company taking the lead on foot and with the Shermans of B Squadron, Sherwood Rangers, firing

An infantry section aboard a Sherman. In winter those sitting on the engine decks got some warmth but those hanging on elsewhere froze. One Wiltshire soldier remarked that: 'It was still better than marching through miles of mud and constantly falling over.'

The road into Kleve. The further the brigade penetrated into the city the greater the level of destruction, not just of trees but buildings as well.

into every house they passed. However, as they moved through the outskirts of Kleve there was little opposition at this stage. The flashes of tanks' main armament spoilt their night vision, and the leading squadron took the wrong road east into the city. Instead of cutting south-east through 44 Lowland Brigade on the Materborn feature, they headed towards the city's southern suburbs.

At 0700 hours, as recorded in the battalion's war diary, 4 Somerset LI was nearing Kleve. 'After hours of slow, stop start crawling along,' the battalion's historian wrote:

> The column moved on and 200 yds. further on the process was repeated. By now we were off the tanks and very much on the lookout for trouble. Dawn had just broken and we could see that we were in the centre of a town that had taken terrible punishment. It had been bombed and there was hardly a house intact. Trees had fallen across the roads which were impassable with huge craters.

Behind the Wiltshires, the rest of 129 Brigade, having advanced on a single route, was strung out in a column over 3 miles long. Unbeknown to the brigade, expecting 'only scattered opposition', they had penetrated deep into enemy positions, some of which had been occupied overnight by the *Fallschirmjäger* reinforcing 84th Division's rear echelons. Lieutenant Sidney Jary, of 4 Somerset LI, confirms that the Germans, still before dawn, were not fully aware of their presence:

> Some way short of the town, shadowy figures of the 15th Scottish Division's soldiers were to be seen on either side of the road. Not a word passed

> between them and my soldiers, which was strange. None of their officers took the slightest notice of us which, as we were driving through their positions directly into the enemy's, was quite extraordinary. At the time I attributed this to simple bad manners. The reader may be surprised to learn that this is unusual on the battlefield, where courteous behaviour is rarely lacking amongst fighting troops. I also wondered if they must have experienced considerable opposition taking Kleve and were now understandably silent ...
>
> After we had moved some distance into the town, the column stopped opposite a side road from which the glow of a cookhouse could just be seen from behind a tarpaulin screen. Assuming this to belong to one of the infantry battalions of 15th Scottish Division, I sent one of the Platoon across to see if their cooks could spare us some hot tea. He quickly returned explaining that, as it was a Jerry cookhouse, he had decided not to ask. Evidently the figures we had seen in the shadows of bombed buildings all around us were the enemy. They, in turn, must have assumed that we were retreating Germans.[7]

Major Beckhurst is quoted in the Somersets' war diary:

> We swarmed into the town, thinking it had been cleared, but instead we had wandered slap-bang into the middle of a German position. We just got to a crossroads around the centre of the town. Then the firing started from all sides. We had to formulate a plan; it was nearly impossible. Finally, all we could do was mop up enemy pockets as best we could.

At 0520 hours 4 Wiltshire reported that D Company, now on foot accompanied by the tanks of B Squadron, had reached a park south of the city centre, with the rest of the battalion 'strung out amongst the chaotic confusion of the ruins of the suburbs'. Here the acting brigade commander, Lieutenant Colonel Kendrick, halted 4 Wiltshire and, believing that 15th Scottish were already in the ruins of central Kleve, ordered the battalion into all-round defence to cover his left rear.

The Wiltshires set about clearing a length of road, rounding up seventy-five prisoners from the ruins of the buildings in the process:

> The difficult job of laying out an all-round perimeter, which was very much extended and, in the bomb-shattered built up area in the dark, was soon under way, and everyone dug like fury ready for any surprise that might come at dawn.

With the three sabre squadrons under command of the infantry battalions, Lieutenant Renders of the Sherwood Rangers was acting as a liaison officer at RHQ:[8]

> We [RHQ] were strung out in a line of vehicles along one of the roads running into the city centre when the fighting started. I was still with the CO's tactical HQ, which had pulled up close to 129 Brigade headquarters of

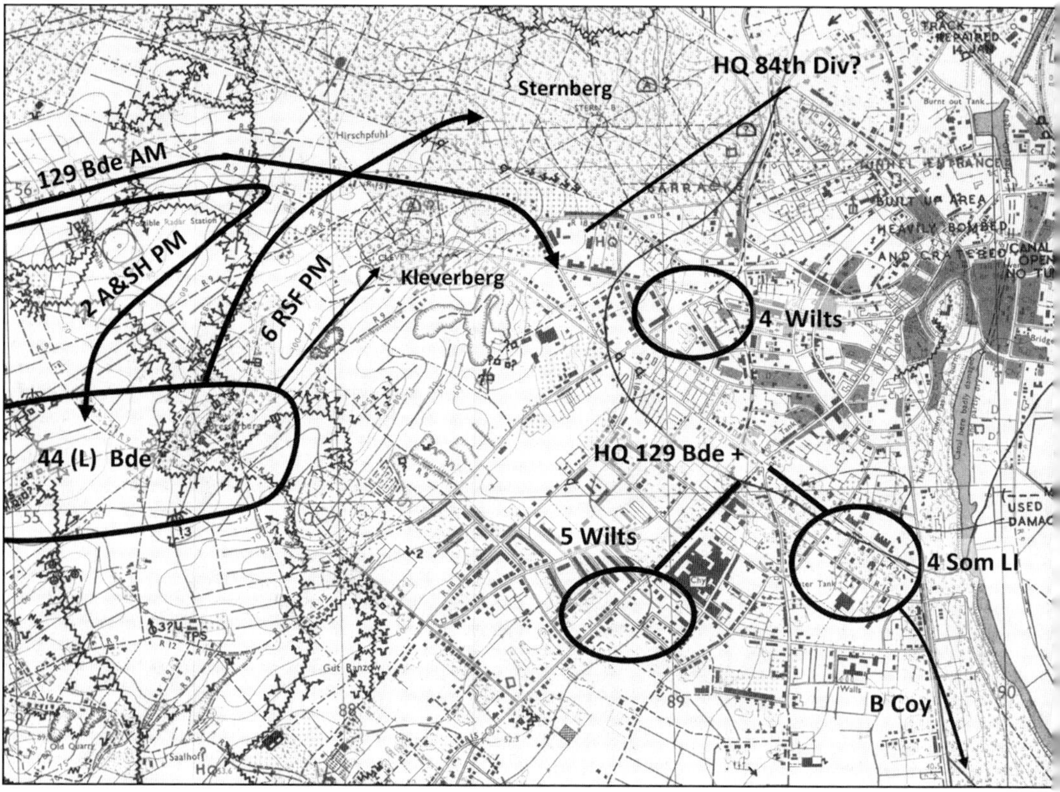

Approximate positions of 129 Brigade's battalions early on 10 February 1945 and 6 RSF's advance to the Kleverberg and Sternberg hills.

> 43rd Division. We had been on the move all night and I got out of the Dingo having been tasked by the adjutant to find the suitable remains of a house in which to get a brew on. When mortar fire started to land any thoughts of tea were quickly forgotten. I made my way back to the relative safety of the scout car. Up ahead, B Squadron encountered an enemy roadblock and there were reports of enemy self-propelled guns as a melee of street fighting broke out between the *Fallschirmjäger* and the 4th Wiltshires.

Private Thornburrow, driver of a brigade headquarters signals vehicle, wrote:

> When the Infantry of 129th Brigade arrived they stumbled across some small pockets of the enemy still clinging to their positions, seemingly unaware of the fact they were now isolated from the main body of their retreating forces. Then, following in the wake of its advancing infantry, 129th Brigade Tac. HQ. convoy came under attack within a few minutes of their arrival in Cleve. This happened as the Brigadier's convoy was moving slowly along a street on the south-west side of the town, when without warning they were suddenly confronted by a German tank – identified as a Panther – which appeared from behind a damaged factory building. The tank took up a firing position in the centre of a T junction approx. 100 yards ahead, but according to what a comrade – who was there in a Defence Platoon Section – told me

later, the Panther Tank must have been short of shells as only three were fired before it reversed and moved away. One of the Panther's shells knocked out a Sherman Tank leading the Brigadier's convoy and a jeep was also hit but not before the occupants had managed to take cover. Fortunately, because of the shortness of the attack the casualties were light.

During this confusion another comrade of the Defence Platoon had run for shelter into a cellar of a ruined building only to emerge almost immediately with several German soldiers with their hands held up high. By the expression on their faces they were only too pleased to surrender and lay down their arms.

Private Pinner, in one of 5 Wiltshires' battalion headquarters vehicles, wrote in his memoirs of a similar experience:

> We had stirred up a veritable hornets' nest, and it soon became apparent that were right behind the German defences, our column coming to a halt in the one passable street, from the far end of which appeared a German tank, making its way leisurely along our column, shooting up each vehicle as it passed.
>
> Fortunately for me the tank was approaching from the other end of the column. Everybody dived out of their trucks, making for cover, of which there was plenty among the heaps of rubble. Len jumped out of our truck on one side … Len was unlucky, receiving a burst of machine gun fire in his left leg. I dragged him into a heap of rubble, which turned out to be a better prospect than I had imagined. Behind the rubble were the remains of a house with both ground and first floors greatly damaged, but remembering that there just had to be a cellar somewhere, I dug around among the debris, and sure enough a trap door appeared. I carried out the normal procedure by carefully lifting the trap door and dropping a grenade into the abyss below, but in so doing destroyed all the bottled goodies stacked on the shelves around the walls of the cellar below.

The Wiltshire Regiment cap badge.

Still unaware that the Scots were not in the city, in accordance with the divisional plan, Colonel Kendrick ordered the rest of the brigade to wheel south, confident that he could push on towards Goch with 4 Somerset LI on the left and 5 Wiltshire to their right. As the defences on the slopes above the village of Materborn had been occupied by German infantry, the Wessex would be advancing south behind the enemy. Essame concluded that 'the arrival of 129 Brigade in Kleve itself had taken them completely by surprise'. Nonetheless,

The road junction where the 5 Wiltshires' transport was 'shot up'. It was taken by Private Pinner later in 1945.

as they made their way through the city's outskirts, they belatedly received the radio message 'Look out for trouble in Kleve'.

As it got lighter the Germans realised that the enemy was among them and started to recover and counter-attack, which ruled out any prospect of an advance on Goch. Having halted his battalion, Colonel Lipscombe, of 4 Somerset LI, gave orders to form a firm base on the head of the column and slowly the tail was moved forward in a running fight at the eastern edge of the town. B Company was

Colonel 'Lippy' Lipscombe, commanding officer of 4 Somerset LI.

ordered forward to secure the road junction where a branch road led through the woods to Bedburg:

> No one can give an idea of the many small battles that took place. The column became split up and many gallant actions were fought against German armour and infantry – eventually we became masters of the situation and something like order was restored to the battlefield.

In their history, 5 Wiltshire noted that: 'The enemy were far from clear what was happening, as amongst the prisoners taken were German staff officers and others who came into Kleve to draw rations for their troops.'

As 5 Wiltshires consolidated their area of Kleve, the enemy tried a Trojan Horse attack with a captured Sherman tank – presumably one of the six reported lost by the Sherwood Rangers that day. Their historian provides a flavour of the fighting:

> An obvious Sherman tank whose commander was standing up with his head and shoulders sticking out of the turret approached B Company positions and beckoned our men to come forward and speak to him. Fortunately, the men of 12 Platoon spotted some German infantry following up behind and opened fire. The 'Trojan horse' withdrew hurriedly, being unfortunately missed by a PIAT bomb. The Somersets' attempts at further progress were completely checked by tanks and self-propelled guns. Brigade Headquarters established itself and was smartly counter-attacked from the west.
>
> A force of one Tiger, one Panther and about ten infantry, probably part of the same body of enemy as had been bothering Brigade Headquarters, put in an attack on B Company positions which faced west. Unfortunately, all the 6-pounders were at this time limbered up in preparation for a move. The attack was beaten off after the infantry had been engaged with small-arms fire, the tanks being out of range of our PIATs. A Company was particularly troubled by sniping and infiltration from the woods, which caused some casualties …

During the course of the day the motor company of 12 King's Royal Rifle Corps, and the battery of 147 Essex Yeomanry, RA, that habitually fought with the Sherwood Rangers made it into Kleve and thickened up 129 Brigade's defences.

15th Scottish Division

Behind 129 Brigade, with two divisions now attempting to use the same single road there was traffic chaos. Throughout the night of 9–10 February the Wessex Division had priority on the road south through Kranenburg but between 0800 and 1000 hours 227 Highland Brigade was to have sole use of the route to mount its belated clearance of Kleve. Brigadier Essame's 214 Brigade, thanks to the stop-start nature of their journey south, was still on the road at 0800 hours, with few places to pull over. The 15th Scottish's divisional historian wrote:

> Unfortunately, this move did not work out to plan. Coming onto the main road from the south, the tanks and other vehicles with the [2] Argylls found 43rd Wessex Division's transport parked so closely along the road and in every side lane that they almost despaired of ever reaching the main road at all. When after endless delays and halts and about-turns the column did reach the road, it had lost all semblance of order …

A combination of the traffic jams and the recce Stuarts of 3 Tank Battalion, Scots Guards, meeting resistance on the Kleverberg en route to the city, despite the earlier passage of 129 Brigade on the same route, meant the advance was very slow. Consequently, as the situation in Kleve was far from clear, the plan was changed. The Argylls would now march on foot through the traffic jams and conduct a relief in place of 8 Royal Scots and 6 King's Own Scottish Borderers on the Materborn feature. This would in turn free up these battalions to advance to the high ground of the Sternberg, west of Kleve. It was not, however, until dusk at 1730 hours on 10 February that the Argylls reached Esperance and the Bresserberg and took over. By this time it was too late to begin the clearance of Kleve.

Meanwhile, during the afternoon Brigadier Cumming-Bruce (44 Brigade) had, however, already ordered 6 Royal Scots Fusiliers to secure the Kleverberg and the Sternberg in order to get a better grip on the high ground overlooking the city. When the RSF advanced they had to cross roads that were still being used by 129 Brigade's transport, which added a level of confusion and delay.

A mobile column of the Carrier Platoon supported by Wasps and 3in mortars was dispatched to the Kleverberg, where the 6 RSF overran some German trenches, and the Wasps secured the hilltop with blasts of flame that set the look-out tower on fire. Meanwhile, the rest of the battalion was advancing on the Sternberg but were halted when the guns of the Wessex Division repeatedly shelled the area, unaware that the Fusiliers were advancing through the enemy-held wood. Tragically, casualties from friendly fire were reported in all four of 6 RSF's rifle companies.

An 88mm Pak 43 anti-tank gun knocked out during Operation VERITABLE.

Symptomatic of the lack of situational awareness between 15th Scottish and the Wessex is this example provided by 4 Wiltshires:

> In the evening D Company received orders to clear some enemy out of a water-tower which dominated the route into town on the western edge of Cleve. When the company was actually on the start line, the Commanding Officer discovered that the Canadians [*sic*] were on the point of doing the same thing from the opposite direction supported by Crocodiles [*sic*]. This proved to be the case and D Company were hurriedly told to desist from pressing their attack. The Canadians duly dealt with the enemy and that particular sector was pacified.

For the 15th Scottish 'it had been a day of frustration':

> The weather was still shocking; the going deeper than ever. Despite the fact that all routes had been 'frozen' to normal administrative traffic for twenty-four hours, traffic congestion had made troop movement almost impossible. Golden opportunities had slipped by in consequence – and all the time the enemy front was hardening. That day two more enemy divisions had appeared …

214 Brigade

It was hardly a better situation for 214 Brigade, where back on the road from Kranenburg the water was 3ft deep and only trucks could get through. General Thomas's tactical headquarters on the road near Nütterden was in the heart of the traffic jam and was for most of the day unable to communicate by radio with Colonel Kendrick's headquarters of 129 Brigade over the hill in Kleve. Consequently, he and all other commanders had little idea of what was actually happening in Kleve and plans were made in ignorance of the true situation in the city.

The Scots' recce regiment eventually found a track that led along the northern edge of the Reichswald. This route showed up on aerial photographs as a straight white line in the forest and had during VERITABLE's planning process been reported by the resistance as a concrete road built to serve the Siegfried Line. It, however, turned out to be a sand track with qualities only marginally better than mud as far as wheeled vehicles were concerned. Major General Ross, of the Welsh Division, agreed to its use by 214 Brigade but it would take most of the day for the traffic chaos to clear on access roads around Nütterden. Consequently, it was not until the afternoon that it was reached.

The Scots were angry about the navigation error that had both put 129 Brigade in western Kleve and stalled 214 Brigade on their road. It is, however, apparent that with the enemy presence on the western part of the Materborn feature and the arrival of leading units of a regiment from 6th *Fallschirmjäger* Division and assault guns from the Arnhem area, they could have could not have advanced on Kleve with so few troops forward. Nonetheless, Brigadier Essame reported that

Brigadier Essame of 214 Brigade photographed following promotion after the war.

there were a series of 'angry meetings throughout the day full of recriminations' between commanders of the Scots and those of the Wessex. It was only late that evening that the leading unit of 214 Brigade, the 5 Duke of Cornwall's Light Infantry, arrived on the Materborn feature.

During the day, thanks to the traffic chaos, the Wessex Division's 130 Brigade were ordered to remain in Nijmegen rather than join the rest of the division in its fight towards its objective of Goch. Thus it can be concluded that road conditions and the resulting traffic jams were the root cause of much of the subsequent loss of tempo on the northern axis, against growing opposition.

Attack and Counter-Attack

Returning to the morning of 10 February, General Schlemm had overnight rushed regiments of three *Fallschirmjäger* divisions to form a line to block the Allies. On the right, in Kleve, was 16th Regiment of 6th *Fallschirmjäger*, which had come west across the Rhine, in the centre was 2nd Regiment of 2nd *Fallschirmjäger* Division, and to the west, further *Fallschirmjäger* to block the 51st Highland Division. These troops were taken from other defensive areas, risking weakening their sectors against subsequent attack. However, with decisions at army group level during 8 and 9 February having been delayed in expectation of an Allied offensive in the Venlo area, this is the only infantry response Schlemm could deliver within his own army resources.

With 129 Brigade and the Sherwood Rangers having found themselves in the suburbs of Kleve around dawn, Colonel Kendrick issued confirmatory orders for the next phase of the operation: the advance south by 4 Somersets and 5 Wiltshires. Shortly after the brigade executed the wheel to the south, daylight revealed the brigade's long column had found itself in a bitterly fought meeting engagement. To their surprise, coming in the opposite direction was a German counter-attack launched by troops of 2nd *Fallschirmjäger* regiment, which had now arrived in strength, supported by *Panzerjäger*. It was soon learned from *Fallschirmjäger* prisoners that they were as equally ignorant of the situation as their British counterparts were.

A Company, 5 Wiltshire, travelled south on the battalion's right towards the road to Goch, threading their way past huge bomb craters, and were nearly out of Kleve when they came under machine gun fire from the woods on the south-eastern outskirts of the town and shell fire from ahead. Their battalion's history records:

> Using the only roads open to traffic, we wound our way forward till the head of the column reached the eastern exits of the town. At this moment a German counter attack, in the form of SPs and paratroopers, came in from the South. No one can fully describe what happened. Small groups stood

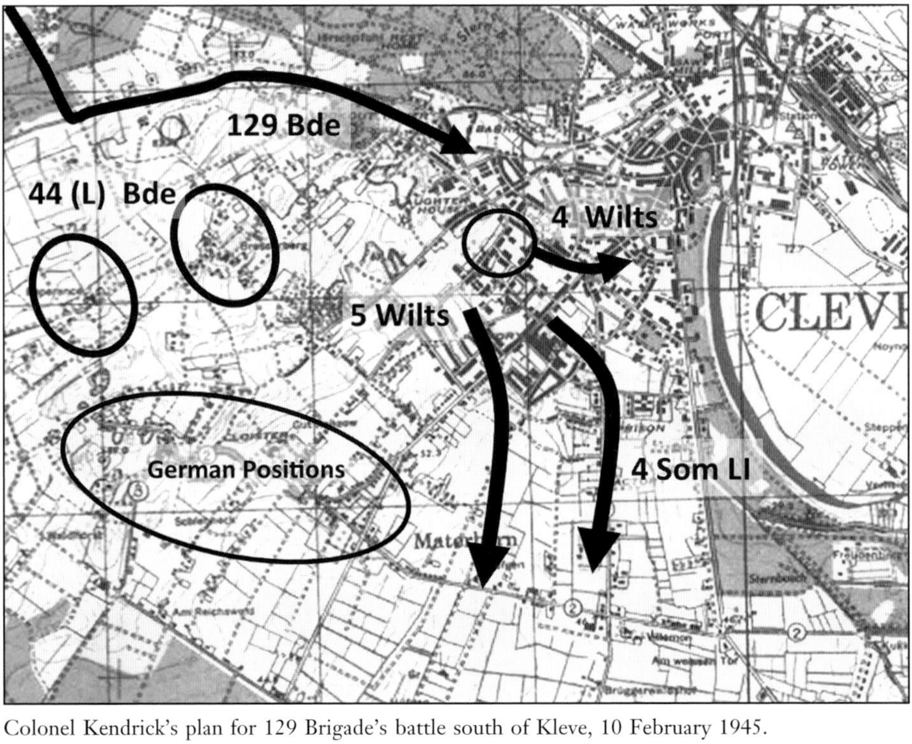

Colonel Kendrick's plan for 129 Brigade's battle south of Kleve, 10 February 1945.

> and fought where they were, forming a thin line with the general direction facing South. German SPs picked off vehicle after vehicle, and we certainly 'bought it'.

The mention of German armour in all accounts gives the impression that there was a significant quantity facing 129 Brigade at this stage in the battle. There were in fact only the remnants of the original five companies of *Panzerjäger* and such limited armour that General Schlemm could release from elsewhere in First *Fallschirmjäger* Army. It was not until midday on 10 February, with the imminent loss of Kleve being reported, that General Blastowitz was convinced that this was the British offensive. Only then did he release the Army Group H's reserve XLVII Panzer Corps to assemble at Uedem, but they would not be able to attack into the Kleve area until the following day at the earliest. In the meantime, the remnants of 84th Division and the two fresh *Fallschirmjäger* regiments in the Kleve area would have to contain XXX Corps.

According to information 4 Wiltshire received from the German labour corps' prisoners and forced labourers, there was a battalion of *Fallschirmjäger* in Kleve and its immediate area. It soon became apparent that the Wiltshires were sandwiched between the various battalions of *Fallschirmjäger* in the city, advancing from the south and those up on the Materborn feature. The counter-attack that A Company, 5 Wiltshire, ran into halted their advance at the junction of the Goch and Bedburg road. The battalion's history continued:

> The leading platoon, No. 8, led by Captain Boucher, leapt from their tanks and, charging into the narrow wood on the left, in a few minutes had accounted for nearly thirty Germans, most of them being taken prisoner. On the other side of the road, No. 7 Platoon, led by Lieutenant Fussey, was achieving the same results. But meanwhile the enemy were attacking from the south with small arms fire and shelling from a self-propelled gun. The Company Commander, Major Dottridge, immediately dispatched his remaining platoon under Lieutenant Mead to counter this threat. But no sooner had Nos 7 and 8 Platoons returned from dealing with the opposition on the left than more enemy moved up to take their place. It soon became apparent that the opposition was more than could be dealt with by one Company, so after sending back a wireless message as to the situation, Major Dottridge organised his men into a defensive position around the road junction. Occasional shelling and small arms fire was kept up by both sides; one enemy SP gun was destroyed, but another soon moved up to take its place.

On account of the craters and the presence of the enemy, the Wiltshires' B Company took a different route from the western outskirts of Kleve, not yet appreciating that the brigade was under a major attack:

> But they had proceeded barely 400 yards when suddenly SP guns opened up on the column, shooting between the houses from the high ground on

Fallschirmjäger were parachutists in name only in the final months of the war. Like the SS, they had lost much of their quality as fighting formations and were typically clothed and equipped with both *Fallschirmjäger* and ordinary items.

An already heavily laden infantry soldier carrying his platoon's anti-tank weapon, the PIAT.

> the right. Immediately two tanks, a jeep and a carrier were 'brewed-up'. The infantry, led by Captain Tarrant and Serjeant Latton, made a dash for the excellent firing position afforded by the rear windows of the houses on the right of the road, and there advancing down the hill across the field in froth of them were German infantry, a magnificent target for the riflemen, and one that was not wasted; the enemy withdrew with heavy casualties.

Lieutenant Renders, waiting with RHQ of the Sherwood Rangers for a liaison task, was to begin as an observer of the battle but soon:

> Around me I could hear the solid bangs of tank fire, the occasional blast of a *Panzerfaust* and the stutter of machine guns. Further up the column, I could see that Shermans from RHQ were attempting to engage a *Jagdpanther*.[9] The German self-propelled gun was using the cover of the facades of

> wrecked houses and the gaps between them to jockey in and out of fire positions. It would suddenly appear in the spaces between the ruins, fire one or two rounds and then pull back out of sight, before appearing at the next gap to fire again. I could hear the growl of its ... engine and the heavy squeal of its tracks, as the 45-ton monster moved behind the ruins looking for more fire positions. Popping my head up over the armoured plate of the Dingo, I squinted across at the gap between what remained of two houses next to our vehicle. Suddenly I found myself looking down the barrel of a bloody great 88mm gun, as the *Jagdpanther* reappeared less than 20 yards away. It had a clear line of sight to where we sat immobilised, with only a rather inadequate 12mm-thick section of the vehicle's armoured shield to protect us. There wasn't even time to think about bailing out.
>
> It was like something out of a slow-motion film and I think I might have got as far as saying 'shit', before I was stunned by the flash of the trace in the back of the armour-piercing round that shot less than a foot over the top of my head. It filled the compartment of the armoured car with a blinding light and I felt its heat before I heard the deafening report of the gun that had fired it. At 4 feet 11 inches, the top of the Dingo is significantly lower than the height of the average tank. Built with stealth in mind, it was a design feature that saved the driver and I from being atomised by the tungsten slug, which broke the sound barrier as it whipped over our heads. Given the range of the engagement, I have always suspected that the *Jagdpanther* was unable to depress its gun sufficiently to hit us. Fortunately, it did not hang around to prove me right or wrong, or to switch to an HE round that would have finished us.

The Somerset's 4 Battalion and 5 Wiltshires had just begun their advance when the leading companies encountered the enemy, coming from the south and west. The weight of the attack was such that the enemy had halted the British advance and as they were both deployed in column for the advance on Goch, to defend themselves they attempted to form all-round defence, amidst the rubble and uncertain situation. This was made all the more difficult as they were under attack by *Fallschirmjäger* from multiple directions.

The counter-attacks drove through the Wiltshire companies toward Colonel Kendrick and Headquarters 129 Brigade, where Lieutenant Renders was waiting:

> As the infantry battled it out among the bomb craters, shells of shattered houses and streets blocked with piles of bricks and smashed furniture, small-arms fire began to crackle around our own position. I saw the tanks of A Squadron [with 4th Wiltshire] move up past us, but there was little I could do, apart from sit in the Dingo and await instructions from the CO. The German paratroopers were beginning to work their way around the column and put in an attack against the brigade headquarters ... Throughout, snipers firing from upper-storey windows kept up a steady fusillade that

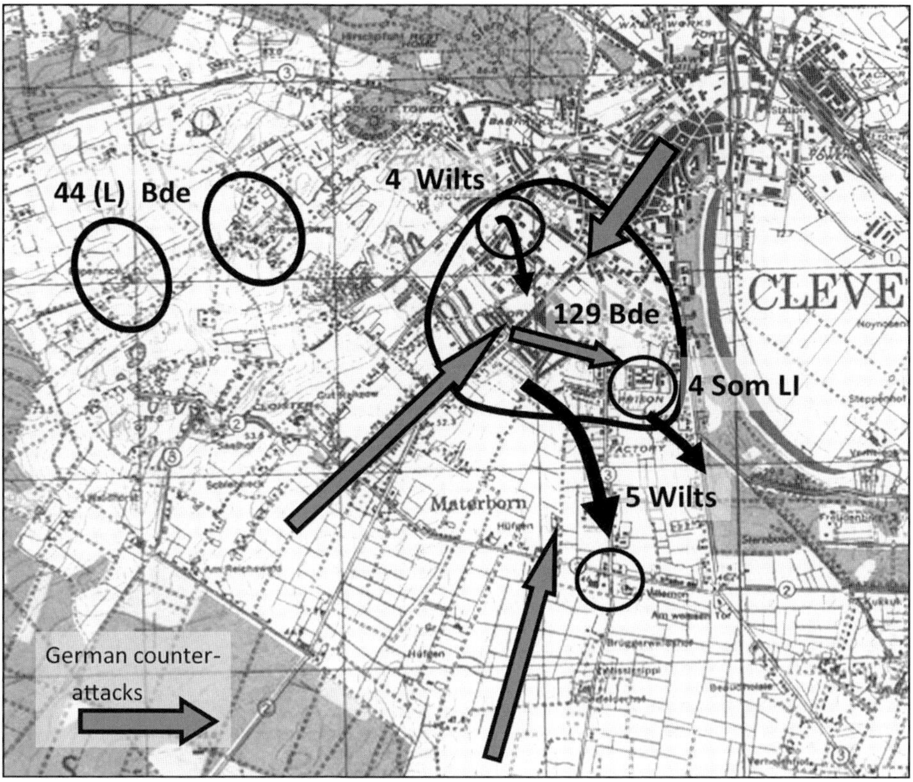

129 Brigade's battle south of Kleve, 10 February 1945.

The long barrel and distinctive design of muzzle brake of the StuG III, despite its low profile, led to frequent misidentification as other German armoured vehicles.

> threatened anyone caught out in the open or exposed in a turret. I felt somewhat helpless sitting in the Dingo, although if I kept my head down below its rim the armoured shields of the vehicle were sufficient to keep out the bullets and my job was to stay put until called for.

Finding themselves at close quarters with the enemy, the brigade's clerks, signallers and staff officers all reached for their personal weapons and fought off the enemy. During the fighting the brigade's staff captain G Ops was killed, but the commander and staff of 129 Brigade were not the only ones to find themselves defending their headquarters. General Fiebig, the commander of the

A Sherwood Rangers' tank in action seen from the cover of a ruined building near the centre of Kleve.

84th Infantry Division, had been caught out by the arrival of the Somersets and the Wiltshire battalions and became personally involved in the fighting. He and his headquarters were, however, lucky enough to escape from Kleve.

Private Pinner, one of the scattered soldiers left behind in a ruined building on the route through the city, following the attack on 5 Wiltshires' battalion headquarters, became a part of a group led by RSM Smith:

> There were noises of men approaching from the rear of the building and I felt that I had to consider my position. I came to the conclusion that if a large body of Germans appeared, and I was discovered, my only option was to surrender ... I watched anxiously from a hole in the wall, and to my great relief there appeared 'Smithy' with a body of which I later established to be cooks and signallers which 'Smithy' had rounded up from somewhere. I quickly made my presence known by calling out '5th Wilts'. I had no wish to be on the receiving end of either a grenade or a volley of shots from nervous comrades!
>
> 'Smithy' soon took control, organising look outs on the first floor, with a 'field' of fire covering all angles'.

Meanwhile, 4 Somerset LI were also under growing levels of attack, having already been split up into small packets as they drove across the southern suburbs. The battalion's war diary reported that the enemy *Panzerjäger* chose 'a part of the column where there were no tanks, drove out and shot up the column. Twelve vehicles (nearly all carriers) were knocked out.' Of the battle, Lieutenant Jary commented:

> What instructors at the School of Infantry would think about the fighting in Cleve I shudder to think. It resembled no other battle in my experience. I had little control and it developed into a section commander's battle. Looking back over the years, it seems militarily totally unprofessional – a real Wild West shoot-out. Tactically, the Germans had every advantage. We were strung out in a long column amid shattered buildings and piles of rubble, with groups of parachute troops attacking from both sides. They could snipe at us and engage us with their Spandaus from dozens of positions totally hidden by piles of rubble. They had the opportunity to concentrate their counter-attacks on the narrowest of fronts but failed to do so. I can only assume that we had the psychological advantage, the circumstances being so chaotic and disorganized. Perhaps, being Germans, they could not overcome their instinct for organization and tidiness.

The citation for Private Tipple's Military Medal provides a feel for that action as German panzers attacked the Somersets:

> The carrier platoon was in action when the position was attacked by a Panther, an SP and some infantry. The Panther came to within 25 yds. of the platoon's position, which began to look desperate. Pte. Tipple, armed with a

In recognition of the severe fight in Kleve on 10 February, officers and other ranks were awarded the Military Cross and the Military Medal respectively.

> PIAT, took his weapon into action. The tank spotted him and firing a round of H.E. at point black range, blew Pte. Tipple and his PIAT to the bottom of the crater. Undeterred, Pte. Tipple, with great courage, crawled up again to the lip of the crater, took up another fire position, engaged the tank, and scored direct hits. Unfortunately, he was unable to knock the tank out, but the blast effect caused it to beat a hasty retreat and it was not seen again.

The Somersets' war diary concluded that after 'confused fighting in the town by the afternoon we were established on the outskirts of the town on the far [southern] side'. At this point the brigade's transport was attempting to get forward to join the battalions. Lieutenant Jones drove around trying to locate 4 Wiltshires but 'found only Germans who shot at him and men that stood on street corners waving by vehicles of friend and foe alike'. Having located the battalion, the Provo Sergeant, Sergeant Welch, was directing vehicles into position when he:

> was approached in a gap in the convoy by several Germans, one of whom was an officer. He thought they were prisoners, so he jerked his thumb to the rear and said 'Go on **** off!' The German drew his pistol and said in excellent English 'You **** off! – at which point some more vehicles were heard approaching and the Germans departed.

With 129 Brigade established in defensive positions in the southern outskirts, despite the presence of roving groups of Germans, this left the ruins of the centre of Kleve in enemy hands, to be cleared by 15th Scottish Division.

The Projector Infantry Anti-Tank (PIAT)

The infantry platoon had fought the 1940 campaign with the Boys Anti-Tank Rifle, but it was already becoming obsolescent due to the increased thickness of armour of the heavier German panzers of the day. Nor was the rifle-fired No. 68 Anti-Tank Grenade useful in battle, It was not until 1943 that the PIAT came into service, by which time an effective shaped charge warhead was available.

The shaped charge warhead relied on the Munroe Effect to penetrate armour, rather than kinetic energy that required a substantial propellant charge, a heavy barrel and the recoil system of an anti-tank gun. The Germans solved this problem with their rocket-propelled *Panzerfaust* and *Panzerschreck* and the Americans with the Bazooka. The British took a different approach based on the spring-powered spigot mortar system used in the Blacker Bombard of the dark days of 1940 and 1941. The shaped charge and the spigot mortar concept were brought together to produce the Projector Infantry Anti-Tank.

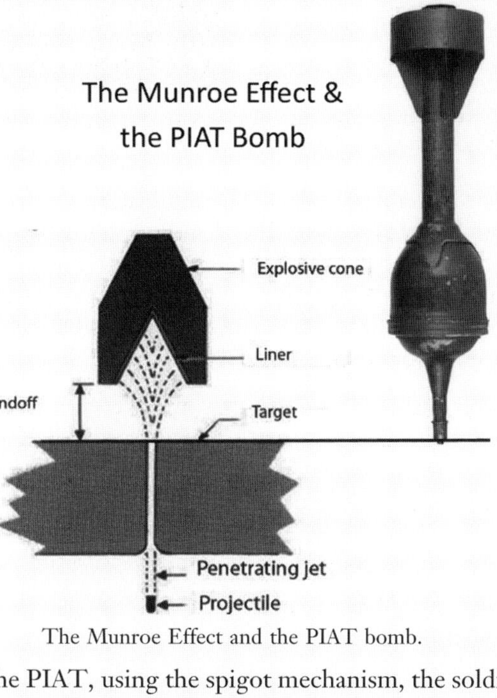

The Munroe Effect and the PIAT bomb.

To cock and load the PIAT, using the spigot mechanism, the soldier had to upend the PIAT, place his feet on the shoulder padding and turn the weapon to unlock the body and then lock the spigot rod to the butt. He would then have to bend over and pull the body of the weapon upwards, pulling the spring back until it clicked into the trigger, thus cocking the weapon. The final step was to lower the body and turn it back to lock it in position. From this explanation it is clear that a tall strong soldier was needed to man the PIAT. It is also obvious that cocking the weapon from the prone position in action was substantially more difficult. Consequently, the two-man crew went into action with the PIAT cocked with only the first bomb to load. Although cocking was a major issue with the weapon, it did not need re-cocking after firing. A small charge at the base of the bomb did this when the round was launched by pushing the spigot back.

A sectionalised PIAT showing the size of the spring.

While the difficulty of cocking the PIAT was a clear disadvantage, there were several points that more than compensated. Firstly, it had a larger (2½lb) warhead than the Bazooka. Secondly, being spring driven, it had no firing signature and, thirdly, unlike rocket systems that had a backblast, it could be more easily be fired from cover, including buildings.

At 32lb and 39in long, the PIAT was neither small nor light, but it had an effective range of 115 yards. It could penetrate 4in (100mm) of armour and take on buildings at a range of 350 yards.

Canadian infantry training in the use of the PIAT. The instructor is demonstrating the loading of the bomb, which would normally be the task of the No. 2.

The PIAT and bomb.

The Destruction of Kleve

For the British soldier, the small Rhineland city of Kleve was the first German urban area they had entered. Not only did the experience of trying to fight their way through it leave its mark, but the levels of destruction principally wrought by Bomber Command shocked them. Even those familiar with the blitzed cities of England commented:

> Hardly anything had survived intact. I'd seen nothing like it, rubble everywhere, houses tumbled into the streets and huge craters caused by blockbusters [*sic*], a lot of them flooded. Most of the cellars survived and had been used by the Germans as shelters from which we winkled hundreds of them out.[10]

Kleve had in fact been first bombed on 22 September 1944 during MARKET GARDEN and several times since, with a big raid on 7 October destroying the historic Swan Tower, the *Schwanenturm*, the symbol of the city.[11] By February 1945, the old centre of Kleve was in ruins and much of the rest of the city badly damaged. The 287 aircraft that bombed Kleve at the beginning of VERITABLE only really finished the destruction of the city and General Horrocks, who probably did not realise that he was looking at the cumulative effect of the bombing, wrote:

> After the war, I used to suffer from nightmares and literally for years these always concerned Kleve. Unfortunately, it was even worse than I had imagined. I had specifically asked for 'incendiaries' to be used, but through some error 1,384 tons of high explosive had been dropped, and the huge craters in Kleve not only held up the German reserves but our own troops as well.

This was no 'error', the bomber barons from Monte Cassino onwards frequently reinterpreted requests from the armies to their own ends – destruction, rather

The historic city of Kleve lay in ruins by the end of February 1945.

than aiding the tactical battle on the ground. Brigadier Essame was excoriating in his criticism: 'What always will rankle in the minds of those who fought at Kleve is the oafish stupidity of the attack by Bomber Command.'

By the evening of 10 February, the first German counter-attacks had been contained and 129 Brigade's situation stabilised but they were still effectively isolated by rising floods, traffic jams and the enemy. Fortunately, the soldiers of the brigade had three 24-hour ration packs but the logistical situation, particularly with ammunition and to a lesser extent fuel, was becoming dangerous, or as Brigadier Essame put it: 'Maintenance was clearly going to be the biggest headache. The enemy had evidently breached the winter dykes on the Alter Rhine, for there was now two feet of water over the main road east of Wyler.' That evening the division's Q staff managed to get one day's supply sent forward 'under special authority from Corps' along the main axis, which this time was effectively cleared of all other traffic.

3rd Canadian Division

With few amphibious vehicles and a growing list of demands on them, the tempo of the 3rd Canadian Division's operations remained low. One unspectacular but thoroughly necessary task was the maintenance and extension of smoke operations on the banks of the Rhine. No fewer than twelve precious Buffaloes ferried forward 120 tons of smoke oil and No. 24 smoke pots a day, plus further equipment and crews to extend coverage.[12] Once landed on the dyke, the fuel was distributed along it by the carriers of the division's recce regiment.

Back on the other side of the Rhine inundations, where the water level crept up on the Kleve road throughout the day, 2nd Canadian Division's engineers built and operated four ferries that ran from Wyler to just beyond the floods at Kranenburg. These ferries were used to transport vital combat supplies forward, bypassing both the floods and traffic jams, and then on their return journey bring back casualties. The route the ferries took was through 8 to 10ft of water, but even so, avoiding sunken hedges and fence posts was the difficult part of the operation. At Wyler, wounded soldiers evacuated from Kleve and the Materborn feature were transferred to vehicles of the field ambulances and taken to the hospitals established in the Nijmegen area.

The 3rd Canadian Division's task for 10 February was to deliver the second phase of the operation. Brigadier Rockingham's 9 Brigade was to take the front forward from the line of Keeken and Mehr captured the previous day to the Spoy Canal. The battalion's objectives were on the right flank for the Stormont, Glengarry and Dundas Highlanders (SG&D), Donsbrüggen and Rindern, and for the Highland Light Infantry of Canada the village of Düffelward.

Preparations for the attack and the wait for sufficient Buffaloes for the two battalions took all morning and the floods prevented the divisional field artillery's

LVT Buffaloes of 79 Assault Squadron RE and smoke operations on the dyke.

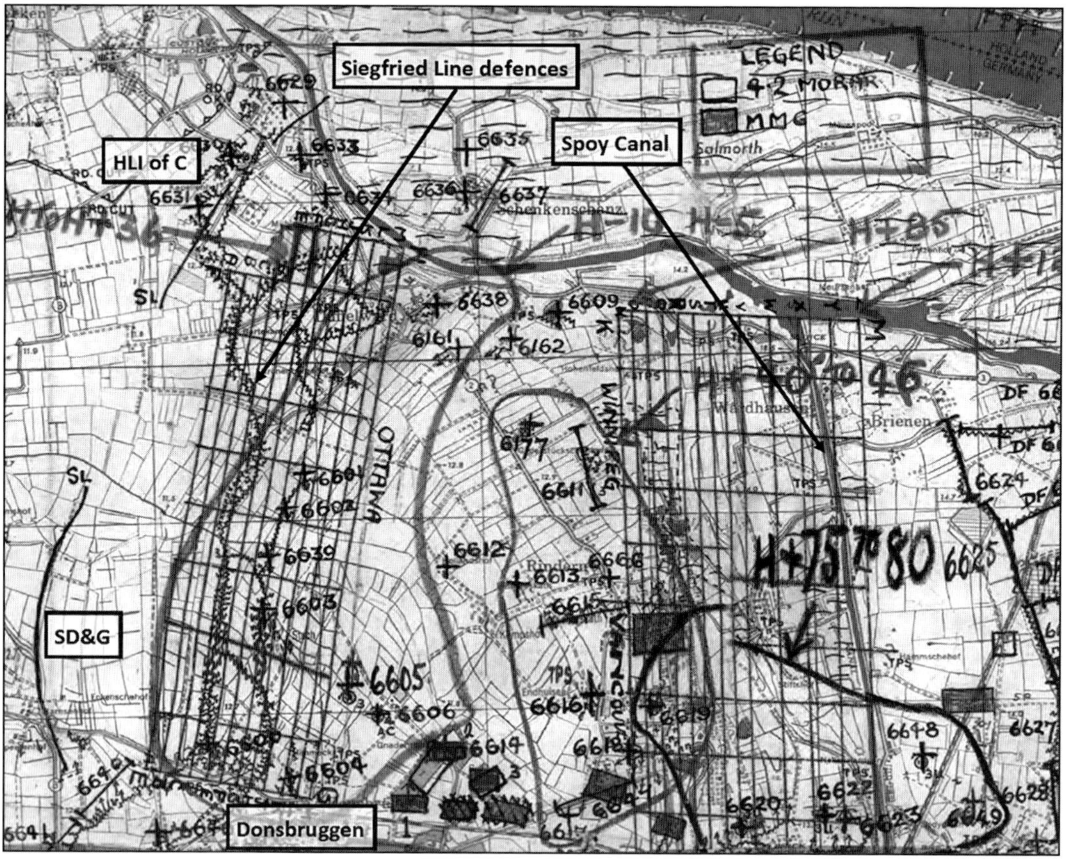

The divisional machine gun battalion's original fire plan to support the advance on 10 February and defensive fire tasks beyond the Spoy Canal.

25-pounder batteries from moving forward to their anticipated positions. Consequently, battalions were told that they would have to rely on their own resources, i.e. their 3in mortars, along with the 4.2in mortars and Vickers machine guns of the Cameron Highlanders of Ottawa.

After waiting in southern suburbs of Nijmegen all morning, the brigade embarked on the Buffaloes near Beek for the 8-mile journey across the southern edge of the inundated area to their first objectives. The SG&D war diary for 10 February records:

0700 Embarking the Buffaloes and Weasels.
1405 Clear of enemy. The first objective for the SD&Gs was DONSBRÜGGEN that day.

A and C companies of the SG&D landed short of their objective and advanced on the village from landward. As C Company approached Donsbrüggen they came under machine gun from the village and the adjacent wooded slopes. C Company dealt with the enemy outpost and the defenders of Donsbrüggen, while 2nd Gordon Highlanders, supported by the Churchills of the Coldstream Guards, advanced on the road from Nütterden. With the Highlanders and Canadians

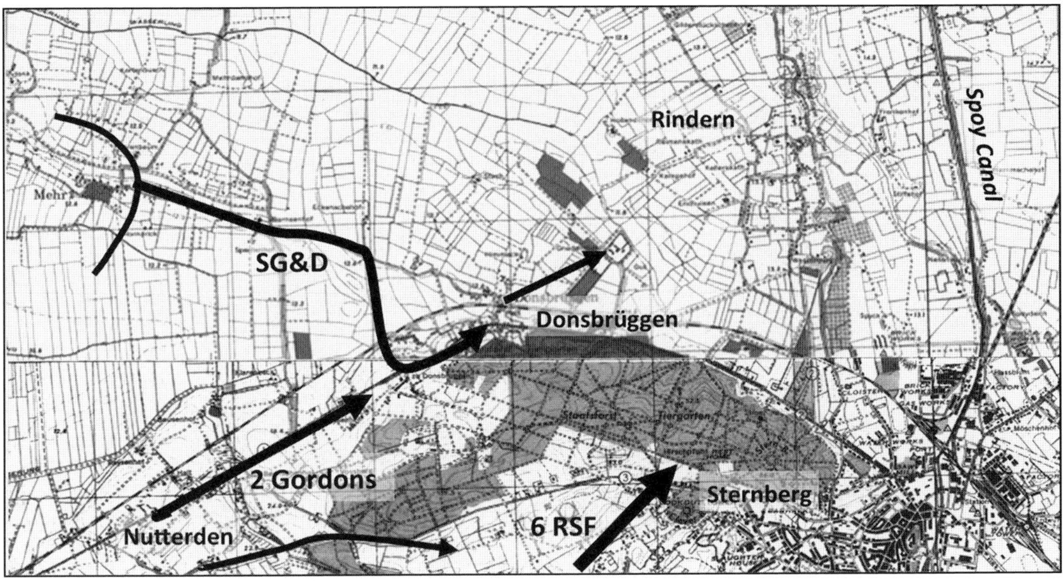

The advance to Donsbrüggen and Rindern.

closing in, the German defenders withdrew without further resistance and C Company cleared the houses in detail. Having completed this, the platoons were pushed out into the flooded country to secure outlying farms on islands of slightly higher ground along with the substantial Schloss Gnadenthal. In sweeping through the area, Corporal Baker single-handedly cleared four houses on the road east of the village, killing four Germans. For his actions he was awarded the Military Medal.

Colonel Rowley went forward with his tactical headquarters to a farmhouse to observe Rindern, but they had been seen and armour-piercing rounds were soon ripping through the roof. Nonetheless, with B and D companies not yet having arrived and C Company clearing up the Donsbrüggen area, the CO launched an attack on the village with A Company. On the approaches to Rindern, the company secured an abandoned Pak 40 anti-tank gun. One Canadian soldier recalled:

> We got in there alright, but they were waiting for us, German parachutists. It was my first experience with that sort of hand-to-hand fighting and there was a good deal of it, with both sides rolling grenades through windows and that sort of thing.

Having overcome a part of the garrison of Rindern, A Company pushed on through the village to the battalion's objective on the Spoy Canal, a further 800 yards east. In doing so, however, 7 Platoon was cut off by fire from a house they had bypassed. Resistance grew and C Company were brought up to join the battle in the village with the aid of a manpack flame thrower.

Colonel Rowley concluded that: 'The boys did very well. We took a lot of prisoners and held them in sort of a barnyard.' The village of Rindern was, however, not fully secured until dawn on 11 February, following a night of fighting with pockets of enemy who fell back from house to house.

Out on the left flank, B Company of the Highland Light Infantry of Canada (HLI of C) made good progress but they were brought to a halt short of Düffelward by well-sited enemy pillboxes and defended houses.

As darkness fell, A Company were sent wading through mud and water across 900 yards of open ground while 5.5 and 4.5in guns pummelled the village. Despite this fire the company was only able to establish a toehold in the village, where they were involved in a miserable and costly struggle. Not only did the Germans

SG&D Highlanders during their long cruise from the outskirts of Nijmegen towards Rindern.

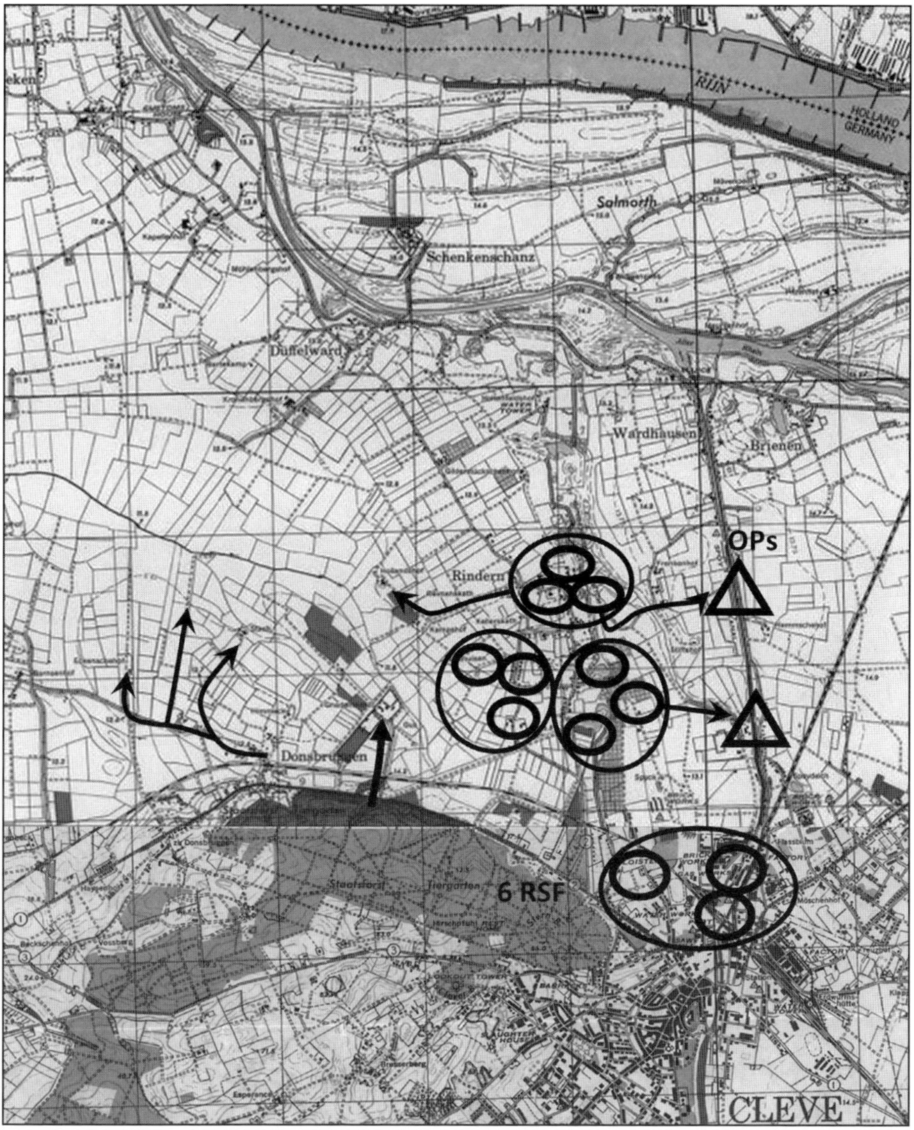

An extract from a map in 9 Brigade's war diary showing SD&G operations at Donsbrüggen and Rindern.

put up a fight but the village was being slowly submerged thanks to the blowing of another dyke. After fighting all night, the village was only finally secure in Canadian hands when A Company was joined by D Company the following morning. Meanwhile, the HLI's other companies were ordered to bypass the village and, at midnight, B and C companies were in possession of their section of the Spoy Canal.

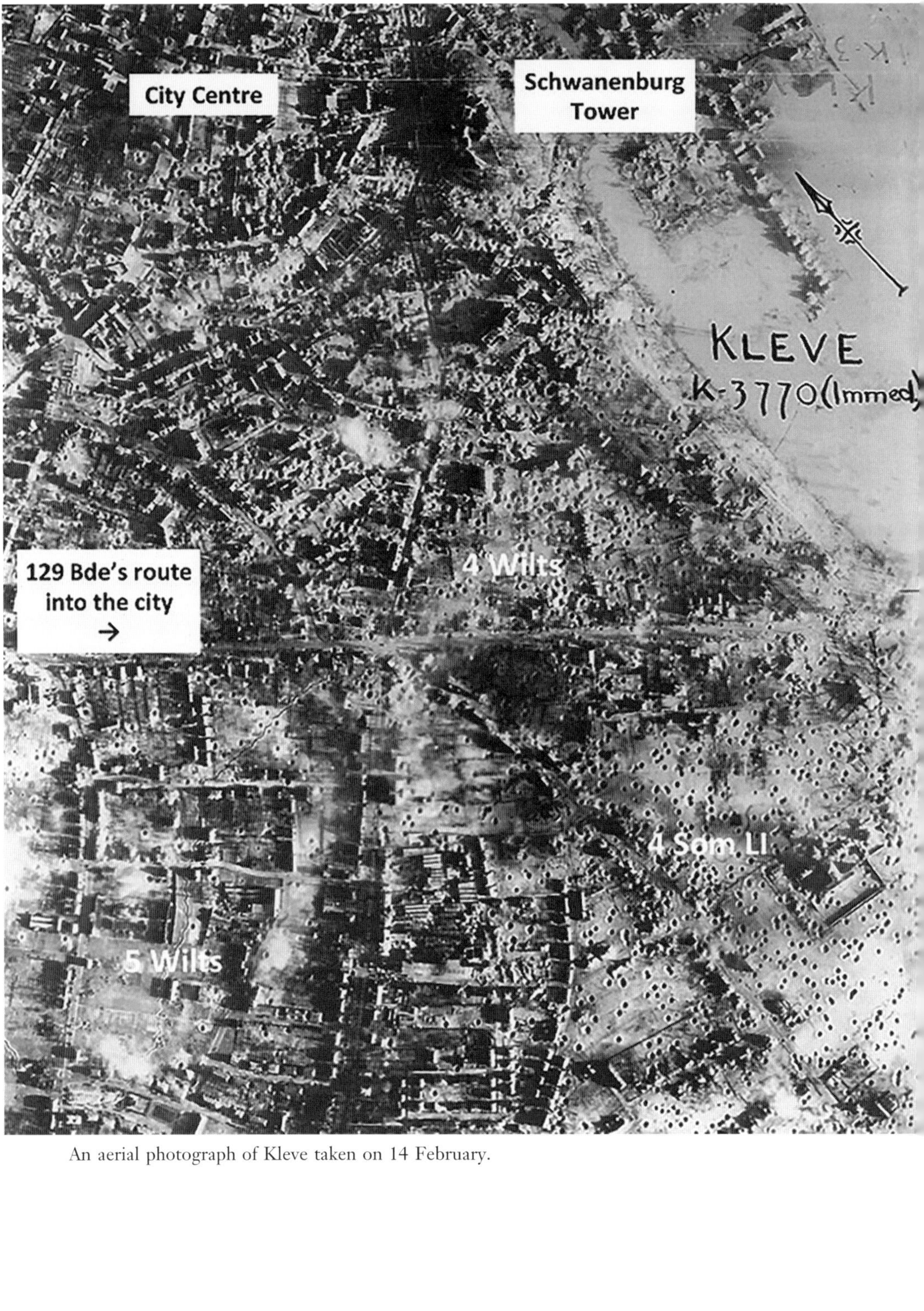

An aerial photograph of Kleve taken on 14 February.

Chapter Ten

The First Attack on Materborn

10–11 February 1945

It was not until late afternoon that the traffic cleared enough for leading units of 214 Brigade to be able to make their way south from Nütterden and through the narrow neck of woods that by now had become the main route to Kleve. The 43rd Recce Regiment led, followed by 5th Duke of Cornwall's Light Infantry and B Squadron, 4th/7th Dragoon Guards, their tanks laden with tree trunks to help with de-bogging. Once up on the high ground they were to follow the edge of the Reichswald in a south-westerly direction, taking the difficult sandy road. There was, however, no alternative and the 43rd Recce Regiment's B Squadron was directed down the track, through the forest towards Materborn. The track proved to be 'scarcely practicable for their unwieldy armoured cars and on approaching Saalhof east of Cloister they struck strong opposition. As a result, through no fault of their own, they jammed the track and hindered the advance of 5 DCLI.'[1]

The task of 214 Brigade was to get on to Goch and to that end Brigadier Essame and Lieutenant Colonel Taylor, commanding the DCLI, would have preferred to bypass the villages, but the German positions in them dominated the ground up to the Reichswald. Thus Saalhof, Cloister and Materborn villages had to be cleared. It was hoped that a vigorous attack would open the way for an advance to Hau just beyond the Goch road. On the basis of this, Colonel Taylor dispatched B Company on a 2-mile advance along the edge of the forest, with the expectation of joining them with the rest of the battalion once opposition in the villages had been dealt with.

By the time the DCLI were clear of the jam on the sandy track, dusk was falling. Colonel Taylor, with his battery commander of 179 Field Regiment, RA, produced a hasty fire plan to soften up Saalhof, with the support of all guns of the divisional artillery that were in range and the battalion's mortars. Also forward was the self-propelled battery of 147 Essex Yeomanry's 25-pounder Sextons attached to the 4th/7th Dragoon Guards. Major Lonsdale's D Company, supported by the tanks, 'swept in to finish the job in house to house fighting'. Lieutenant Colonel Taylor wrote:

> The Germans fell back into Materborn. Before pursuing them, I formulated a plan whereby we could keep one company [B Company] on the move by by-passing the village between the road and the edge of the forest. This decision had been prompted by the fact that ... not a shot had been fired at us from those sinister-looking woods. We were a wonderful target.

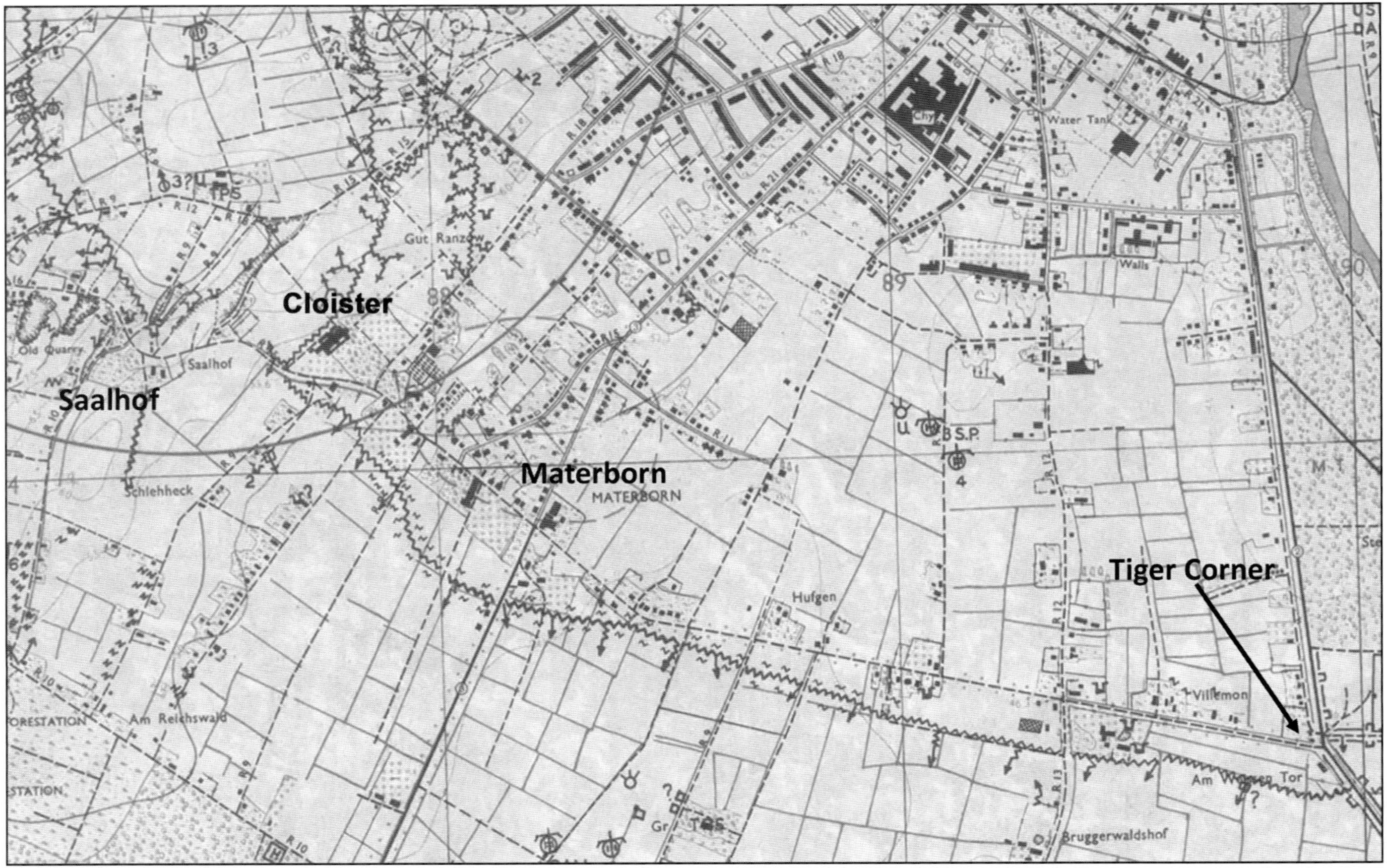

An extract from the tactical overprint map showing the now occupied defences around Materborn village.

Lieutenant Colonel George Taylor, the highly successful commanding officer of 5 DCLI.

> There was just time to brief the company in the fast-fading light. They were to take the road near the corner of the forest, just south of Hau. The ground was too soft for vehicles or tanks to accompany them. Meanwhile, we hoped to catch the enemy off balance by smashing through Materborn with the tanks and, using the road, press on to link up with B Coy. But despite the Germans' night defeat in Saalhof, they were better organised than we thought, and were reinforced with tanks and support guns.[2]

The attack on Materborn had 'seemed doomed to failure from the start. One of the tanks carrying one of the three C Coy platoons refused to start; then, just when the advance was nicely under way on the road leading to the village, the Germans opened up with their 88s.' The commanding officer continued:

> The men crouched on the cold, inhospitable armour plating of the tanks tried to make themselves as small as mice as the tracer and shrapnel flashed and crashed around them. The first tank [the troop commander's], carrying Lieut Bruce Jones and his men of 15 Platoon, burst into flames after taking

The cap badge and shoulder insignia of 5 DCLI.

two bazookas' hits. And to add to our misery the heavy rain that had begun soon after that attack started turned into snow.

While C Company were attacking Materborn frontally, D Company had been ordered to work their way around the right flank and to attack the village from the south-west but they fared no better:

After crossing a series of water-filled ditches in the dark and fighting for hours, the men were soaked to the skin and nearly dropping from fatigue, mostly the effect of the previous night. Discretion, I decided, must be the better part of valour. I called the whole thing off. The battalion had to be rested and fed and then we could make a better job of it on the morrow.

Colonel Taylor ordered C and D companies to fall back for the night into defensive positions beyond the large monastery buildings (marked Cloister on the maps), halfway between Saalhof and Materborn. B Company had, as ordered,

A Sexton 25-pounder self-propelled gun of the type attached to British armoured brigades.

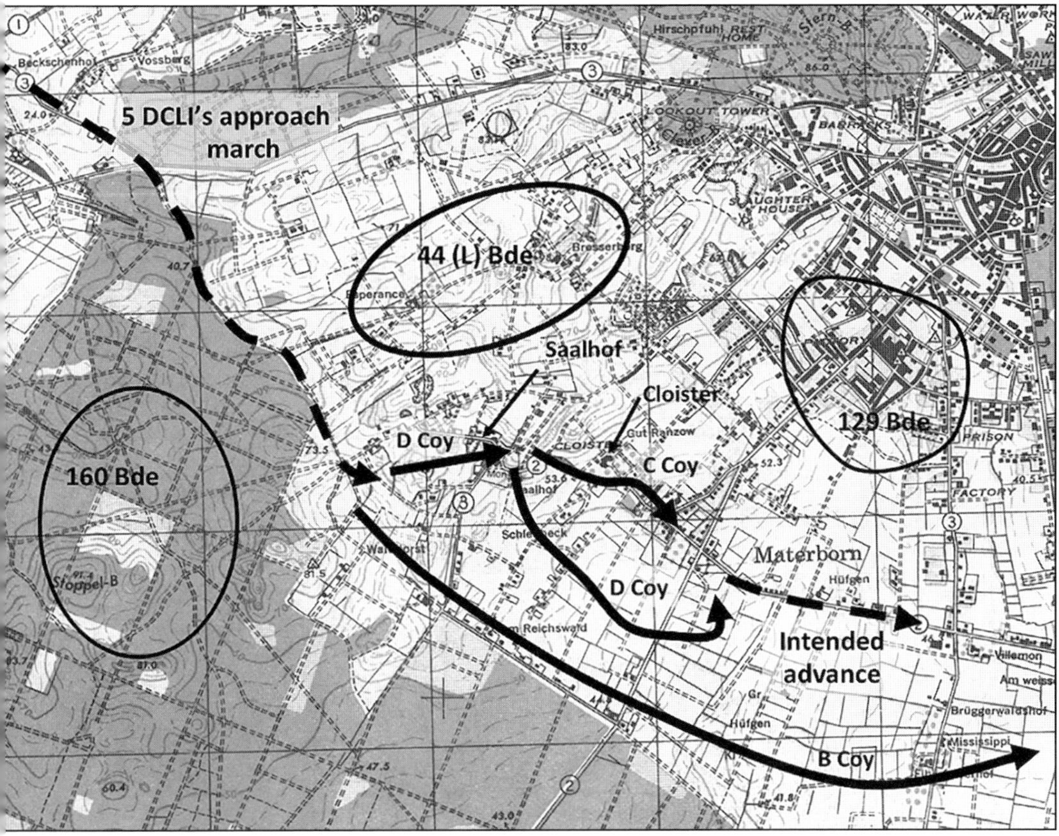

Colonel Taylor's plan for the capture of Materborn and the advance to 'Tiger Corner' on the evening of 10 February.

penetrated 2 miles along the edge of the Reichswald towards Hau. The regimental historian described the company's night-time excursion:

> Meanwhile B Company had made good progress. They had set out on their ... march just as it was getting dark. The going was slow, for they were in enemy country, they carried heavy kit and they had had no sleep for forty-eight hours. The route, along the edge of the forest, involved the passage of innumerable wire fences, no easy obstacles for a heavily encumbered man to negotiate in the dark, certainly not in silence. At first progress was helped by artificial moonlight over another part of the battlefield, but when this was turned off it became very dark and they had much difficulty in locating their objective, one of several roads cutting right across the axis of advance. In the continued search for the road to Hau parties of Germans were met, shots were exchanged, and the company became split. Nos 11 and 12 Platoons (Lieutenants Yarker and Acton) laboured across 2,000 yards of sticky ploughland, thinking the rest of the company were ahead of them. They eventually reached the Cleve–Goch road on which lay the company's objective but they searched along it for some way without finding any signs of the remainder of their company. The platoon commanders discussed

The Sten gun was carried by most NCOs in a platoon rather than the rifle.

> this situation and came to the sensible conclusion that a weak force such as theirs would stand no chance in their present exposed position once their whereabouts became known to the enemy. They therefore decided to withdraw about 500 yards to a farmhouse which they had noticed during their advance, and which offered some prospect of defence.

Lieutenant Acton described the cautious approach they made to the buildings at Verelenhof:

> As we approached the farm Lieutenant Yarker and six NCOs, all armed with stens, went forward to see if it was occupied. They were challenged when

The No. 18 manpack radio set in use during training earlier in the war. Its sensitive valve technology was prone to damage by rough handling and wet conditions. Add to this variable-quality batteries and a relatively short range, infantry radio communication was generally poor.

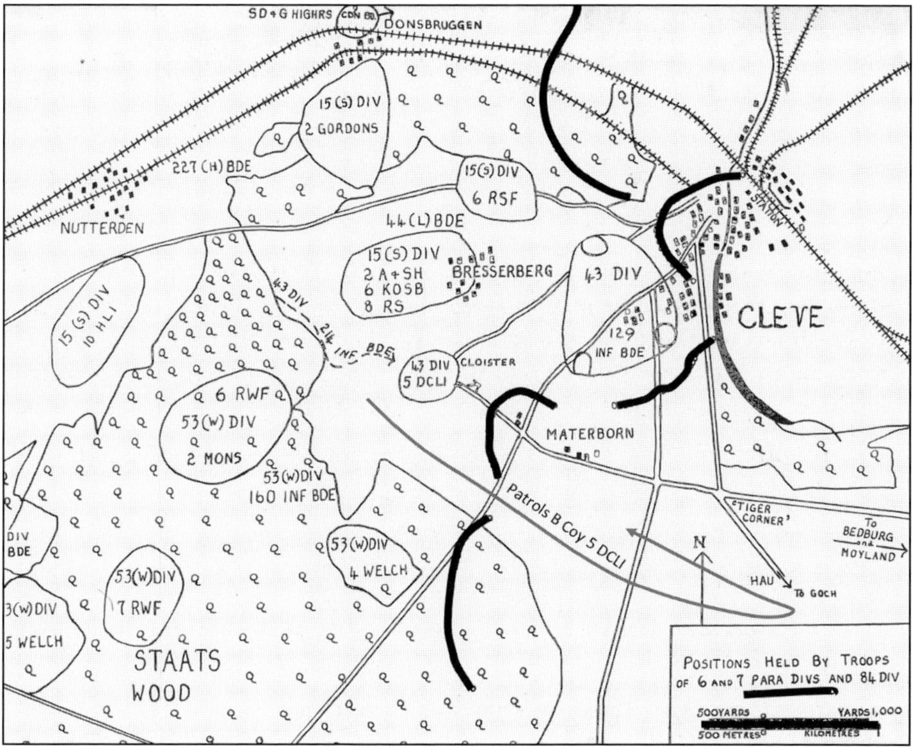

Brigadier Essame's map of the situation in Kleve overnight on 10–11 February 1944.

> they were about 20 yards from the building. The challenge appeared to come from a window and was repeated. Immediately all seven stens fired at the window; there was no repetition! We entered the farm and found a captain and about a dozen men. They offered no resistance, in fact some of them were asleep. There was no sign of the man who had challenged us; further investigation proved that the challenge had come from a loud speaker set in the window. The prisoners told us that they were the staff of an observation post for heavy artillery. The telephone then started to ring. This put us in rather a spot. We dared not allow the officer to answer it; on the other hand, none of us spoke good enough German to bluff it out. We therefore let it ring, hoping that they would only send a line party to investigate. We could easily deal with them. The most welcome sight in the farm was a mug of hot coffee. This was the usual ersatz stuff, but a drink was never more appreciated.

It was not long before a strong group of Germans approached the farm, and the two platoons were lucky to get away amidst a fusillade that fortunately did no harm. Lieutenants Acton and Yarker were lucky to get back and join the rest of the battalion.

Meanwhile, according to Colonel Taylor, B Company HQ, had returned:

> They had reached their destination, but their communications had failed and they had lost touch with Battalion HQ and I was very anxious about their fate. Fortunately, Major Hutchins, after waiting for some time and seeing no sign of a battalion breakthrough, had wisely decided to come back. Without tanks or anti-tank guns, the company would have been in an extremely vulnerable position.

Brigadier Essame noted that by 0300 hours B Company had returned to the battalion in Saalhof and Cloister, 'bringing back with it fifteen prisoners and considerable though confusing information'.

Chapter Eleven

The Advance from Kleve

11 February 1945

The previous day the 43rd Wessex Division's 129 Brigade had found itself in the southern suburbs of Kleve, where they were vigorously counter-attacked and virtually surrounded by *Fallschirmjäger* from various divisions that had been rushed to the defence of the city. The traffic jam that resulted from this enemy action and the precipitate committal of the Wessex reduced the tempo of operations on VERITABLE's northern axis down to a crawl. It was not until the late afternoon of the 10th that the 15th Scottish Division, having shaken themselves free of the traffic jams, partly cleared the wooded high ground west of the city. It was dark by the time 214 Brigade also got through the traffic jams between Kranenburg and Nütterden and was able to start moving up onto the eastern extremity of the Materborn feature and start to advance on Goch. By nightfall, with serious enemy resistance and very difficult ground condition, neither the Scots nor the Wessex had achieved their objectives. Consequently, XXX Corp's intent for the 11th was for the Scots to relieve 129 Brigade and complete the clearance of Kleve, while the Wessex, with 8 Armoured Brigade under command, were to thrust south towards Goch, as the first phase of a breakout into the Rhineland.

Before the 15th Division arrived in Kleve, the *Fallschirmjäger* reinforcements started to push out into the suburbs occupied by 129 Brigade. One position they encountered was held by RSM Smith, a true warrior character, and 'a motley bunch of clerks, signallers, cooks and drivers' from 5 Wiltshires. Private Pinner recalled:

> During the morning, our first floor look-outs reported large numbers of Germans approaching across what had once been the gardens of our ruined dwelling. We manned whatever vantage points gave us a clear view, and we waited with bated breath, trying not to make the slightest sound. At last the enemy came into full view, and there appeared to be some 50 or 60 Germans coming our way. 'Smithy' was beside himself with delight 'teach the buggers a lesson – let them get closer until I give the order to fire'. At a range of some 50 yards we let fly with every weapon at our disposal. The result was devastating, the surviving Germans fled; leaving many dead behind on the ground, which 'Smithy' insisted counting – 29 dead he reported with a great deal of satisfaction.[1]

Private Pinner's photo of the area in Kleve where he fought with 'Smithy's' 'motley bunch'.

15th Scottish Division

Despite Hitler's insistence that Kleve be held at all costs, after 'sporadic and confused fighting during the night', by the morning of 11 February the majority of the city's defenders had fought their way out, leaving only isolated detachments to provide opposition to the Scots. Even though there was no longer organised defence in Kleve, General Schlemm had managed to produce a defence based on 6th and 7th *Fallschirmjäger* divisions around the city to contain the British.

General Barber's plan in greater detail was for 227 Brigade to continue its advance from Donsbrüggen via the main road into Kleve and clear the northern part of the city. Once relieved by 46 Highland Brigade, 44 Brigade would continue its operations on the high ground to the west of Kleve, take over the southern portion of the city from the Wessex and complete its clearance in detail.

The relief in place of 44 Brigade on the northern end of the Materborn feature took place overnight, and the first recorded action of the day was the dispatch of what has been described as a company-sized reconnaissance patrol towards Kleve at 0700 hours. This speculative advance by 6 KOSB, however, very quickly ran into trouble, once again in the Sternberg area, into which the enemy had re-infiltrated during the night. The 8 Royal Scots Fusiliers and their Churchills from 4 Tank Grenadier Guards (6 Guards Armoured Brigade) were brought forward and the combined effect of an artillery bombardment and fire from the tanks prompted approximately 100 of the *Fallschirmjäger* defenders to surrender. The RSF remained around the watch tower on the Sternberg to prevent any further enemy infiltration, while Brigadier Cumming-Bruce ordered 8 Royal Scots and 6 KOSB into the city. By 1030 hours they had taken over most of the southern suburbs from 129 Brigade and set about clearing their sector of the ruins of Kleve. There was little ground opposition beyond 'mopping up' but clearing acres of rubble was a slow process, with most of the brigade's casualties inflicted by German artillery fire.

Operations of 15th Scottish Division, 11 February 1945.

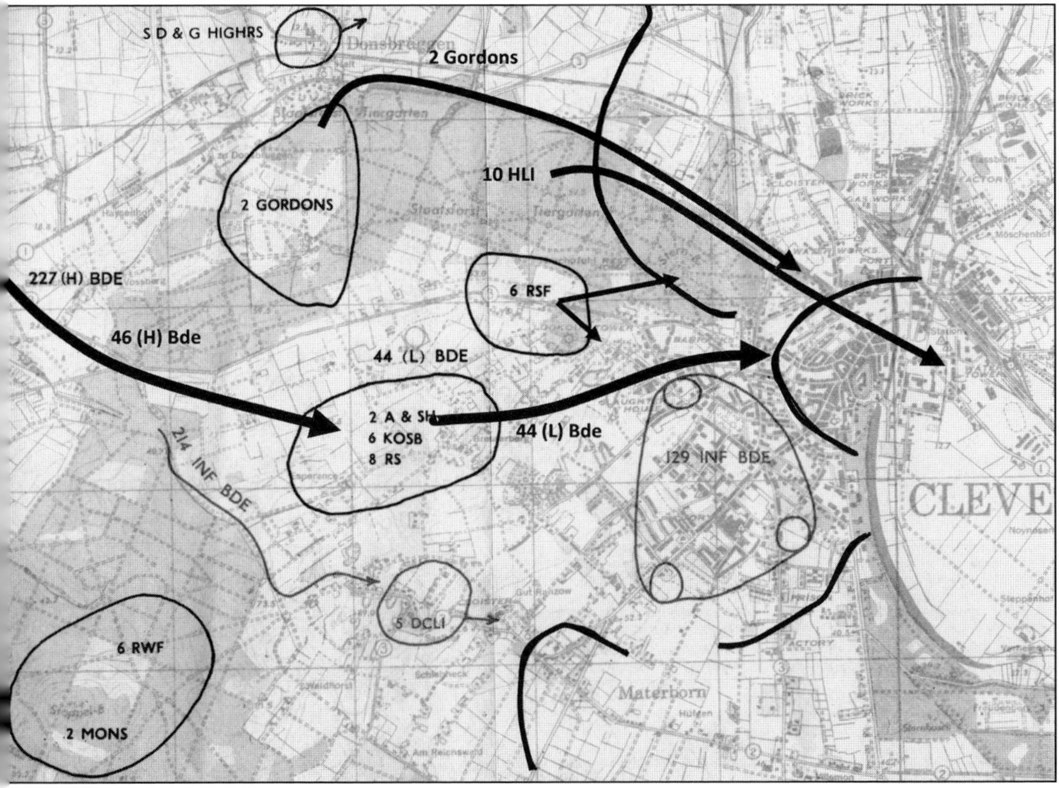

Meanwhile, 2 Gordons (227 Brigade) and the Left Flank Squadron, 3 Tank Scots Guards, continued their advance to Kleve on the main road from Donsbrüggen but they too struck opposition almost immediately. A Churchill was knocked out by a *Panzerfaust* fired from the steeply rising wooded hillside to the right, where 'stiffish' opposition was reported. The Gordons' battlegroup then proceeded to clear the feature with the assistance of a troop of Churchills. By early afternoon the Gordons and the attached tanks of the Scots Guards had reached Kleve, where Lieutenant Colonel de Winton Wills set up his headquarters in the cellars of a boot factory. The city had been bombed flat, so movement was difficult in the centre but the guards' forward squadrons soon reported that not only had they cleared the northern sector up to the canal, but also that they had taken a bridge almost intact over the canal west of the railway station. By 1530 hours they had established a bridgehead across the canal and the bridge itself had been repaired.

This was the report that 10 Highland Light Infantry and the Scots Guards' Right Flank Squadron had been waiting for all day. Their task was to pass

2 Gordons clearing the slope on the way to Kleve on 11 February – along with a captured goat.

Sir Edward de Winton Wills, commanding officer of 3 Tank Scots Guards.

through the Gordons' bridgehead and to clear the city east of the canal. As dusk fell and with time pressing, the HLI drove into Kleve. Their sudden and noisy arrival precipitated what the divisional historian described as a 'moment [when] there was all the makings of a promising battle between the HLI and the Scots Guards on one side and the 44th Brigade and the Grenadiers coming up from the south'. However, with the aid of a single Crocodile from C Squadron,

141 RAC, the eastern part of the city was secured with little trouble and the final act of the day was to push 15 Reconnaissance Regiment's patrols through the ruins and east along the road to Emmerich.

The 15th's divisional historian noted that such was the level of destruction in the city it was 'hard to find anywhere for the soldiers to get out of the rain and snow'. Rather than return to leaguers to the rear, the guards' squadrons, to avoid traffic jams and groups of isolated enemy infantry, bivouacked amidst the ruins among the infantry companies.

Throughout the day the flood waters continued to rise in both Kranenburg and in Kleve, despite blowing a 165ft stretch of dyke near Nijmegen to release the flood waters downstream. This it had been calculated would drain the Rhine flats of an estimated 2 million gallons an hour back into the River Waal, but in response the Germans created another breach upstream that more than compensated for the outflow of water further west. Consequently, there was no relief for

Infantry of 227 Highland Brigade mounted on the tanks of 3 Tanks Scots Guards.

the logisticians, who had to sustain the fighting in Kleve despite the flooded road. In addition to the Canadian engineers' ferry service, increasing numbers of Royal Army Service Corps DUKW companies were summoned to support the logistic effort. The historian of 6 Guards Armoured Brigade reported that this was a success, albeit, he noted, helped by finding a large German ration store. Consequently, quartermasters were able to concentrate on bringing forward fuel and ammunition, of which 'there was no shortage of either'.

The Canadian Advance to the Spoy Canal Continues

Out on the inundated Rhine floodplain, the previous day had seen the committal of Brigadier Rockingham's 9 Canadian Brigade, which duly took the advance forward to the line of the Spoy Canal. On the right flank, the Stormont, Dundas and Glengarry Highlanders (SD&G) had secured Rindern, which was finally fully in Canadian hands around dawn on 11 February. A serious counter-attack launched by *Fallschirmjäger* in at least company strength from Kleve, fell on C Company at 0930 hours but fortunately by this time the SD&G had been joined by their support weapons and reorganised, so were in position to defend their gains. The enemy fought hard to break into the southern part of the village but failed, with the guns of the divisional artillery coming to the aid of the SG&D.

Meanwhile, the Highland Light Infantry of Canada had fought an even more protracted battle for Düffelward, adjacent to the Alter Rhine dyke and a good 2 miles short of their objective on the Spoy Canal. Despite the Germans' isolated

A DUKW of 297 Transport Company RASC and a Buffalo. Note the smokescreen.

A Canadian infantry platoon embarking on an LVT.

position on the dykes and the imminent loss of Kleve, they fought determinedly amidst the rising waters. It was not until early afternoon of the 11th that D Company, aboard increasingly scarce serviceable Buffaloes, advanced to Wardhausen on the Spoy Canal. Resistance here was limited and the village was secured without loss at dusk.

With Kleve finally in XXX Corps' hands and the Canadians poised to outflank the defences beyond the city, we must return to the Wessex Division.

43rd Wessex Division

Meanwhile, 129 Brigade to the south of the city, having been relieved of defensive responsibilities by the Scots, adjusted their positions with a view to resuming the advance towards Goch. The 4 Somersets moved to some high ground on the south-eastern outskirts of Kleve, which took most of the day to clear thanks to German reinforcement. Lieutenant Jary, of 18 Platoon, 4 Somersets, finally dug in, but:

> Below us, about 1,200 yards to our front, was a church with a small copse a few hundred yards beyond it. Through binoculars I could see the rear of a *Wehrmacht* open Volkswagen protruding from behind the church tower.

The shoulder flashes of 4 Somerset LI. The single infantry red bar indicates that 129 Brigade was the division's senior brigade. XIII was the Somersets' old regimental number.

> I studied this for a full two minutes before a pair of camouflage nets behind the church suddenly came into focus. Further examination revealed six of these, each covering a 105mm German field gun. There, laid out before me like a sand table exercise, was a six gun field battery with the observation post in the church tower. No doubt the Volkswagen belonged to their Forward Observation Officer.

This was well beyond the range of platoon weapons and there were no supporting arms in the area. Jary, however, used his company's No. 18 Set and spoke to the battalion's affiliated battery commander who, armed with the grid reference and bearing, tasked a troop of 25-pounders:

> Within a few minutes we heard a short rumble of artillery fire to the west and within a few seconds four shells burst between the church and the copse. I instantly reported ... that they had fallen 200 yards south-east of the church. Within a few minutes a second salvo straddled the church. This I also reported.
>
> Sergeant Kingston then pointed to the copse, where a magnificent sight met our eyes. Six gun teams, horses and limbers, came at full gallop towards the gun position behind the church. In record time the German gunners had secured their 105s to the limbers and the whole battery retired in good order before Geoff's third salvo erupted on their gun position.

On 11 February 214 Brigade was to resume its stalled advance to the south-west towards Hau with the Cornwalls and the 7th Somersets, with 129 Brigade also under Brigadier Essame's control as General Thomas was sick, 'laid up in his caravan'. The division's objective remained opening the way to Goch.

Colonel Taylor's task for 5 DCLI was for a renewed attack on the village of Materborn. He deployed A Company on the right and C to the left, along with the support of the Shermans of B Squadron 4/7 Dragoon Guards. H Hour was at 1400 hours when the two companies leading the attack were to break into the village. The big difference between the previous night's failed attempt, which was a quick attack, and the second attempt was that it was a deliberate attack, well supported by the fire of the divisional artillery, supplemented by guns of the

The German 105-mm LeFH18 was the workhorse of the German divisional artillery.

AGRA. In short, the German defenders would be neutralised to a far greater extent than was the case the previous evening. The commanding officer wrote:

> Our attack went like clockwork. Covered by artillery fire and supported by the tanks of 4th/7th Dragoon Guards, we went forward in style. With C Coy keeping the Germans busy on the left, A Coy penetrated on the right, and quickly took half the village. B and D Companies then leap-frogged through to complete the task.
>
> Such was the precision of the attack, that the enemy were unable to put up much of a fight. We swept through, taking prisoners and a considerable amount of equipment. Our own casualties were light.[2]

'Sweeping through' this time with generous artillery support actually took two and a half hours, during which time A Company, having advanced further than C, was under fire for a time by its own artillery. Both companies reported 'little opposition' and the battalion recorded that a Panther and an SP were reported as being knocked out, thirty prisoners taken, and that the rest of the enemy again withdrew quickly.

Eric Gethyn-Jones, padre of the 43 Recce Regiment, in his diary for Sunday, 11 February, illustrated the continuing traffic problems through the Materborn gap. In attempting to get to forward elements of his regiment:

> ... my LAC (light armoured car) took two hours to cover 1,000 yards – mud and terrific traffic – cup of tea with the tank *walhas*. Tried to go through the Reichswald ... tried four routes but failed ... Afterwards walked back to RHQ – much quicker and safer than car!

In theory the next phase of the revised brigade plan could be put into action immediately; an advance led by 7 Somerset Light Infantry to capture the hamlet of Hau via 'Tiger Corner', a distance of some 4,000 yards.[3] The battalion's C Company followed the DCLI into Materborn in order to take over the advance

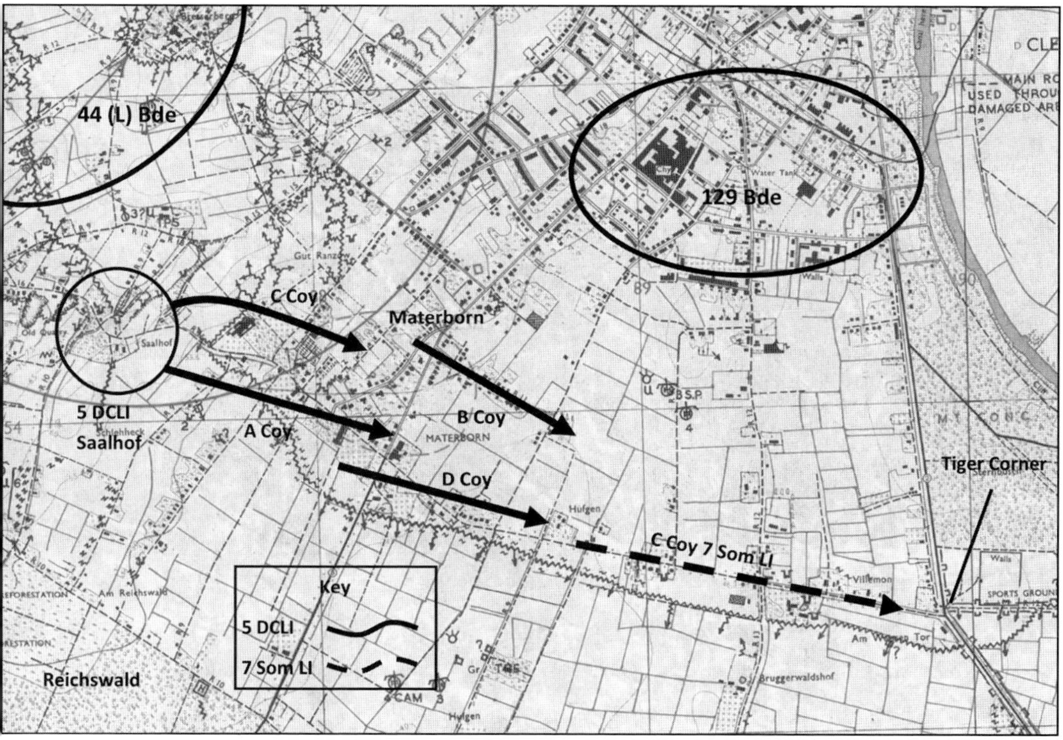

The 5 DCLI's second attack on Materborn, 11 February 1945.

as expeditiously as possible but in the confusion of houses and gardens, pockets of enemy had been missed, which had to be cleared before the company could occupy its start line. This delayed H Hour from 1630 by half an hour.

As the shells of the artillery fire plan burst in front of C Company on a road junction that became known as 'Tiger Corner', 'as soon as the situation seemed reasonably secure, they went forward. They advanced quickly for 1,000 yards until within 400 yards of the Goch road where they should turn south.'

At this stage, both the DCLI and Somersets mention German refugees and note that 'they felt no pity after the misery which they had seen in France and Holland'. Most were rounded up, separated from prisoners of war and secured in Materborn church until the fighting had moved on. In the meantime, those digging in felt no compunction at taking doors from German houses to use as the basis of overhead cover.

Meanwhile, C Company, 7 Somersets, were approaching 'Tiger Corner', with 13 Platoon leading, supported by a troop of A Squadron, 4/7 DG's Shermans. An air observation patrol had already reported armoured vehicle movement around the junction on the artillery radio net and engaged the area with the fire of medium guns. As the last rounds fell, 13 Platoon reported that they could see a knocked-out Tiger, burning near the crossroads. This 'Tiger' was actually a *Jagdpanther*. The regimental history records that:

> At the same moment they came under heavy *spandau* fire, and 88mm shells from further SPs started to burst in the trees over their heads – throwing out

The Auster air observation aircraft piloted by gunner observers was hated by the Germans and for its lack of vulnerability, despite its slow speed. It was known as the 'Iron Tommy'.

The *Jagdpanther* knocked out at 'Tiger Corner', with the Materborn church in the background.[4]

> shrapnel and great mushrooms of black smoke. No one was injured. The tanks got to work on the *spandaus* and saturated them with fire from their Besas [*sic* .30 calibre Brownings], while the platoon leapfrogged forward using the houses as cover – the tanks, in order to do their job properly had to spend long periods stationary. Major Durie set his three-inch mortar section to work on the SP guns. Slowly the vanguard group secured the crossroads.[5]

The Shermans confined to the road one behind the other suffered casualties. The third tank was hit and set on fire by the German *Panzerjäger*, 'followed later by hits on the leading and second tanks, which were able to withdraw'. It was by now getting dark and the rain turned to sleet as Lieutenant Colonel Reeves ordered the advance to be resumed without the close support of B Squadron's tanks, which had gone to the rear to replenish fuel and ammunition. For the infantry it was a both tiring and bone-chilling night. 'It was so cold that the covering Bren gunners had to use two fingers to operate the triggers, and gunners were changed at frequent intervals.'

7th Somerset LI's advance on the night of 11–12 February 1945.

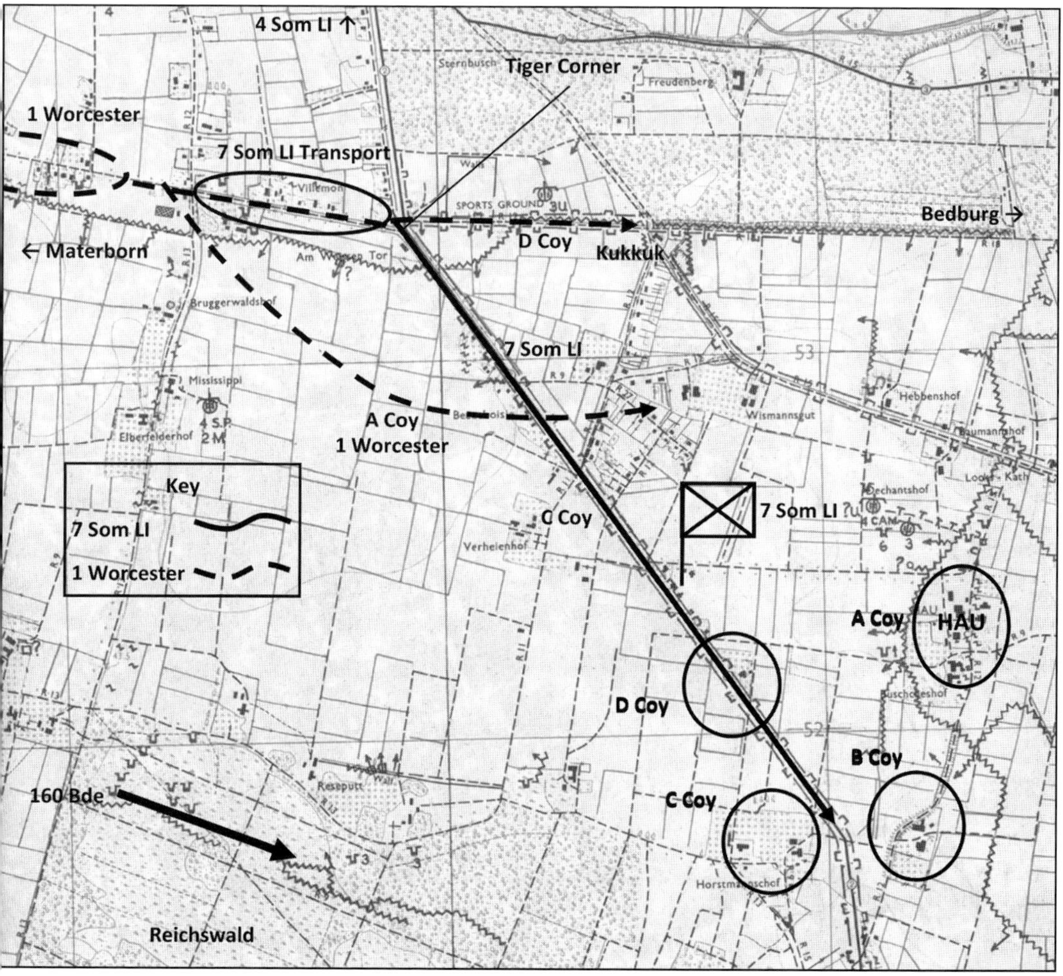

From 'Tiger Corner' the road is dead straight in a south-westerly direction for a mile. There was little cover for the Somersets from the 'Spandaus [that] seemed to answer every move, spitting lines of red and blueish tracer past them in the darkness',[6] other than the ugly tree trunks at regular intervals. Another problem as the companies advanced along with their FOOs was that radio communication with the battalions supporting artillery battery became intermittent as night set in. Calls for illuminating shoots were among those that went unanswered, necessitating largely unsuccessful attempts to set houses on fire with 2in smoke bombs. The leading platoons, however, after finding some *Tellermines* in the verges, were relieved to find that the further they went they saw mines intended for their pre-dug holes still stacked in crates beside the road, obviating the need to call for the flail tanks following the brigade.

Without more than the odd catnap since they left Nijmegen forty-eight hours earlier, the Somersets were now exhausted and clearly the enemy were not much better off. In these circumstances, and under pressure to 'get a move on', Major Durie, with his objective still 1,000 yards off, took a risk. He decided he needed:

> to wake his own men from their fatigue – there comes a time when a man is too tired to be afraid, and any risk is better than that. He gave 15 Platoon the order to lead straight down the road dealing only when opposition showed itself from the scattered farms and houses – if there was mopping up, it would be done by the troops following.

This was successful and at 0200 hours, having covered 1,000 yards, C Company was at the bend south of Hau. Here they spotted evidence of the passage of

By 1945 the *Tellermine*, which was first introduced in 1935, had undergone numerous developments and was still an effective anti-tank mine but it could also be fused as anti-personnel device.

significant quantities of armour into the nearby Reichswald. Not only that, some of the prisoners taken among the farms along the edge of the forest were for the first time identified as members of 15th *Panzergrenadier* Division, who complained that they were supposed to be 1,000m behind the front and protected by *Fallschirmjäger*. Also taken was 'A brand new German half-track that drove up the road and was captured intact by 14 Platoon'. This identification confirmed the intelligence warnings that had been descending the chain of command from First Canadian Army and XXX Corps: XLVII Panzer Corps was on the way north.

Meanwhile, A Company, next in order of march, had swung left off the road and into Hau at 0230 hours with 8 Platoon leading the way. They assumed that the village was strongly held and the enemy alert, but:

> They found a line of zig-zag trenches, unmanned, covering the whole western side. Here 9 Platoon was dropped off with the role of providing covering and cut-off fire across the top of the village in the darkness. The leading platoon reached its first farm and found the door locked. Lieutenant McKinlay made an entry through a window and was killed instantly from inside; his batman was wounded in the side but got back to the Company Commander. A PIAT was sent up and the house was surrounded, at the same time the other farm was found empty. 7 Platoon set to work on the two village streets and by 3 a.m. the objective was secured though mopping up continued till 4.30. One Captain and twenty other prisoners were taken in the village, and at Lieutenant McKinlay's farm one man was shot on the ground floor, and another Captain and four men were captured upstairs. One of the Captains – a fine Aryan specimen – had in his pocket a photo of himself being decorated by Hitler.

Infantry in the more open country of the Rhineland, February 1945.

B Company swung further left to its objective, taking further surprised German prisoners, concluding thirteen hours of fighting that saw 7th Somerset Light Infantry capturing their objectives and reporting being 'firm' at 0930 hours. The risks the battalion had taken overnight had paid off but the presence of prisoners from XLVII Panzer Corps, however, indicated that there was more hard fighting to come, and German reaction built steadily. Fortunately, the serious enemy counter-attacks only started in the early afternoon of 12 February, by which time 7 Somersets were dug in and well prepared.

While the protracted fighting for 'Tiger Corner' and Hau had been taking place, 214 Brigade's third battalion, 1 Worcesters, had been left well to the rear, 'halted for another uncomfortable night at Nutterden'. During the afternoon of the 11th, the Worcesters had marched up from reserve and were planned to advance east on the road to Bedburg from 'Tiger Corner'. The battalion's historian noted that:

> Those who slept at all were awakened at dawn [on the 11th] by the crash of artillery in the immediate vicinity and opened their eyes to see that the harbour area had become gun-lines overnight. There seemed to be no likelihood of a move before midday, so everyone washed, shaved, fed and rested.

A XXX Corps ambulance attempts the floods in Kranenburg to evacuate casualties from the fighting around Kleve.

> In the afternoon we moved off again and passed through the northern edge of the Reichswald. Progress was very slow and when we finally debussed at Materborn it was already dark.'[7]

With movement confined to roads this was far from simple; the Worcesters had to wait for the DCLI to capture Materborn and for the Somersets to have vacated the area of 'Tiger Corner'. They waited most of the night, but the Somersets' transport remained parked up on the road awaiting the capture of Hau. The road was essential if a conventional advance was to be made by the battalion supported by tanks. However, as the night wore on with no sign of the road being cleared, Colonel Hope-Thomson 'decided to feel his way forward during the hours of darkness and to establish a base from which to complete the task at first light':

> B Company advanced about 1,000 yards along the road and occupied a cross-roads known as 'Tiger Corner', so called because of a tank clash there earlier on, the clash being testified by the remnants of one Sherman and two Tiger tanks [*sic*]. A Company passed through and turned south-east and occupied a cluster of farm buildings from which they extracted a handful of prisoners with little trouble. D Company were later passed through B Company and advanced on a built-up road junction called Kukkuk, about 500 yards ahead.

Signalman Stan Proctor, manning the Worcesters' rear link on the brigade radio net, recorded in his signal log a SITREP sent by the commanding officer. 'Enemy posn strongly held. Have tried both flanks but unsuccessful. Enemy has road covered by SP guns and infantry. Cannot use own sheldrake owing to posn of own troops.'[8] Any further advance would have to wait until after dawn on 12 February.

Morning, 12 February

The opening phase of Operation VERITABLE to force the Reichswald Plug had been far from the dash into the Rhineland that the Allied planners had hoped for. The thaw had left the ground saturated, and the floodplains inundated with melt and rainwater flowing down the Rhine. Not only were ground conditions facing XXX Corps appalling, but with Operation GRENADE stalled thanks to the damage to the Roer dams, they would face the undiluted efforts of the German reserves for twenty-five days before the Ninth US Army was able to join the battle.

Over the previous four days, 51st Highland Division had fought through the Germans' forward position, the Siegfried Line defences in the Reichswald and out onto the Maas floodplain, crossing the River Niers to capture Gennep on VERITABLE's southern axis (see map on page 228). Meanwhile, in the forest, advancing alongside 15th Scottish, 53rd Welsh Division had reached the Stoppelberg in the north-east corner and had swung south-west to clear the remainder of the Reichswald. With Kleve secure, a new phase of the battle was beginning but the Allies were still struggling to generate momentum. The corps' plan was for 3rd Canadian Division and 15th Scottish to advance south-east into the

Rhineland, with their objective being Kalkar. The 43rd Wessex Division, the fifth of XXX Corps' divisions in action so far, had forced its way off the Materborn feature and was advancing south-west along the face of the Reichswald towards Goch with the tanks of 8 Armoured Brigade.

With General Blastowitz having waited to be convinced that First Canadian Army's attack on the Reichswald was the Allies' main effort, on 12 February General von Lüttwitz's XLVII Panzer Corps had begun to arrive to confront XXX Corps. In their move north from positions east of the Maas in the Roremond bend area both of these already severely reduced divisions were hamstrung by a lack of fuel and consequently only dribbled forward from Geldern overnight on 11–12 February. Initially at least General Wilck's 116th Panzer Division fielded a small *Kampfgruppe* based on a company of panzers, which were joined by the eight surviving *Jagdpanthers* and sundry *Jagdpanzer* IVs of *Panzerjäger Abteilung* 655.

Signalman Proctor recorded a revealing intelligence report that was circulated on 214 Brigade's radio net on the morning of 12 February:

> 0946 52D [code for 5 Wiltshires] attacked this morning by 16 Para Regt – shot up and enemy gave it up. 5 officers & 174 ORs [PW].
> Offrs. State men had no food for 3 days & were in no fit state to fight.

During the night 7 Somersets had reached Hau and were digging in in expectation of counter-attack. Behind them, much delayed thanks to being tied to a single road, 1 Worcesters had reached a point just beyond 'Tiger Corner'. Here they waited for dawn before launching an attack on the hamlet of Kukkuk, which

The *Windhund* symbol of the 116th Panzer Division.

General Heinz von Lüttwitz, commander of XLVII Panzer Corps.

Schwere Panzerjäger Abteilung 655

Mobile units were hurried to the Reichswald as the realisation dawned on the German chain of command that VERITABLE was not a feint attack. Among the first to arrive was *Schwere Panzerjäger Abteilung* 655 (655 Heavy Anti-Tank Battalion). These *Panzerjäger* were in addition to 84th Infantry Division's vehicles of their own *Panzerjäger* battalion. Ten or fourteen StuG IIIs, IVs or Hetzers were concentrated in 2nd Company. The other companies had towed anti-tank and anti-aircraft guns.

At this stage of the war, only one of *Schwere Panzerjäger Abteilung* 655's three companies was 'heavy'. 1 and 3 Companies were equipped with the 26-ton *Jagdpanzer* IV 70 (V), which was known as the Guderian *Ente*.* It mounted the 75mm KwK L70 gun as fitted to the Panther tank. The theoretical strength was fourteen *Panzerjäger* per company, but the actual numbers deployed to face VERITABLE cannot be confirmed.

Introduced into service during 1944, the *Jagdpanzer* IV was an effective weapon system but by this point in the war, as seen on this abandoned vehicle in the ruins of a village, the muzzle brakes fitted to earlier versions had been removed on the *Jagdpanzer* IV 70 (V).†

* *Ente* is German for a duck and colloquia language for a joke. It is said that due to the heavy gun sited well forward, the front heavy vehicle waddled like a duck and was a bit of a joke; hence its nickname. General Heinz Guderian was Inspector General of the *Panzertruppen*, and despite his reservations about the vehicle he was included in the nickname.

† This was due to the dissipating effect of the muzzle brake obscuring the fall of shot and the gun being hull mounted, which absorbed the recoil significantly better than a turret.

The battalion's No. 2 Company with fourteen 45-ton *Jagdpanther* was, however, up to strength. Its vehicles mounted the powerful KwK 43/3 L71 88mm gun as fitted to the King Tiger. Despite its high profile to accommodate such a large gun, its sloping armour afforded a high level of protection.

The battalion also had two *Bergepanthers* (recovery panthers) and a platoon of *Flakpanzer* IV based on the Pz.IV chassis.

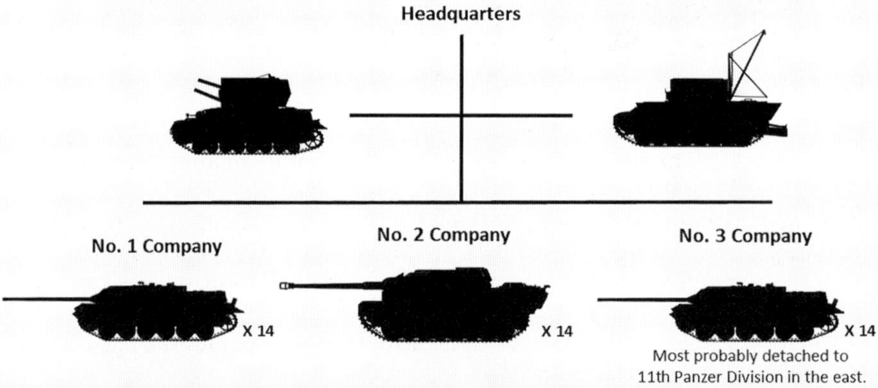

ORBAT 655 *Schwere Panzerjäger Abteilung* 655.

The *Bergepanther* and the *Flakpanzer* IV (2cm *Flakvierling* 38) '*Wirbelwind*'.

This battalion represented a powerful reinforcement for the 84th Division but presumably they experienced the same problems operating on the muddy tracks of the Reichswald as British armour. The forest was, of course, not an environment where the long range of the two guns could be used and, without a turret, in close-range engagements traversing was slow. In thick country, if the *Panzerjäger* were to be the core of a defence, they would need the protection of determined infantry, which was seldom the case in the Reichswald. For these reasons *Schwere Panzerjäger Abteilung* 655 was less than fully effective but once out into the open Rhineland performance was much improved.

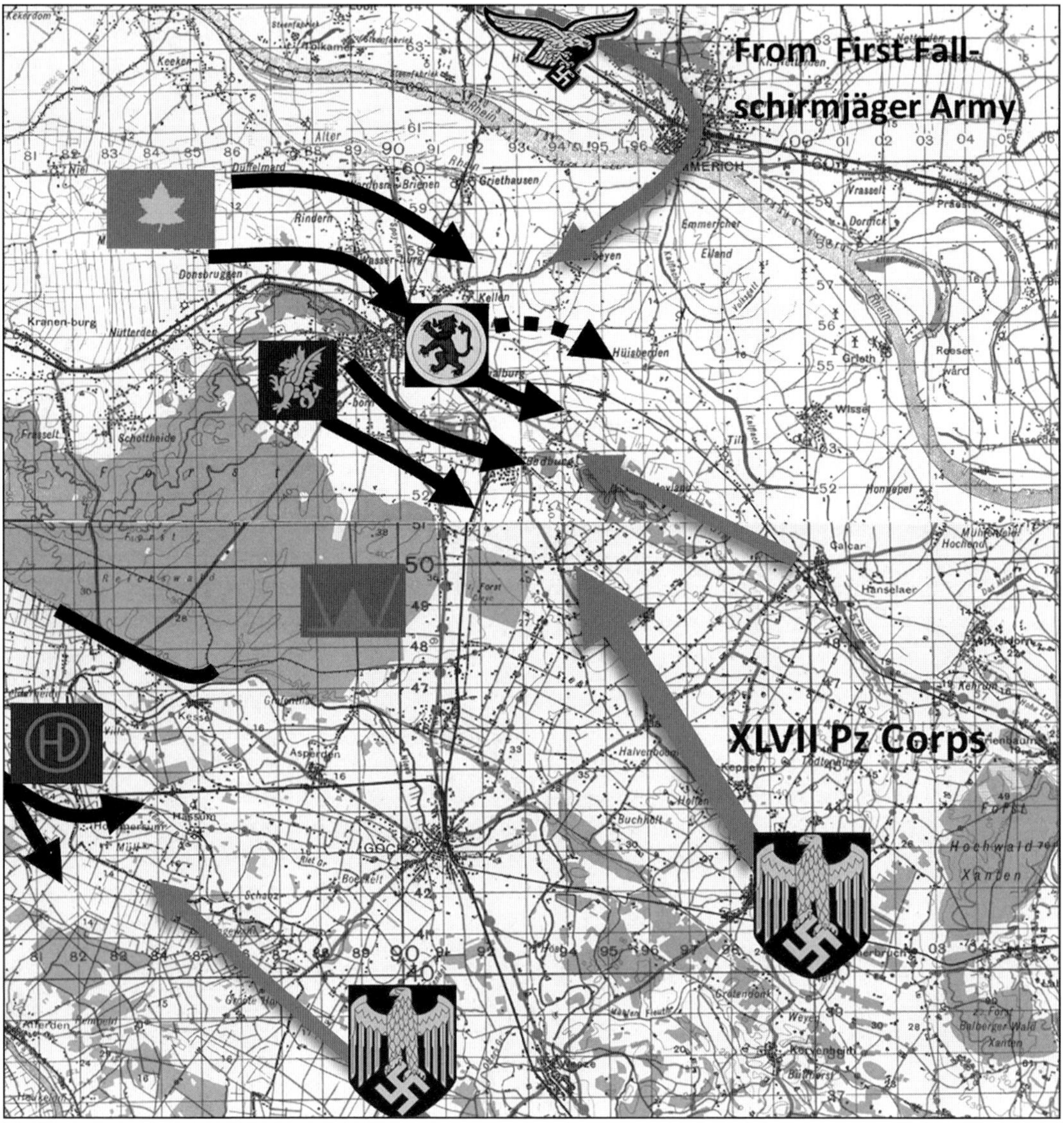

The general situation on XXX Corps' front, 12 February 1945.

they were to use as a firm base for their advance east along the road to Bedburg (see map on page 219). The battalion's A and D companies began their part in the operation as dawn was beginning to break. Lieutenant Pullen, commanding a platoon in D Company, described the action around 'a prominent house':

> Lieut. Crossingham was ordered to take 7 Platoon [A Company] into the building by the direct route. That Platoon advanced until it was about 50 yards from its objective when the firing of *spandaus* and very lights forced it to ground; tracked vehicles were heard moving. Major Elder decided to use 16 and 18 Platoons [D Company] in a right flanking movement, the plan being to move through A Company which had attained its objective, then

> along a row of houses which led to Kukkuk, clearing them in the process. 16 Platoon, under Capt. Huxter, cleared the first four or five houses, then 18 Platoon, which I commanded, passed on to deal with the remainder and secure the Company objective. It was my first experience of house clearing and seemed to consist mainly of firing the contents of a Bren gun magazine through the windows, battering the front door with a pick-axe, and wandering through the house firing an occasional round just to lend colour to the situation.
>
> Whilst clearing the last house in the row I saw what appeared to be the dead body of a German soldier, but several vigorous prods with a bayonet made it wake up and it immediately became a very frightened body indeed. He had gone to sleep amongst friends and woken up a prisoner – my first. His Luger pistol afterwards proved very useful.
>
> Finally, the large building: the enemy had fled and it was taken with two rounds from a Sten gun. In the cellar a German paratrooper greeted Sergt. Lawlor with the words in perfect English: 'Hello, I have been waiting two hours for you.'

The Worcesters' next objective was a crossroads on a ridge of high ground short of Bedburg. Colonel Hope-Thomson had been promised the support of the divisional artillery, a total of seventy-two 25-pounders, as well as the fire of one of the AGRAs. He was, however, told at 0715 hours that due to the delays in starting his advance, he had lost the guns of the AGRA for three hours while they were supporting 51st Highland Division. It also transpired that not all the Wessex Division's other batteries could be called on. Lieutenant Goddard explained the absence of the fire of the eight 25-pounders belonging to his battery of 112 Field Regiment, RA:

> Although the main axis to Nijmegen was impassable due to enemy flooding of the Rhine the Regt was ordered forward at 05.00 hours on the 12th. It took four hours to get the guns out of the quagmire of the gun positions.

The history of 94 (Hants & Dorset) Field Regiment provides more information on the battle with the mud and extricated themselves from their gun position:

> A mile further on the track crossed a flooded field and here one gun after another was bogged and had to be unhooked and winched yard by yard, till firmer ground was reached. The regiment took three hours to pass over this eighty-yard stretch.

Lieutenant Douglas Goddard, Command Post Officer, 220 Battery, 112 Field Regiment, RA.

Ahead of them 112 Field Regiment was now forward on firmer ground, as recalled by Lieutenant Goddard:

> The move through Kleve, now clear of enemy, was made under intense shell-fire ... The Regiment came into action near the newly captured town of Materborn and was immediately immersed in two fire plans ... Luftwaffe jet planes attacked the gun positions with rockets but amazingly there were no casualties.[9]

A gunner in the Wessex Division's anti-aircraft unit was not so lucky, as recalled by Padre Gethyn-Jones:

> That same day, during a dive-bomb attack near RHQ [43 Recce Regt], a gunner manning a nearby anti-aircraft gun had his nose, lips, chin and eyebrows removed by a bomb splinter – as cleanly as though he had passed through a bacon slicer. We carried him, fully conscious, to the MO.

As a result of the artillery's difficulties in providing the accustomed weight of fire, Colonel Hope-Thomson on his own initiative made what would have been at the time considered a brave decision. Realising that with reports of XLVII Panzer Corps approaching, time was crucial if he was to be in position to meet them. Consequently, he elected to carry on with the attack with the limited fire support of his six 3in mortars and such guns as became available. At 0815 hours the Worcesters' advance began with B Company on the left clearing through woods

43rd Wessex Division's operations south-west of Kleve during 12 February 1945.

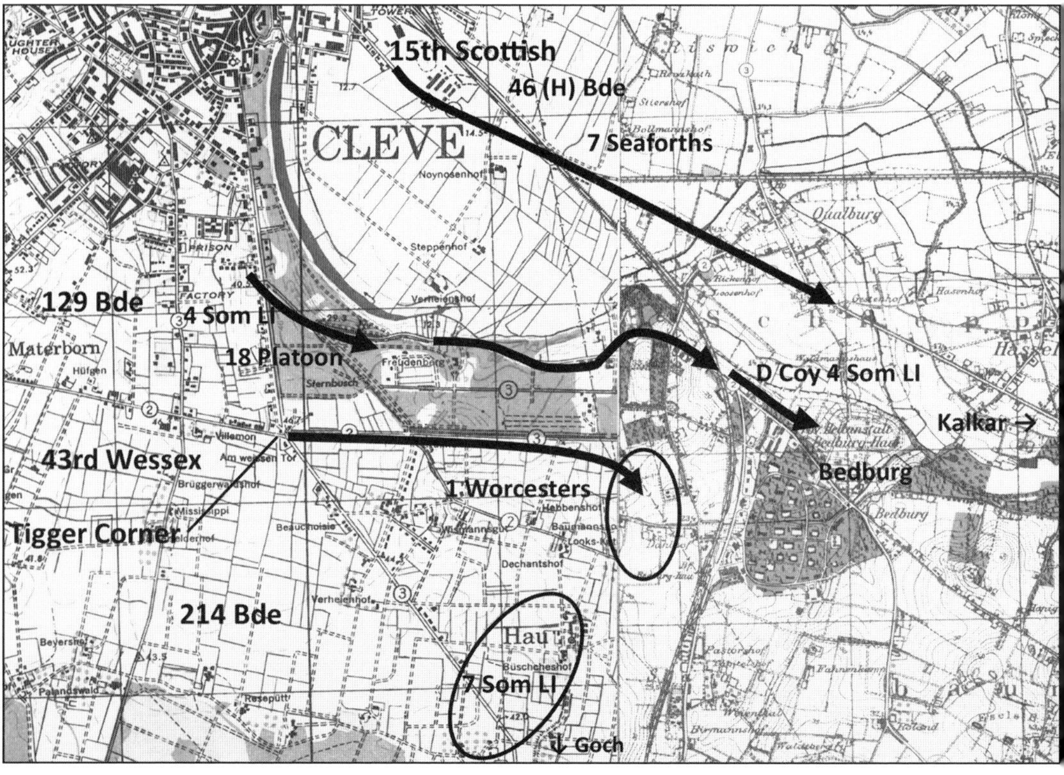

and C on the right in more open country, supported by a troop of 4/7 DG's Shermans from the road in the centre:

> B Company passed through D Company and entered the wood to the north of the road, meeting little opposition with the exception of one sniper who inflicted a fatal casualty and delayed the advance some thirty minutes.

Meanwhile, C Company was also on the move and 'in accordance with the Company Commander's (Major Clover) policy fired at everything which might contain enemy'. The supporting troop of Shermans joined in engaging identified opposition in buildings and set several houses on fire with tracer rounds from their hull and co-ax machine guns or high explosive shells. Moving quickly alongside tanks, C Company approached the ridge at 0930 hour. Here they 'consolidated on the forward slope overlooking the cross-roads' and Bedburg. As a result, in full view of the enemy, 'They were severely shelled as they were getting in but received only two casualties – one NCO killed and one man wounded.'

> All this activity, and particularly the smoke from the burning houses, drew the enemy's attention. He must have suspected another thrust westwards from the ridge, for from midday onwards he shelled the area with venom and intensity until late evening, during which time life was distinctly unpleasant.

It was clear from this reaction that the Germans feared that the Worcesters' thrust into their defences would be exploited later in the day, but the battalion was out on a limb and driving a deeper salient west on a narrow front would be dangerous. Other battalions, both Wessex and Scots, were to advance and come up into line. When this began, as the Worcesters' historian commented, 'The sound of … engagement could be distinctly heard, and our area quietened considerably.'

The Capture of Bedburg

The Germans were wrong in anticipating a continuation of the attack by 214 Brigade. Instead Headquarters XXX Corps had ordered an advance from Kleve on two parallel roads astride the Wetering stream, a little over 1,000 yards apart, running south-west to Hasselt and Bedburg. The former was to be the objective of 15th Scottish and towards the latter General Thomas committed the West Countrymen of 129 Brigade. The previous day the brigade had had a brief opportunity to rest and reorganise in the suburbs of Kleve and were now to advance through the woods on the left flank, sweeping past the Worcesters to capture Bedburg.

Late on the evening of the 11th orders were given for 4 Somerset Light Infantry to lead the brigade's advance the following morning, with Major Freddie Cooke-Hurle's D Company the forward company and Lieutenant Jary's 18 Platoon out in front. Jary recalled that:

> Information about the enemy in the area was vague; so vague indeed that there seemed a distinct possibility of a fluid situation existing that could be turned to advantage. I asked Freddie if 18 Platoon could fight without

Lieutenant Sidney Jary, commander of 18 Platoon, 4th Somerset Light Infantry.

> small packs until we had consolidated at Bedburg. If we could leave them on the Company transport with our picks and shovels we could certainly move faster ... After some discussion, he finally agreed and 18 Platoon with considerable relief loaded their small packs into the 15cwt Bedford.[10]

Earlier in the day there had been reports of amour and infantry in strength immediately in front of D Company's start line but by the time the advance began it would seem that they had withdrawn thanks to the Worcesters' advance threatening to cut them off. Consequently, 18 Platoon got off to a good start, advancing through the woods in single file to their first objective, a schloss at Freudenberg. After half a mile they came across an abandoned roadblock consisting of a mined crater in the road and pressed on to the schloss, which was unoccupied. Continuing the advance east along the road, 18 Platoon were sniped at from the trees to the north. This gave Lieutenant Jary 'every encouragement to keep up a cracking pace which in turn discouraged the opposition who retreated before us until we came to a cafe on the right of the road':

> Some bursts of *Spandau* fire came from a stone farm building to the left of the road. Corporal Cheeseman's Section went to ground and returned the fire with their Bren. Parachute troops they may have been, but those few bursts from the Bren made them run back further down the road to Bedburg. I urged Corporal Cheeseman to keep on their tails. His Section had led the advance since we left Cleve and, as a good section commander, he asked that one of the other sections should now take over. He was quite right. I should have relieved them long before.
>
> Leaving Corporal Cheeseman's Section to give covering fire, I sent Corporal Proctor with his Section to seize the stone farm building and Sergeant Kingston with his Section to seize the cafe. I went with Corporal Proctor. We seized the stone building with no difficulty and from small windows high in the thick walls saw the *Spandau* detachment retreating about 200 yards to our front.

No. 18 Platoon had been halted around the cafe and stone building for about ten minutes while clearing the buildings and reorganising, but Lieutenant Jary knew he needed to keep the enemy on the move in order to retain the initiative. Coming up in line with the Worcesters, ahead of them, beyond the railway line, they could see a large hospital building in the trees south of Bedburg:

> 200 yards short of the wood a railway track ran across our front with a level crossing on the road. Fearing that the retreating parachute troops would

> make a stand on the edge of the wood, I increased the rate of advance, joining Lance-Corporal Porteous in the forward section.
>
> Running across the level crossing, I suddenly found myself face to face with a German platoon complete with MG34. Fortunately, the gun was mounted on a tripod, which was unusual, and could not be traversed in our direction. From a drainage channel on the left of the road, a parachutist leaped up swathed in a camouflage veil. Pointing his *Schmeisser* at me, from about 10 yards' range, he fired a whole magazine of about thirty rounds. It was like watching a slow running silent movie. I didn't hear the chatter of the *Schmeisser* but I do remember seeing the stream of empty cartridge cases fly from the German gun. Miracles do indeed happen. One 9mm bullet went through my beret, missing my head literally by a hair's width. Another went under the epaulette of my jacket, penetrating the webbing cross brace of my equipment and grazing my right shoulder. A third bullet ricocheted off the surface of the road and disintegrated, the jacket finally lodging in the palm of my right hand. Then came the anti-climax. The German looked at me in amazement, threw away his *Schmeisser* and, with a shrug of the shoulders, surrendered. My natural elation was short lived. Behind me lay Lance-Corporal Porteous shot through the heart.

Some of the German defenders ran across open fields and were 'cut down by rapid rifle and Bren fire' from the Jary's leading section, which now lined the railway track. Thereafter the remainder of the enemy promptly came over the level crossing with their hands up.

While reorganising, a 20mm light flak gun fired directly down the road from the wood. One of the shells wounded Major Cooke-Hurle in the leg and he was evacuated on the company jeep. Lieutenant Jary took over command of the company and: 'Still obsessed by the fear of the enemy taking a stand on the edge of the wood, I urged the Company forward in one last charge, which took us about 200 yards into Hospital Wood.' The hospital proved to be a facility for some 500 patients with mental illness.

The Bren gun was the British infantry section's light machine gun.

D Company dug in with 16 and 17 platoons forward and 18 Platoon with Company HQ about 150 yards to their rear, having taken fifty-seven prisoners:

> The Company's left flank rested on the main road on the far side of which was a cottage ... As the house had not been cleared, Sergeant Kingston, now commanding 18 Platoon ... went to investigate and noticed a door leading to some steep stone steps into a cellar. Filled with rough wooden bunks, it had obviously served as an air raid shelter ... Suddenly from under a pile of blankets leapt the only fanatical German paratrooper we encountered in the entire battle. A large man, he seized Jack Lee around the throat in an attempt to strangle him. Private Flude rose to the challenge. In a bound he was down the steps and, with a mighty lunge, transfixed the German on his bayonet ... The German was indeed unlucky as it was the only occasion throughout the campaign on which 18 Platoon's bayonets were blooded: we usually used them to open food cans.

With D Company reorganising beyond the railway line, 4 Somersets' three other companies exploited the success with the support of Sherman tanks and were soon on their objectives around Bedburg; digging in before dark. Some years later, Lieutenant Jary justifiably reflected on 18 Platoon's success on 12 February 1945:

> The advance from Cleve to Bedburg, a classic light infantry operation, was 18 Platoon's battle. Throughout Operation Veritable the average rate of advance by our Army was one 1¼ miles per day. The Platoon had advanced 3 miles in a morning, brushing aside all opposition, until it shot its bolt on the railway level crossing at Bedburg. We had no artillery or armoured support and no other troops were involved, not even 16 or 17 Platoons. I like to think that Sir John Moore smiled on it.[11]

With 46 Highland Brigade advancing on Hasselt to his left and the Worcesters in position to his right, and 'with events now turning his favour', Colonel Lipscombe brought up the rest of the battalion. '... the other three rifle companies carried out successful attacks on their objectives. By evening the whole area [of Bedburg] was in our hands.'

For his part in directing 4 Somerset's overall operations during 12 February, which was a highly successful advance, Colonel Lipscombe earned a bar to his DSO.[12] Lieutenant Jary had already earned the MC back in November 1944.

15th Scottish Division

The previous day had seen the Scots taking over the southern part of Kleve from the Wessex and completing its clearance, including forming a bridgehead in the eastern part of the city beyond the River Kermisdahl river. As a part of XXX Corps' opening move into the Rhineland, a mobile column from 46 Highland Brigade, based on 7 Seaforth Highlanders, was ready to be released on the road to Hasselt. Under command of Colonel Hunt, they were to advance parallel to 4 Somerset Light Infantry 1,000 yards to the south, with an H Hour of 1100 hours (see map on page 219).

The Seaforth's battle group, known as HUNTFORCE after the commanding officer, assembled around the ruins of Kleve railway station but it was not until 1300 hours that 'HUNTFORCE moved through CLEVE to start adv towards CALCAR'. The infantry were mounted in the Kangaroos of 1st Canadian Armoured Personnel Carrier Regiment. Supporting them were the armoured cars of the 15 Recce Regiment, the tanks of No. 2 Squadron of the Coldstream Guards', a battery of 25-pounder Sextons and a platoon of engineers. As they moved forward to the start line, the third Churchill in the column ran over a mine in the rubble and 'they were delayed by a full two hours while a passage was being cleared'. While the rubble and mines were being removed, the armoured cars were feeling their way forward and based on their information there was another

A troop of Churchill tanks of 4th Coldstream Guards drive along a badly damaged street in Kleve on 12 February 1945.

delay at the outskirts of Kleve, as described by Major Binsted, commanding B Company:

> Recce had reported a small pocket of enemy around the Rly [railway] crossing SE of KLEVE on the CLACAR Rd . . . The tanks were very loath to lead so it was arranged that they would get off the rd and shoot us into the area. We went sailing on in the Kangaroos.

Of this incident early on during the advance from Kleve, the divisional historian recorded that:

> Immediately the column met small groups of the enemy. At the same time reconnaissance patrols reported that the enemy in some strength were holding Qualburg, a village just beyond the level-crossing and less than a mile and a half from the station. B Company, the vanguard of the Seaforth, drove straight for Qualburg in their Kangaroos.

They reached to 'about 500x – 600x past the LC [level crossing]' and approached Qualburg. Here at around 1330 hours, they ran into what was in effect an ambush. No fewer than four Kangaroos were knocked out by enemy infantry with *Panzerfausts*, backed up by *Jagdpanzer* IVs of 3rd Company of *Panzerjäger Abteilung* 665. Headquarters 46 (H) Brigade commented that:

> Although Kangaroos were used in this operation they were not considered a great success owing to their inability to get off the roads making deployment on a wide front impossible. In this way they became easy targets for shelling and mortaring when halted one behind the other on the road.

A Kangaroo photographed while supporting 15th Scottish Division.

The ambush was well sited near to the Wetering river and the surrounding sodden fields, and the Germans had successfully halted the advance on the single road that was the Seaforth's axis. The battalion's war diary recorded: 'The area was held in strength and every house had to be cleared.' Major Binsted continued:

> I gave orders to 'detank'. How terribly vulnerable one feels getting out of Kangaroos, but we had the satisfaction of knowing we were right amongst the Bosch . . . For the first hour I thought the company had 'had it' but the bravery of the few at last began to turn the tide . . . How one has to scream and swear at men to get them to do anything when you are up against it.

Meanwhile, Lieutenant Woodall with the Coldstream's supporting Churchills:

> Immediately ordered his troop Sergeant to tow the Kangaroos off the road as they were completely blocking it, while he engaged the SP, scoring two hits on its side. He then contacted the infantry and edged the tanks forward to continue the advance – a performance which earned him the MC.[13]

Major Binsted noted that: 'After about 4 hours after the start of the battle we had cleared about 400x–500x of the village and the situation was well in hand.' B Company took sixty-five prisoners and counted twenty-five enemy dead. 'The cost was wretched, my 2ic, CSM best Pl comd and about 22 chaps. It seemed much more at the time':

> D Coy were passed through us at this stage and how pleased I was as everybody was all done. We went back that night and reorganised on the rly crossing and it did nothing but rain, rain, rain.

The 15th Scottish Division's battle area.

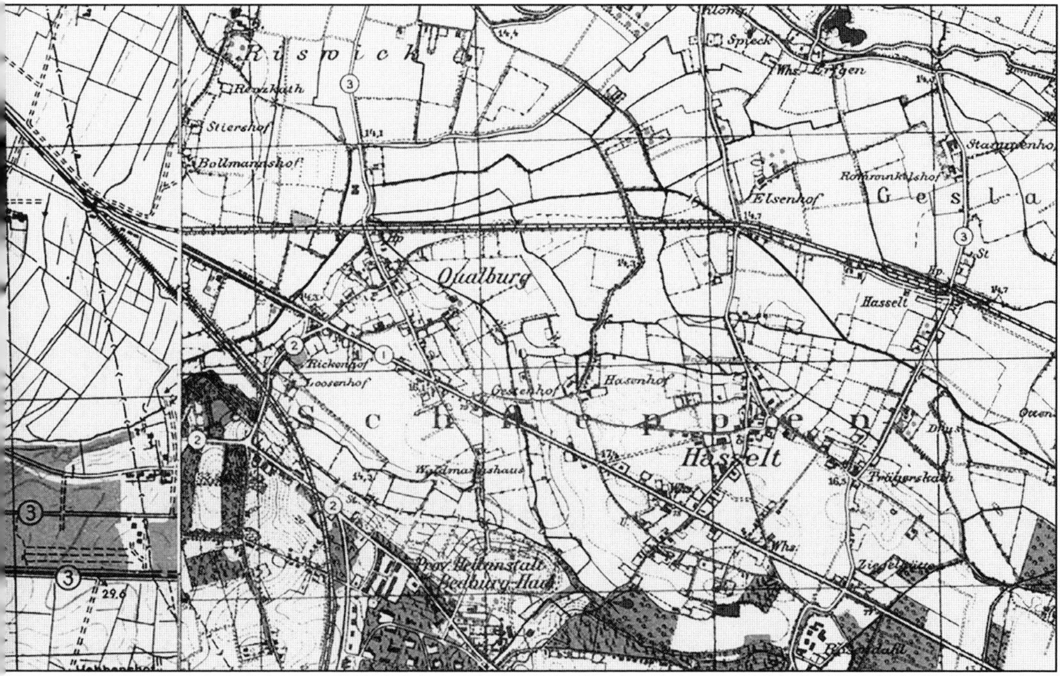

Soldiers of 2 Gordons and 4 Tank Coldstream Guards in Kleve. Clearing the city of enemy pockets took several days.

B Company had broken through the enemy's main defences, but according to the battalion's war diary 'after a sticky time got the area cleared, killing 25 and capturing 65 P of W and wounding quite a few.'

The war diary continues: 'Enemy shelling and mortaring of area became heavy but "D" Coy passed through "B" Coy and in their Kangaroos reached HASSELT', an advance a further 1,000 yards along the main road. 'Here they found the enemy in strength and were under heavy mortar and shell fire with the enemy determined to fight on this axis.' The advance had been led by Lieutenant Milne's Churchills. The Guards Brigade's historian wrote:

> ... at the next village, Hasselt, the enemy again opened fire, this time from houses on the northern side of the road. The infantry began to clear the houses and the tanks to engage two SPs which were shooting up the road ...

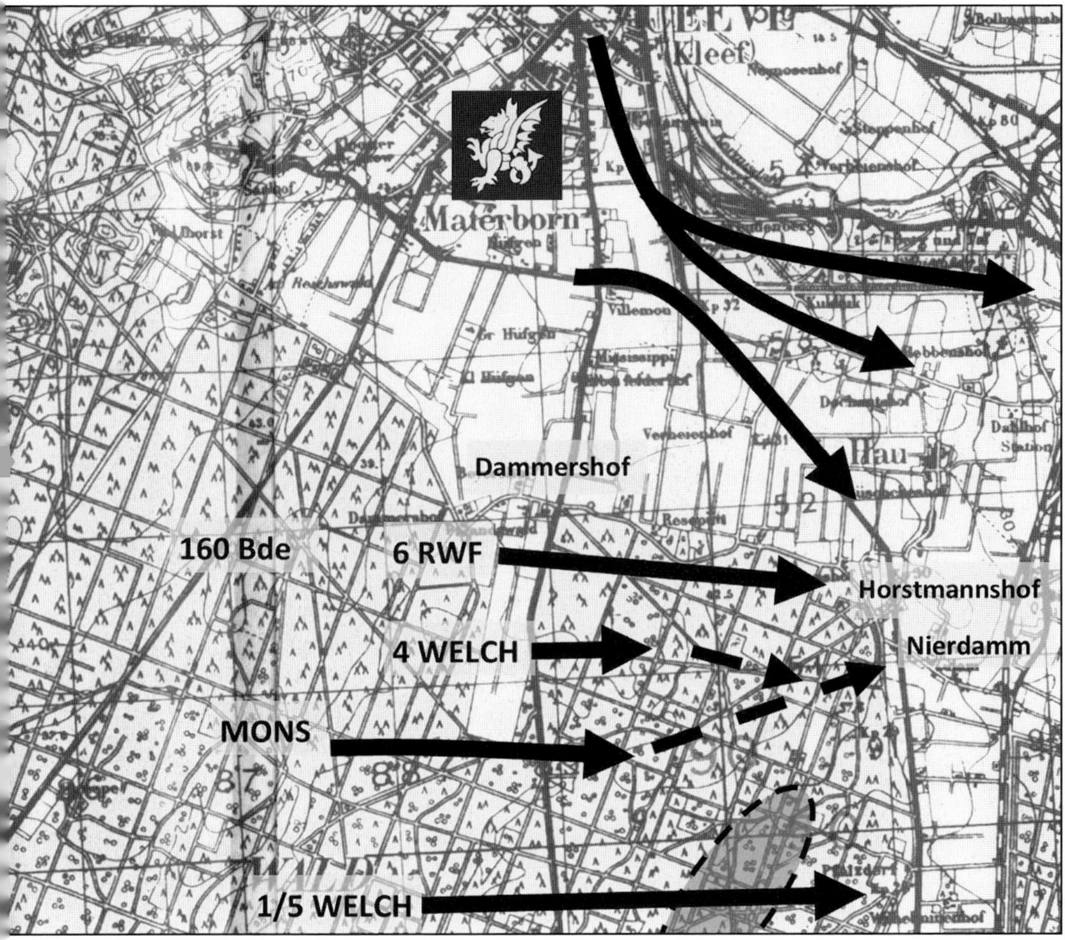

The advance of 160 Brigade of 53rd Welsh Division, on the morning of 12 February 1945.

With the Rhine flood waters rising, the company out on its own and under heavy artillery and mortar fire, Colonel Hunt ordered D Company back to join the rest of the battalion in defensive positions between the level crossing and Qualburg. Patrols were tasked to the north to make contact with 129 Brigade in Bedburg.

Reconnaissance of the Niers

Meanwhile, on 43rd Wessex's right flank, 7 Somerset LI had expanded their grip on area they had captured overnight with patrols and contacted 53rd Welsh Division's units on the edge of the Reichswald. Following the Brigade's successes that morning, B Squadron, 43rd Recce Regiment, supported by tanks of 8 Armoured Brigade, was ordered forward through 7 Somersets. Their task was to report on the line of the upper River Niers some 1,000 yards ahead. Padre Gethyn-Jones noted that 'The 12th was a bad day':

> B Squadron lost three cars and three supporting tanks in the first probe forward towards Goch. The two remaining cars managed to turn and withdraw, with several of the crew members of the 'brewed-up' LACs clinging to

Shoulder insignia of 43rd Recce Regiment.

> them. Later, a volunteer came with me and, under cover of a Red Cross flag, we brought in the bodies of Corporal Viggars and Trooper Ward without any interference or reaction from the Germans. There was no sign of the other missing members of the car crews.

The padre buried the five soldiers of 43rd Recce killed that day but even in battle, while completing the record of field burials he fell victim to petty politics when a Roman Catholic padre from divisional headquarters called into RHQ:

> and enquired whether any of the men were Roman Catholics. I replied that I had not yet checked; two of them were reinforcements who had only arrived a few days earlier. We went through their AB 64s, and found that Trooper Ward, one of the recent arrivals, was an RC. The Padre reported me for having taken prayers over a Roman Catholic. I was hauled up before the 'beaks' and received a large size in rockets for contravening King's Regulations in taking a C of E service over a Roman Catholic – the correct procedure was to bury the body, and then report the map reference to the nearest RC chaplain. This, to my mind (particularly when they were my men) seemed callous and unchristian, and I fear that I continued to take the normal burial service and commendation over my men, and later reported the map reference of the grave of any Roman Catholic to Divisional HQ for the information of the Divisional RC chaplains.

Kleve

While 4/7 DG were fighting with the Wessex Division, the remainder of 8 Armoured Brigade remained in Kleve awaiting their turn on the roads of the

A Daimler armoured car of C Squadron, 43rd Recce Regiment, which had replaced the Humber.

waterlogged Rhineland. Lieutenant David Render, of the Sherwood Rangers Yeomanry, recalled occupying the ruins of houses:

> The distinctive smell of German soldiery that seemed to permeate all their dugout, vehicles and barracks also pervaded the cellars. The stink of Jerry was something we all commented on and it seemed to emanate from a combination of sweat, leather, the strong black tobacco they smoked and the carbolic soap they washed with. I have often wondered what we smelt like to them.[14]

During the 12th, 3rd Canadian Division's 9 Brigade completed its advance through the floods beyond the Spoy Canal to Kellen, the North Nova Scotia Highlanders' final objective, which lay to the north-east of Kleve. The village was duly secured without fighting by early afternoon, completing the Canadians' capture of the floodplain. Thereafter, 7 Brigade took over the defence of Kleve to enable the 15th Scottish and 43rd Wessex divisions to concentrate on offensive operations. Thus, for 44 and 227 brigades, this relief marked the end of the battle for the Reichswald and action for the time being. While they were out of the fighting 'resting', conditions for them remained far from comfortable, with continuing supply difficulties and, amidst medium batteries' gun positions, the subject of overs from enemy counter-battery fire.

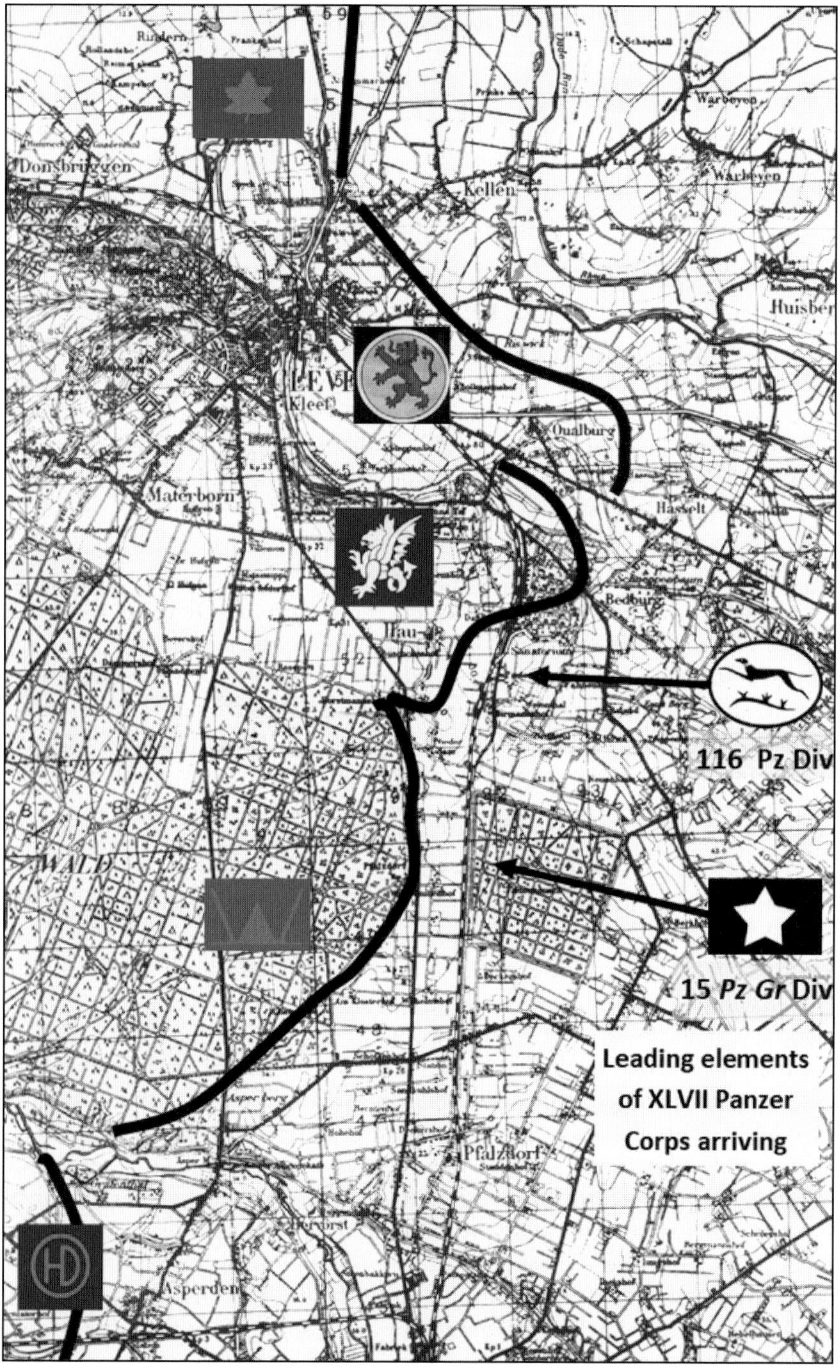

XXX Corps' situation at mid-day on 12 February 1945.

Chapter Twelve

Counter-Attack

12 February 1945

General Horrocks' concept of operations for XXX Corps had all along been for a speedy advance into the Rhineland, before the Germans could react and the battle become what he described as 'another bitter slogging match'. The thaw and the resulting ground conditions rather than effective resistance by General Fiebig's 84th Infantry Division had slowed the advance and had bought time for First *Fallschirmjäger* Army's reserves to be committed. Elements of 6th *Fallschirmjäger* Division crossed the Rhine from Twenty-fifth Army to fight in the battle for Kleve, and initially a regiment of 7th *Fallschirmjäger* Division came north from the Geldern area to confront 51st Highland Division. Slim though these reinforcements were, they were balanced by the problems XXX Corps had in developing momentum. The ground conditions continued to confine armour to roads and decent tracks, while behind the advance roads were flooded and supply routes became virtually impassible, which together reduced the tempo of operations during the first four days of the battle to that of wading through mud.

German Reaction and Plans

Field Marshal von Rundstedt's headquarters had only belatedly released his reserve, XLVII Panzer Corps, with the code word '*Ziethen*'[1] at 1745 hours on 10 February. General von Lüttwitz's corps was located to the south in hides in the Mönchengladbach area, in accordance with the German estimate that the Second British and Ninth US Armies would attempt to break into the Rhineland, the former via a crossing of the Maas in the Venlo area. Now confident in the knowledge that thanks to the blowing of the valves in the Roer dam, Ninth US Army could not attack across the river for at least ten days, XLVII Panzer Corps could be safely sent north to reinforce General Schlemm. Despite the delay in identifying the presence of 'missing' British divisions, the weather, ground and *Wehrmacht* resistance around Kleve bought time for most of von Rundstedt's reserves to be deployed.

The distance of between 20 and 35 miles from their dispersed hides to the Reichswald, during which they were subject to some air interdiction, was not XLVII Panzer Corps' only deployment issue. The Russian capture of the Ploesti oil fields in the east, the Allied bombing of synthetic oil production plants and transport networks, plus depletion of strategic reserves during the Battle of the Bulge, had produced a fuel crisis. Consequently, the vehicles of 116th *Windhund* Panzer and 15th *Panzergrenadier* divisions had to await the arrival of scarce fuel before they could begin their march north to confront XXX Corps.

The star badge of the 15th *Panzergrenadiers* was stencilled on the division's vehicles.

Meanwhile, in First Canadian Army's area north of Nijmegen, the front was quiet. Consequently, General Blastowitz was progressively dispatching as many reinforcements as he dared from elsewhere in Army Group H, starting with several battalion-sized *Kampfgruppen* from 2nd *Fallschirmjäger* and 346th Infantry divisions.

As 84th Infantry Division's strength diminished and it lost such grip as remained, at Hitler's insistence XLVII Panzer Corps was ordered to recapture Kleve and the Materborn feature. Even though he passed these orders on, Lutwitz and General Schlemm's realistic aim was to shore up the First *Fallschirmjäger* Army's front by holding XXX Corps long enough to give the projected defensive line between Moyland and the Kleve forest some substance.

By the night of 11–12 February 116th *Windhund* Panzer and 15th *Panzergrenadier* divisions were beginning to arrive east of the Reichswald. Both of these divisions, already severely reduced by the fighting in the Bulge and suffering paucities of every kind of equipment and manpower, continued to be hamstrung by the lack of fuel. Consequently, they only dribbled forward from Geldern overnight into contact with XXX Corps. Initially at least, General Wilck's 116th Panzer Division fielded a *Kampfgruppe* based on a company of *Windhund* panzers, which were joined by the eight surviving *Jagdpanthers* and sundry *Jagdpanzer* IVs of *Panzerjäger Abteilung* 655 and his own infantry under Major Brinkmann. The new half-track mentioned being captured during the night (see Chapter Twelve) probably belonged to newly arrived troops of this *Kampfgruppe*.

General Schlemm ordered von Lüttwitz to take over the south-western part of the Reichswald and the adjacent approaches to the Materborn feature. As we have seen, *Kampfgruppe* Brinkmann was to rebuff the Wessex Division's advance overnight on 11th–12th on the 'Tiger Corner'/Hau axis, which the Germans perceived as the immediate threat, along with the 53rd Welsh Division in the northwest part of the Reichswald. In more detail, Wilck's panzers were to attack from the northern side of the Kleve forest, while 15th *Panzergrenadiers*, commanded by *Oberst* Wolfgang Maucke, would be launched south of the forest and into the Reichswald, which the Welsh were still clearing. As had been the case during the Allied attacks, the ground across which these two attacks took place heavily influenced the differing outcomes of the fighting for the two divisions.

Colonel General Gerhart Wilck, commander of 116th Panzer Division.

XXX Corps' Difficulties

In many respects the Germans were by 1945 used to fighting at a material and physical disadvantage, but 'General Winter' was now denying XXX Corps' accustomed luxuries of superior fire power, numbers of troops and plentiful combat supplies in comparison with those of the enemy. Up to this point those Allied officers reporting on the progress of the battle stressed that the main enemy had not been the Germans but the mud and floods. Now, however, with the arrival of serious German reinforcements the divisions of XXX Corps faced an altogether more serious challenge.

The part played by the Allied air forces, particularly the RAF's 2nd Tactical Airforce, had up to this point already been heavily constrained by the weather. With observation, electronic warfare and ULTRA warning that German formations were on the move, it was an intensely frustrating time for the airmen. As a series of frontal systems swept in from the west there were two main factors that

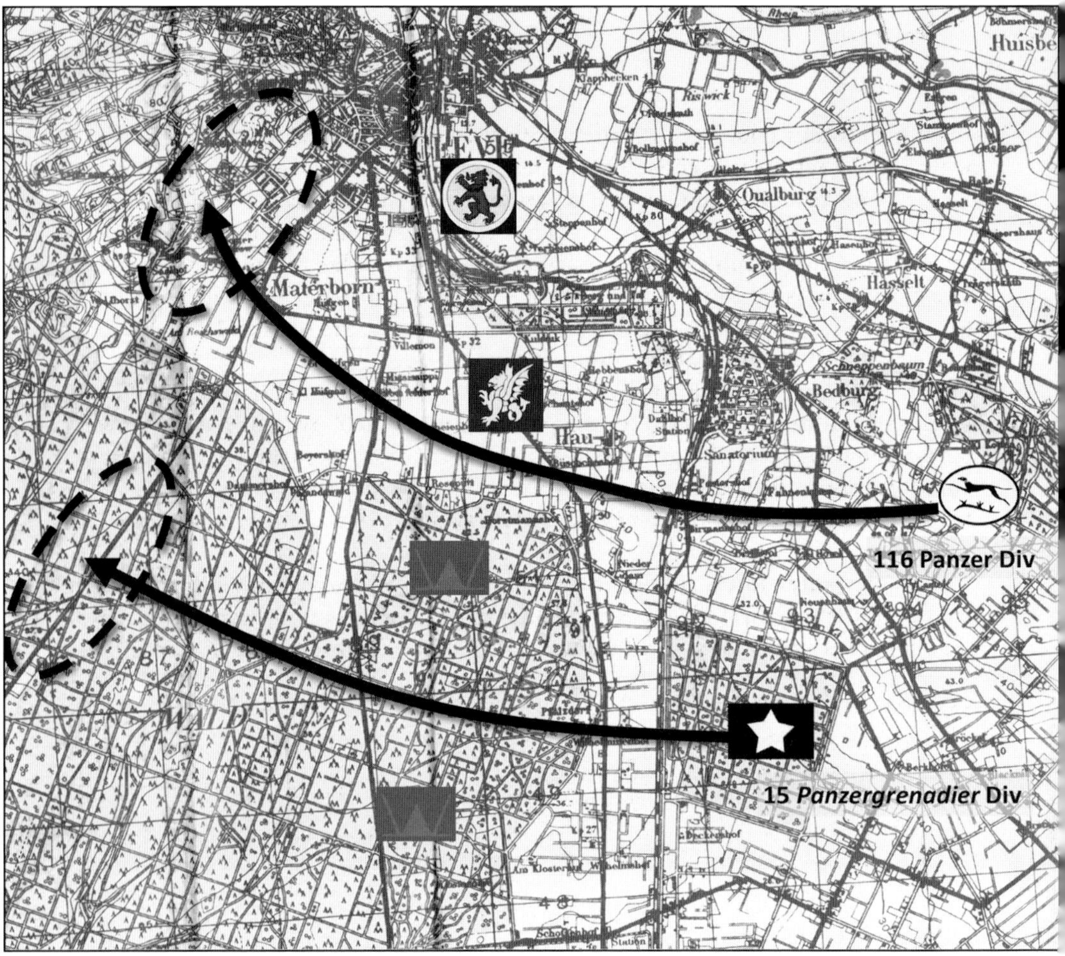

General von Lüttwitz's outline plan for the counter-attack.

caused difficulties. Firstly, being unable to identify targets thanks to low cloud, fog and heavy rain (even with radar and other navigational aids available in 1945), and secondly, flying conditions at the airfields the aircraft were operating from up to 120 miles to the rear were often different to breaks in the weather over the battle area.[2] Of these two factors the former was the more important part of the equation. Combined with the long hours of darkness, the overall weather conditions resulted in intermittent interdiction of German reserves and a reliance on observed artillery fire in the close battle.

With limited air support the four AGRAs under command of XXX Corps, plus 2nd Canadian AGRCA, which together with the seven divisional artilleries fielded approximately 1,000 guns of all types, theoretically provided a crushing weight of fire. Moving the guns, however, from their initial positions west of Nijmegen and the Groesbeek Heights and then taking their turn on the two roads south was, as already recorded by Lieutenant Douglas Godard, a slow process that often disrupted plans. For instance, 'On 12 February, as 7 Medium Regiment, RCA moved forward, it found that the single road available was flooded and only its 60-cwt trucks could get through.' Without its command vehicles and those of its FOO there was a considerable delay in getting the regiment into action. Even having reached the new gun position up on the Materborn feature on the 13th the difficulties were not over. The war diarist recorded that 12 Medium Battery RCA had trouble getting its guns into position due to the muddy terrain. The battery enlisted the assistance of an armoured bulldozer but still could only get one gun into position. The other guns were left on the road and a whole new area was found for the battery the next day.

Not only was it difficult to move the guns, but with rates of consumption of all types of artillery ammunition totalling 80,000 to 100,000 rounds a day, delivering sufficient shells to the gun positions was an enormous challenge. Delivery of ammunition on the inadequate roads using vehicles capable of wading through the floods meant that lower-priority users had to wait their turn for combat supplies.

With the water levels on the main supply route through Kranenburg having risen considerably by 11 February, sustaining troops in action beyond the flood became a pressing issue as virtually the only vehicles divisions had that could get

A Canadian medium gun in action with a stack of shells prepared for a barrage shoot.

through were the amphibious Weasels, although their carrying capacity was small. Consequently:

> . . . the DUKW companies which had been at the call of corps were moved forward and eventually took over the task of the 10-tonners. The short period before the DUKWs were available was however sufficient to cause such further damage to the already overburdened road surface as to make the rapid establishment of an alternative axis, south of the Reichswald Forest [by 51st Highland], more than ever imperative. In order to limit the turn-round distance of the DUKWs from the field maintenance area through the

A column of DUKWs makes its way along a flooded road between Nijmegen and Kleve.

> floods to Kleve/Materborn, a DUKW transhipment point was established in Nijmegen where the amphibians were tailboard loaded from normal 3-ton vehicles.
>
> 30 Corps, using the DUKWs established forward of the flooded stretch a skeleton FMC stocked only with petrol, compo ration packs, and ammunition main natures so as to maintain troops isolated by the waterlogged axis. To meet essential needs beyond the resources of this emergency installation and to provide for the evacuation of casualties, divisions were each allotted about two sections of DUKWs for use as required.

Royal Army Service Corps soldier Driver Heathfield-Robinson, of 297 General Transport Company, RAOC, drove a DUKW for sixteen hours a day during this period, taking supplies forward and visiting the casualty clearing station of 129 Field Ambulance on the way back. This unit took over the handling of all the casualties from the three divisions fighting off the Kleve road supply route beyond Kranenburg, amidst the Rhine flood waters:

> At Kranenburg, due to the floods, the casualties had to be brought out of first-floor windows, a tricky job with stretcher cases. The night journeys were the worst, as what looked like normal hedgerows were in fact tree tops and houses were under water ... During our night journeys if we used our headlights to get our bearings, the Germans would open up with their 88mm guns, but due to the slow speed of the DUKW in water, approximately 8 MPH, the shells would land well in front of us.[3]

Being unable to see roadside ditches was another difficulty, as this Morris gun tractor found out.

For 6 Guards Armoured Brigade, the supply situation in Kleve continued to be eased by a German supply depot near the barracks in the northern suburbs from which 'the whole brigade increased its stocks of sugar, jam, treacle, flour and meat. It was unfortunate that no 3-tonners were up at the time and the booty had to be removed by scout car – vehicles totally unsuited for transport of stores in bulk.'

The *Windhund* Attacks

The weight of *Kampfgruppe* Brinkmann's attack fell on the Wessex Division's 214 Brigade at Hau and to a lesser extent on the ridge overlooking Bedburg. In the case of the latter, 1 Worcester's war diarist reported heavy enemy shelling and their deployment of a coordinated anti-tank defence 'with a view to a likely enemy counter-attack possibly by 116 Panzer Div on Bn front'. Divisional and AGRA FOOs were deployed forward and the Vickers guns of the Wessex Division's machine gun battalion, 8 Middlesex, were also positioned to create a strong defensive front. At Hau 7 Somersets also reported that its forward companies 'were heavily pounded by artillery and mortars' and further reported a series of attacks throughout the day.[4] Those in the morning were most probably reconnaissance, but the main attacks fell on 7 Somersets during the afternoon, by which time Brigadier Essame had fully coordinated 214 Brigade's defence. Brinkmann had simply not arrived in time to be able to launch a counter-attack while the Somersets and Worcesters were still reorganising and digging in.

The *Kampfgruppe* now consisted of three of *Windhund*'s four weak infantry battalions. On the left, 1st Battalion, 156 *Panzergrenadier* Regiment (I/156 PzGR), supported by a mix of eight to ten Panzer IVs and Panthers, was to attack west along the northern edge of the Reichswald, while on the right the first objective of I/60 PsGrs, supported by the six surviving *Jagdpanthers*, was 7 Somerset's forward positions around Hau. II/60 PzGrs were the reserve.[5]

Now that the Germans were out of their dugouts and counter-attacking, their losses mounted. Hitherto, the Allied artillery bombardment certainly did much to neutralise the German defensive positions, and providing the attacking infantry were on the enemy positions soon after the last shells detonated, their casualties would be relatively light. XXX Corps, however, across the VERITABLE battle area took thousands of prisoners per day, stunned and demoralised by the bombardment. As the Germans were very well dug in, their casualties in comparison were light but, as in Normandy where the Germans came out to deliver their habitual counter-attacks that both their tactical doctrine and Hitler demanded, casualties were heavy. The following account by the Somersets illustrates the building of those attacks and ultimately the cost to the Germans:

> All day on the 12th February, the forward Companies, particularly 'A' and 'B', were heavily shelled and mortared . . . Two of their supporting Sherman tanks were also knocked out by 88s, but the one mounting the long 17-pounder, it was called 'Hellz-a-Poppin', survived all day and, in fact, was still with us at the end of the war.

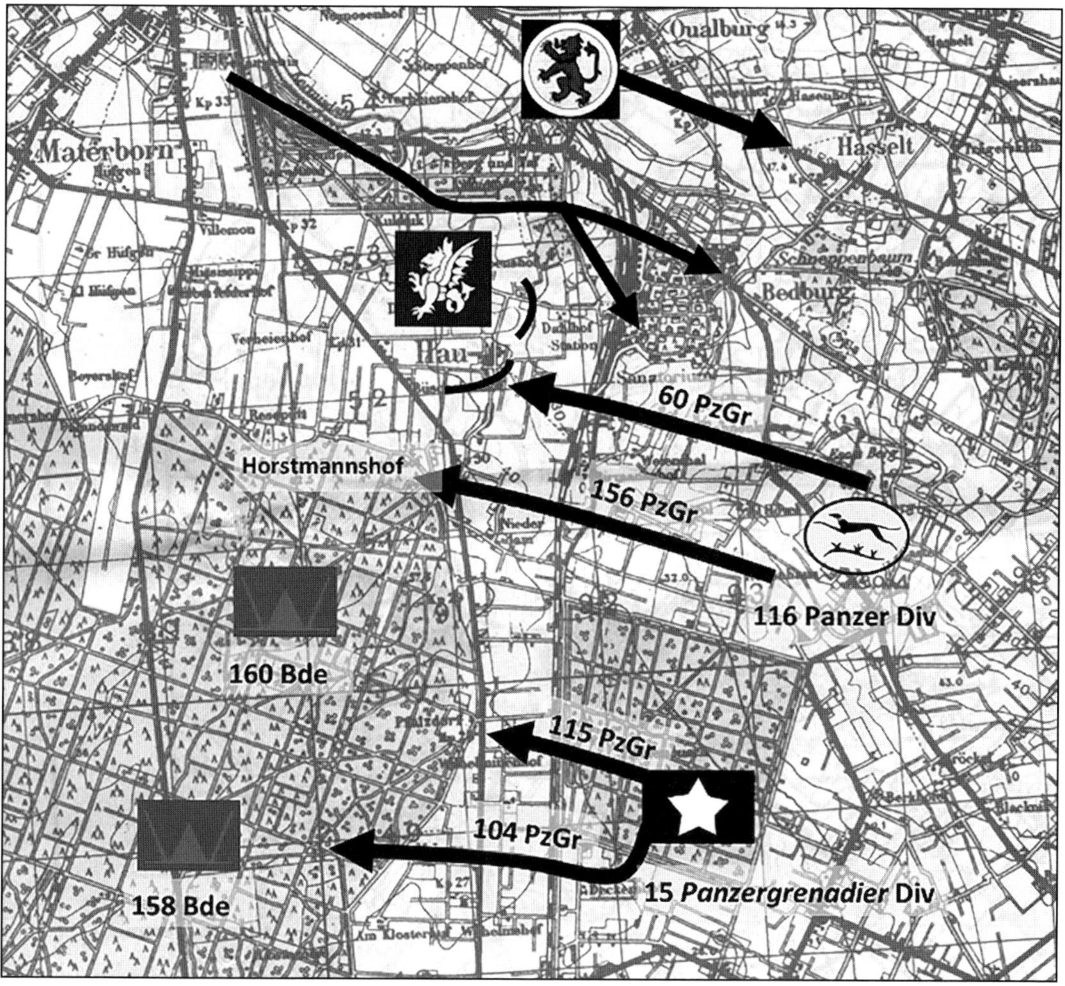

The counter-attack of XLVII Panzer Corps on 12 February 1945.

At 1448 hours 'B' Company was counter-attacked by two companies of infantry supported by three Panther tanks, one of which was destroyed by 'Hellz-a-Poppin'. At 1500 hours 'A' Company, using Brens, caught a recce patrol of eight enemy on their front, and not one of them escaped alive. At 1717 hours 'A' Company was very suddenly attacked by a force of a weak battalion in number.

Three times, in all, the enemy formed, or launched, a counter-attack; three times our outposts passed the word to their Companies, and the Company Commanders to the Commanding Officer. Simultaneously the mortar and gunner O.P.s flashed the target area back to their gun positions. The infantry manned their weapons and waited. In 'A' Company Major Roberts had placed his two machine guns (of the 8th Middlesex) with his forward platoons and they caught the enemy in flat, open ground. Before the machine guns and Brens fifty or sixty casualties were mown down, the assault wavered and turned. A distant thunder told that the guns had heard; salvo

> after salvo screamed overhead, as the Germans retreated, they were caught by the weight of our artillery defensive fire; shells rained down barely 5 yards apart. Great was the slaughter. The attack was obliterated.

The Panther being knocked out is noted at various times in several battalion, regimental and formation war diaries ranging from 1000 hours through until late afternoon. This was almost certainly the work of Sergeant Stone of L Troop, 59 Anti Anti-Tank Regiment, RA, who received the Military Medal for his action against the panzers supporting I/60 PzGrs on 12 February:

> Throughout all the battles since the beginning of this campaign this NCO has shown initiative, bravery and leadership of the highest order ... In February 1945 during the heavy and bitter fighting around Cleve, Sergeant Stone as No. 1 of a 17 pounder S.P. Valentine took his gun under heavy shellfire across open country in full view of the enemy and destroyed a Panther tank at 500 yards range. Although his own position was then drawing fire Sergeant Stone continued firing his gun at infantry positions and was largely responsible for breaking up an impending counter-attack. His fine fighting spirit and great devotion to duty have at all times been most marked.

The engagement was with the awesomely destructive 17-pounder APDS round. The account was not, however, entirely one way, with two Sherman 75s being knocked out during the fighting.

The cost to the German *Windhund Panzergrenadiers* on the afternoon of 12 February was indeed heavy and capped by a loss of ten precious AFVs. Among the mortally wounded was Major Brinkmann.

At the same time as the attacks on Hau, I/156 PzGrs was being launched towards the north-east tip of the Reichswald and the hamlet of Horstmannshof. From there the *Panzergrenadiers* intended to continue the advance on the Materborn feature, but they ran into the leading company of 4th Welch, which had just arrived, and unlike 214 Brigade had not had time to dig in. The historian of the 4th Welch recorded that:

> On reaching a track meeting point near the extreme North-East edge of the Forest the leading Company was violently counter-attacked, driven back and its commander killed. The Commanding Officer (Lieut-Colonel Frisby) rallied the Company and with it, and another, cleared the area and restored the situation.

Having reached the north-west tip of the great Reichswald forest, 156 PzGr's attack faltered and was halted. They had also been broken up by massed artillery and anti-tank fire along with that of the 8 Middlesex's machine guns enfilading them from the area around Hau.

Counter-Attack by the 15th *Panzergrenadiers*

The northerly pincer of XLVII Panzer Corps' counter-attack was delivered by *Oberst* Maucke's 15th *Panzergrenadiers*. He was to attack into the Reichswald

A 17-pounder Valentine Archer of the Wessex Division's anti-tank regiment driving through the floods at Kranenburg.

from the area south of the Kleve forest with his much-reduced battalions supported by a company of *Sturmgeschütz*. Here he would face the Welsh Division, whose plan for 12 February was a resumption of the previous day's advance. The Welsh historian wrote:

> The Divisional plan for the 12 February was for both leading battalions to press forward to the eastern edge of the Forest, with the 71st Brigade mopping up in the rear of the 158th. The latter brigade was to make every effort to capture the [Niers] river bridge north of Asperden.

In the north of the forest 160 Brigade extended its grip on the northern edge of the Reichswald as far east as Horstmanshof, where, as already recorded, they were counter-attacked by *Kampfgruppe* Brinkmann.

A Panther knocked out during one of the counter-attacks.

Oberst Maucke's attack was carried out by four battalions with 115 PzGrs on the right and 104th PzGrs on the left, supported by artillery, mortar fire and a number of *Sturmgeschütz* assault guns. It fell astride the brigade boundary on 6 RWF (160 Brigade) and on the right 1/5 Welch (158 Brigade). In not dissimilar ground conditions to that of the Wessex Division, 'The attack was beaten off' partly by well-directed artillery and partly by small arms fire which the defending infantry withheld until the attackers were within about 300 yards. This caused serious losses to the enemy, who withdrew in disorder.

Sergeant Machin of 1/5 Welch described an attack at 1615 hours:

> The enemy made a real blunder in deciding to counter-attack B Company. It was a gunner's dream as they came on in extended order and exposed their left flank to D Coy some 300yds to the south. Both companies opened up with their Brens, Vickers and Besas. It was too much for the Boche, who broke ranks, leaving some thirty casualties behind. During the night the gunners went to work on the Bosch with a vengeance …

The divisional historian continued his account:

> About the same time small parties of the enemy operating further South attempted to infiltrate into the East Lancashires' positions, but they were

> mopped up by a platoon from the reserve company and a troop of tanks. Just before dusk some 200 Germans were seen opposite the positions of the same Battalion and it looked as if a counter-attack was about to develop. The enemy were, however, dispersed by artillery fire and by the unit carriers which were brought up to a position from which fire could be opened 'mounted'.

The attacks by XLVII Panzer Corps had, as General Schlemm expected, failed to get anywhere near recapturing the Materborn feature or Kleve. Allied intelligence was forewarned of the approach of von Lüttwitz's command, and the Wessex Division was able to rush forward supporting arms and weapons to produce a sound defence by the time of the counter-attack. General Wilske complained that his *Windhund* division had been rushed into battle incomplete and directly off the line of march with precious little time for battle procedure. By the time they attacked the Wessex Division the result was almost a foregone conclusion when they came up against a solid front lavishly supported by artillery.

Soldiers of the Royal Welsh Fusiliers advancing through the Reichswald.

For 15th *Panzergrenadiers* it was a different matter. Their encounter with the Welsh Division was characteristic of a meeting engagement; one in which they were rushed into, but were outnumbered and outgunned, and lost heavily in battle at close quarters.

XLVII Panzer Corps' attacks had, however, achieved General Schlemm's realistic aims. They had brought the advance of the Wessex Division on Goch to a halt and curtailed the Welsh Division's aims to form a second pincer on Goch. At a considerable cost in men, and equipment, particularly to 15th *Panzergrenadiers*, they had bought time for all available reinforcements to concentrate on the battle.

The intelligence staff of the 43rd Wessex Division were not impressed by the scale of the attacks during the 12th, noting in their evening INTSUM that: 'The Corps [XLVII Panzer] probably has more ambitious plans for tomorrow and it must be reckoned with that the recapture of the Materborn feature is amongst

German prisoners taken in the Rhineland being searched by British military policemen.

Transport of the 43rd Wessex Division and 8 Armoured Brigade on the outskirts of Kleve on the road to Goch.

them.' A German officer during questioning later asserted that the Germans had a very different view of the day's fighting: 'There was no more talk of major counter-attacks, but a defensive stalemate had been temporarily achieved.' The stalemate did not last long as the following day General Horrock's XXX Corps resumed its fighting advances east into the Rhineland.

With those words it can be said that the battle for Kleve and the breakout into the Rhineland were over, and the fighting was already morphing into VERITABLE's next phase. With the leading troops of XXX Corps beyond the 'Reichswald Plug' into more open country, General Crerar could deploy General Simonds' II Canadian Corps to join the fighting to capture of the nodal Rhineland towns of Goch, Kalkar and Uedem. The battle, however, ground on in the same very difficult circumstances for a further month. The thaw in late January and early February had condemned the soldiers of XXX Corps and II Canadian Corps to fighting in appalling ground and weather conditions with all that implied. Matters were made infinitely worse due to the Ninth US Army's Operation GRENADE being stalled at the River Rorer, consequent on Bradley's failure to capture the dams in a timely manner. Thus, British and Canadian soldiers faced all that the Germans could throw at them to halt operations that despite everything opened the way to final victory.

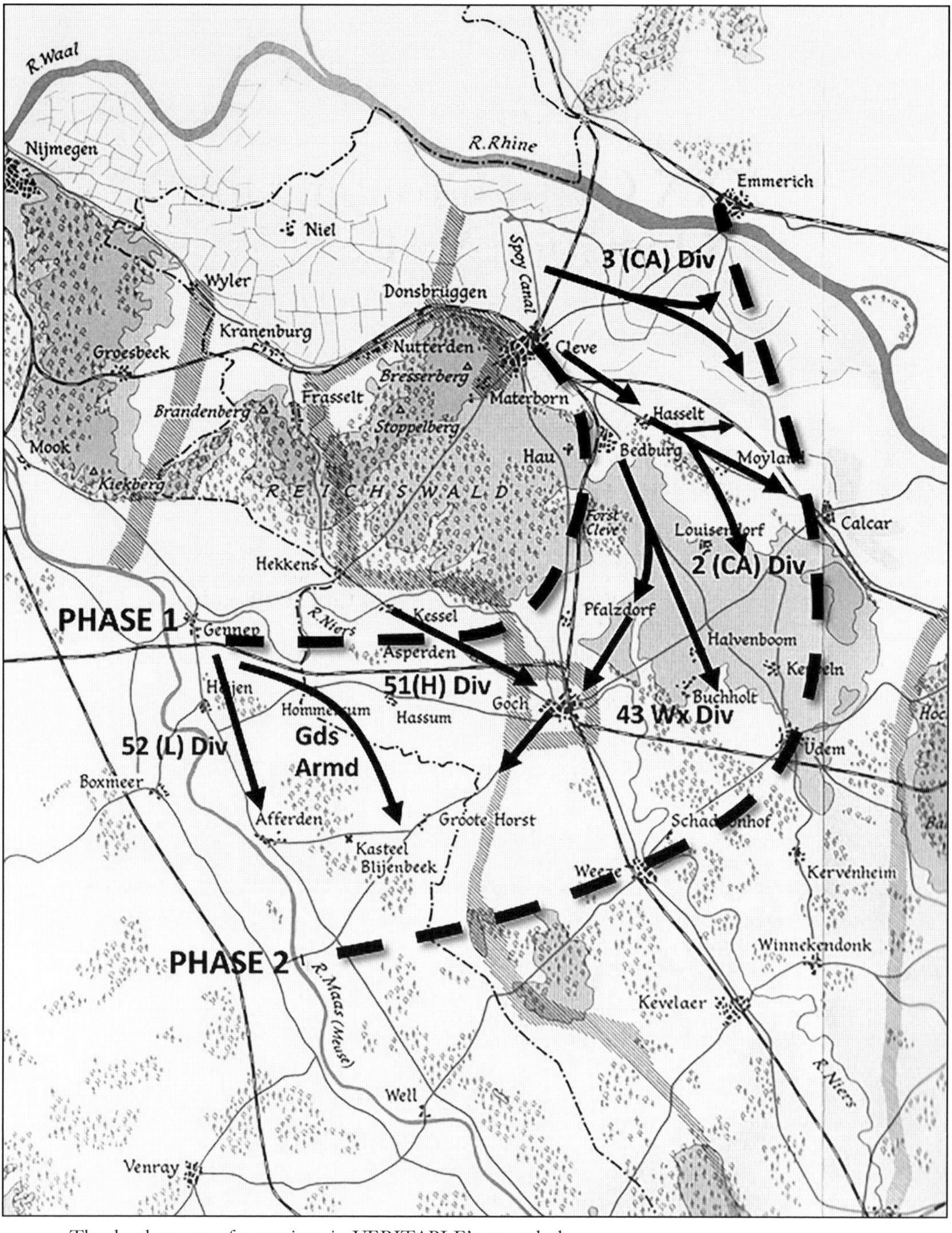

The development of operations in VERITABLE's second phase.

Appendix I

XXX Corps Grouping for Operation VARSITY

Phase One

(Taken from XXX Corps Operation Instruction No. 47.)

	Under Command	*In Support*
(a) Guards Armd Div	Det 4 Svy Regt	64 Med Regt
(b) 15 (S) Div	2 HCR 6 Gds Armd Bde 86 Fd Regt (SP) 147 Fd Regt 198/73 A Tk Bty (SP) 234/73 A Tk Bty (SP) Det 100 Radar Bty Det 4 Svy Regt 'H' Flt 662 AOP Sqn Tp 356 SL Bty	22 DGNs 141 RAC less 'A' Sqn 6 Aslt Regt RE less 82 Sqn 1 Cdn APC Regt less one sqn 49 APO Regt 84 Med Regt
(c) 43 Div	8 Armd Bde less one regt plus one sqn 13/18 H 73 A Tk Regt less two btys Det 4 Svy Regt 'C' Flt 662 AOP Sqn	121 Fd Regt
(d) 51 (H) Div	107 RAC 6 Fd Regt 146/63 A Tk Bty (SP) Det 4 Svy Regt 'C' Flt 662 AOP Sqn Det 100 Radar Bty Tp 356 SL Bty	'D' Sqn 1 LOTHIANS 1 FF YEO less 'D' and 'C' Sqns 42 Aslt Regt RE less 16 and 617 Sqns 79 Med Regt
(e) 53 (W) Div	34 Armd Bde less 107 RAC 19 Cdn Fd Regt (SP) 56 Cdn A Tk Bty (SP) Det 4 Svy Regt 'A' Flt 662 AOP Sqn Det 100 Radar Bty Tp 356 SL Bty	W DGNS less 'A' Sqn 'A' Sqn 141 RAC 82 Aslt Sqn RE 72 Med Regt
(f) 2 Cdn Div	One sqn 13/18 H 'A' Flt 660 AOP Sqn	One tp 'C' Sqn 1 LOTHIANS One tp 617 Aslt Sqn RE 4 Cdn Med Regt

(g) 3 Cdn Div	13/18 H less one sqn 'C' Flt 660 AOP Sqn Tp 557 SL Bty	617 Aslt Sqn RE less one tp 'C' Sqn 1 LOTHIANS less one tp 11 R Tks less 'C' Sqn 5 Aslt Regt less 26 Sqn 7 Cdn Med Regt 803 Pnr Smoke Coy Two Pls 810 Pnr Smoke Coy 112 Pnr Smoke Coy
(h) CCRA	3 AGRA 4 AGRA 5 AGRA 9 AGRA 27 LAA Regt 4 Svy Regt less dets 356 SL Bty less three tps 557 SL Bty less one tp 660 AOP Sqn less three flts 662 AOP Sqn less three flts 1 Cdn Rocket Unit	106 AA Bde *Under Op Control* 2 Cdn AGRA

NOTES:

(i) The following troops do not come under command 43 Div till 1500 hours D Day.
4/7 DG
NOTTS YEO
One Sqn 13/18 H (from 2 Cdn Diy)
8 MX Regt (from PEPPERPOT)
Two btys 73 A Tk Regt (Towed) (from PEPPERPOT).

(ii) 43 Div will take under command 147 Fd Regt [Essex Yeomanry – 8 Armd Bde] during their move forward.

(iii) Guards Armd Div will take under command 86 Fd Regt during their move forward.

(iv) 2 HCR will come under command 15 (S) Div on arrival in assembly area and revert Gds Armd Div at a later stage.

A DUKW in action during the Rhineland Campaign.

Appendix II

Topography of the Battle Area

The ground across which the battle was fought is described in the Canadian Historical Section report:

The topography of the area of intended operations presented some unusual difficulties. A study of the map will show that 40 to 50 miles southeast of Nijmegen, at Duisburg, and at Venlo, the Rhine and Maas flow in a northerly direction some 20 miles apart. Gradually they approach and begin to swing to the west so that at Mook (7251) the Maas, now turning due west, is only 6 miles south of Nijmegen on the main channel of the Rhine, which here becomes the Waal. Immediately west of Nijmegen the two rivers are connected by the Maas-Waal Canal, while farther south a smaller stream, called the Niers, runs parallel to them through the intervening plain. The front line followed the course of the Maas as far north as Cuijk (7249) and thence ran northeast and north close to the German frontier to meet the Waal some 3 miles east of Nijmegen. It will be appreciated that to reach the forward assembly areas all formations except 2 and 3 Cdn Inf Div had to cross the Maas, and in many cases, the Maas–Waal Canal as well. Some had to pass through the built-up area of Nijmegen and all had to wheel through more than ninety degrees to line up opposite the enemy's defensive positions.

Both the Maas and the Rhine run through low plains which were inundated during December. By January most of the floods had receded but the ground was left mucky and covered with scattered pools. Further obstacles were abandoned channels, ditches, marsh and backwaters. The most outstanding geographical feature is the Reichswald, a large diamond-shaped forest 9 nine miles from east to west, and 5 miles from north to south, lying between the town of Cleve and the German-Dutch frontier. There are some clearings and a few farms in the forest. The Materborn ridge, some 200 to 250 feet above sea level, extends from Cleve in a southwesterly direction along the northern edge of the forest, commanding a flat and featureless countryside. The trees are mostly pine of fairly recent growth, planted four to seven feet apart and divided into blocks by narrow rides. Southeast, the Hochwald and Balberger Wald lie to the west of Xanten. The rest of the country between the rivers is low and gently undulating with a number of small woods. Movement over cultivation was interrupted only by occasional tree-lined fields, rises in ground, and small ditches along the fields. The rolling nature of the country and frequent coppices made covered approaches possible, but in the predominantly wooded areas movement off the roads was difficult. An abundance of cover among the trees was limited only by the season of the year. In such country the view was often obstructed even from the eminences which themselves were nearly all wooded. During the long quiescent period prior to 8 Feb, the Canadian outposts were on relatively high ground overlooking much of this future field of battle and, with the like advantage of being also largely wooded, and affording excellent cover for even the larger formations involved.

Two main roads run southeast from Nijmegen, one along the east bank of the Maas through Gennep to Venlo, the other across the German frontier north of the Reichswald to Cleve where it divides. The northern branch continues to Calcar and Xanten and thence southeast towards the Ruhr; the other runs southwards to Goch and on through Weeze and Kevelaer to Geldern. Other roads from Cleve run northeast to Emmerich on the Rhine, southeast to Uedem and southwest through the Reichswald to Gennep. Fortunately, most of the civilians had been evacuated from the considerable number of small towns scattered about this corner of Germany.

During January the weather had been cold with considerable snow and ice but early in February a thaw set in. It was realized that any prolonged operation after severe frost was likely to churn up the ground very badly. Further, it was clear that the Rhine could be flooded by blowing the winter dykes, although complete breaching was considered impracticable. In addition, it had to be borne in mind that if the Americans did not succeed in capturing the Roar dams before they were destroyed, their failure might have far-reaching effects. All these hazards had to be taken into consideration in the planning and the risks accepted.

Part of a corps headquarters sited in the woods around Groesbeek is well cammed-up, despite the tree cover.

Appendix III

Confirmatory Conference Notes

At General Crerar's conference on 4 February, he again outlined his plan and enlarged on it as follows:

In Phase 1 – of the 'break-in' attack against the very strong Reichswald defences – Lt-Gen Horrocks will employ 15 (S), 51 (H) and 53 (W) Divisions, 3 Cdn Div and a portion of 2 Cdn Div. Each division will have strong armoured support. This assault, weather permitting, will receive maximum assistance from the air. It is the intention to retain the greatest practicable element of surprise and definite and detailed steps have been taken to that end. The programme of fire support decided upon by Lt-Gen Horrocks, (and so, positive indications of time and place of attack) will not be revealed until 'D' Day, and a few hours before the attack goes in. On the other hand, from D-3 onwards, it will be increasingly difficult to conceal from the enemy the necessary forward assembly, in the Nijmegen area, of the large assaulting force. While, therefore, it would be otherwise desirable to delay 'D' Day until weather conditions promised full air support, if this situation does not obtain on 8 Feb, the attack will go in, anyway, and with fire support from ground weapons only. One thing that must not be allowed is time and opportunity for the enemy fully to prepare his defensive arrangements and every day and hour that passes after forward assembly commences, increases this risk.

If weather is suitable, the air support which will be afforded this operation will be on a maximum scale. In direct support of the assaulting divisions, will be the Second Tactical Air Force with a potential of 1,000 fighters, or fighter-bombers, 100 medium day, and 90 medium night bombers. 84 Group, R.A.F. – which is that portion of the Second Tactical Air Force operationally and directly linked to First Cdn Army, will provide the 'close-in' support. Bomber Command will attack targets in the immediate battle area with up to 1,000 heavy bombers and support is also expected from the medium bombers of Ninth and the heavy bombers of Eighth US Army Air Forces.

Ground fire support will be provided by over 1,200 guns, of which more than one third are mediums, heavies and super-heavies. The resources of 79 Armd Div will be fully utilized, including 'Crocodiles' (flame throwers), 'Flails' (mine destroyers) and Armoured Personnel Carriers – such as first were utilized by the Canadian Army South of Caen, last August. The Canadian Rocket Projector Battery will also be employed.

As I intimated, I cannot forecast, with any degree of reliability, the time which will be taken to complete 'Veritable', after it is launched. If everything broke in our favour, weather, ground, air support, enemy dispositions and reactions – I would not be surprised if armour of 30 Corps reached the Geldern-Xanten line in a few days. On the other hand, if conditions are against us, I see three 'set-piece' operations, one for each Phase, and the battle may well last three weeks.[1]

A 240mm gun of 3 Super Heavy Regiment RA photographed on 8 February 1945. With a 22-foot barrel the gun fired a 360-pound shell out to a range of 2,400 yards.

German, Canadian and British Ranks

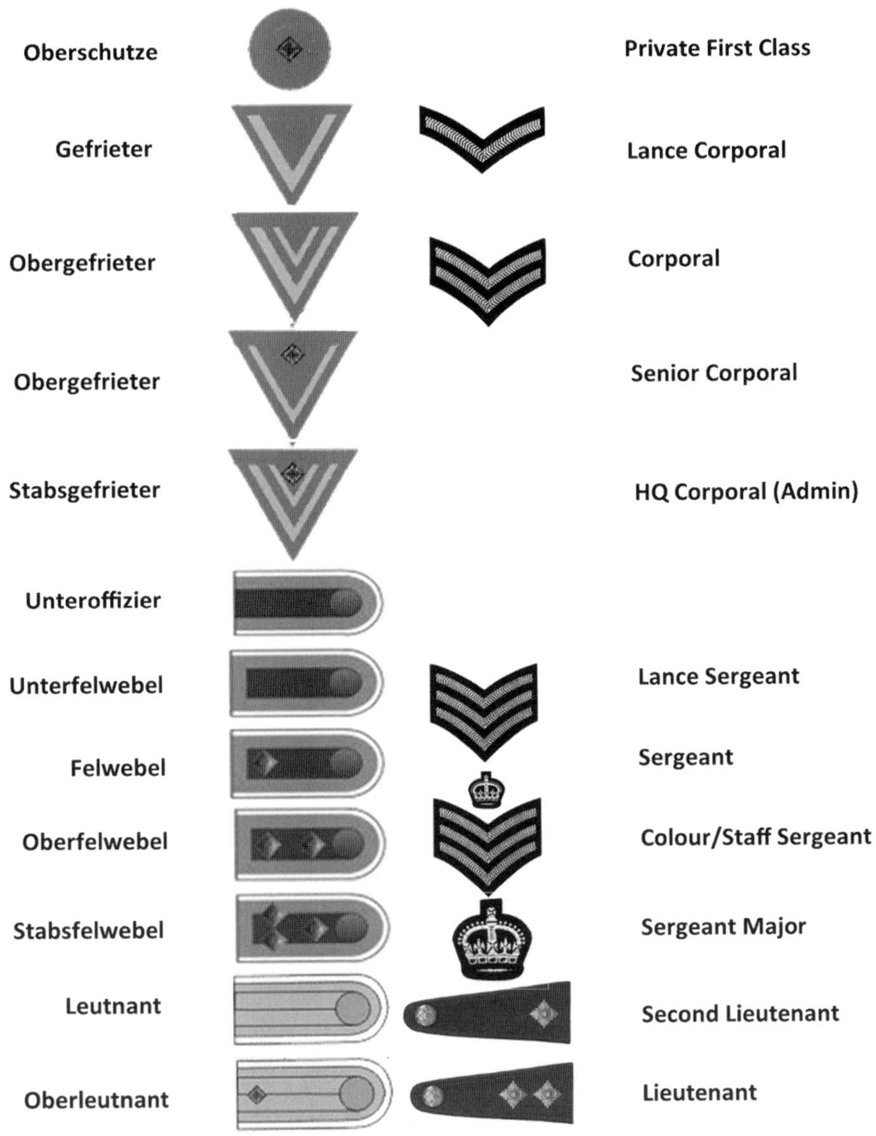

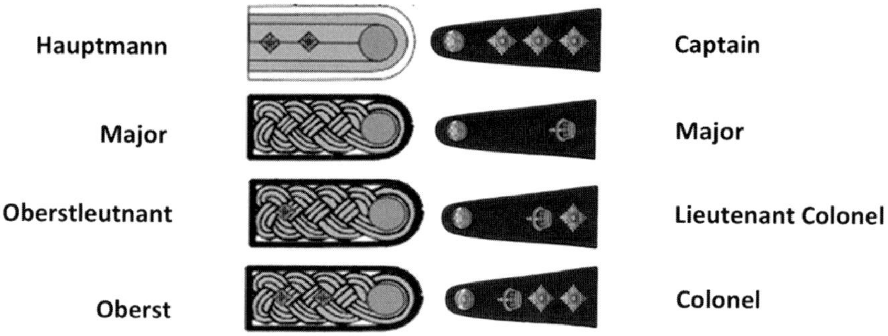

The braided collar and epaulets of a *feldwebel*.

Appendix V

The Numbering of Infantry Platoons

Unlike today when platoons are numbered in British battalions in companies A to C sequentially from 1 to 9, the 1943 the system was significantly different, with the numbering starting in Headquarter Company and Support Company, followed by the rifle companies A to D.

Headquarter Company
No. 1 Signal Platoon
No. 2 Administrative Platoon

Support Company
No. 3 Mortar Platoon
No. 4 Anti-Tank Platoon
No. 5 Carrier Platoon
No. 6 Assault Pioneer Platoon

Rifle Companies

A Company	B Company	C Company	D Company
No. 7 Platoon	No. 10 Platoon	No. 13 Platoon	No. 17 Platoon
No. 8 Platoon	No. 11 Platoon	No. 14 Platoon	No. 18 Platoon
No. 9 Platoon	No. 12 Platoon	No. 15 Platoon	No. 19 Platoon

British infantry moving forward through VERITABLLE's mud.

Notes

Chapter 1: Autumn and Winter, 1944–45

1. Combat supplies include fuel, ammunition and food.
2. Operation WYVERN was a XXX Corps plan made during October. The new Canadian corps plan made in November was named VALEDICTION.
3. The first shipping only reached Antwerp on 28 November following the clearance of the Scheldt. Reliance on road convoys from distant Normandy continued for some weeks.
4. Stacey, Colonel C.P., *The Victory Campaign* (Queen's Printer, Ottawa, 1960).
5. Ibid.
6. 'Advocate', *From Normandy to the Baltic with 44th Lowland Brigade of the 15th Scottish Division from D Day to the End of the War in Europe* (C.H. Wasers Druckerei, Holstein, Germany, 1945).

Chapter 2: XXX Corps' Planning and Preparation

1. 52nd Lowland was a pre-war Territorial Army division, with the 15th being formed as a part of doubling the TA.
2. 6 Guards Armoured Brigade, and the other tank brigades, were renamed 'armoured' in late 1944.
3. G.J.B. Watkins, *From Normandy to the Weser, The War History of the Fourth Dorsets* (Henry Ling, Dorchester).
4. Essame, Major General H., *The 43rd Wessex Division at War 1944–1945* (William Clowes and Sons Ltd, 1952).
5. The PEPPERPOT shoot was the concentration of all available weapon systems to deluge a target area with fire for a relatively short but concentrated period.
6. The better accuracy and lesser danger area for a 25-pounder allowed the infantry to approach far closer to their fire than the rockets.
7. First Canadian Army War Diary. 'British and Canadian Sappers in the past few weeks have constructed, widened and improved approximately 100 miles of road. For this purpose about 20,000 tons of stone J 20,000 logs and 30,000 pickets have been used.'
8. Quoted in Canadin Military Headquarters report No. 155.
9. Smith, John, *In at the Finish, North West Europe 1944–1945* (Minerva Press, 1995).
10. This was probably snow that had drifted into the anti-tank ditch and had yet to melt.
11. Eisenhower, *Crusade in Europe* (Hutchinson, 1948).

Chapter 3: The Siegfried Line and the Defenders of the Reich

1. The defences of urban areas would also serve as strongpoints if the British attacked across the Maas on the direct route to the Rhine.
2. Post-war analysts visiting the Reichswald counted about seventy concrete structures in the forest, mostly small. Even the seven larger ones were too small to accommodate the larger anti-tank guns of 1944–45, Most of these mounted machine guns.
3. This is a myth. The stoutly built German houses tended to have half cellars, the small windows of which being just above ground level coincidentally served as loopholes. The cellars were mainly used for shelter from shelling.
4. A proportion of the soldiers were from 1st *Wahn* Battalion. This was a psychiatric unit for men recovering from battle exhaustion. Subsequently, soldiers from the 2nd and 3rd *Wahn* battalions also joined the division when it was reconstituted in the autumn and winter of 1944.

5. There is some dispute over the issue of *Jagdpanzer* IVs to 655th. One authority states that these vehicles were only issued after the battle of the Rhineland, while others theorise that these issues were in fact replacements.

Chapter 4: The Opening Bombardment

1. Lace, Brigadier F.D., war diary CRA, 2 Cdn Inf Div 1 February 1944.
2. G (Training) HQ BAOR, *Battlefield Tour – Operation Veritable* (BAOR, Germany, 1947).
3. 4th (Durham) Survey Regiment was a pre-war Territorial unit from Gateshead. They were XXX Corps troops for most of the North-West European Campaign. The other regiment was 2nd Canadian Survey Regiment, also corps troops, in their case, II Canadian Corps.
4. Blackburn, George, *The Guns of Victory* (McClelland & Stewart Inc., 1997).
5. This is believed to have been Colonel Stacey, head of the section and author of *The Victory Campaign, the Canadian Official History of the NWE Campaign.*
6. Historical Section, *Report 155, Operation Veritable: Maas and the Rhine, The Winter Offensive between the 8–25 Feb 45 (Preliminary Report)*, Canadian Military Headquarters.
7. BAOR, *Battlefield Tour – Operation VERITABLE* (BAOR, Germany, 1947).

Chapter 5: VERITABLE Begins

1. G (Training) HQ BAOR, *Battlefield Tour – Operation Veritable* (BOAR, Germany, 1947).
2. 5th Canadian Infantry Brigade after action report.
3. Movement Light was provided by RA searchlight batteries reflecting their beams off a cloud base. The angle had to be right to illuminate the enemy rather than friendly forces.
4. Hammerton, Ian C., *Achtung Minen! The Making of a Flail Tank Troop Commander* (Book Guild, 1991).
5. Martin, Lieutenant General H.G., *The Fifteenth Scottish Division 1939–1945* (Wm Blackwood & Sons Ltd, 1948).
6. National Archive, WO 373/53.
7. Despite War Office instructions in the 1920s that in the spelling of serjeant, the 'j' was to be replaced by a 'g', many regiments continued to use it in both long form and abbreviations.

Chapter 6: Closing up to the Siegfried Line

1. War diary, C Squadron 141 RAC.
2. Smith, John G., *In at the Finish: North-West Europe, 1944–45* (Minerva Press, 1995).
3. Crocodile squadrons usually, as in this case, operated as half squadrons, with three troops commanded by the OC and two by the 2iC from command tanks.
4. Hammerton, Ian C., *Achtung Minen! The Making of a Flail Tank Troop Commander* (Book Guild, 1991).
5. National Archive, WO 373/53.
6. War diary, 3rd Tank Scots Guards.
7. 2 A&SH's history.
8. Martin, Lt Gen H.G., *The Fifteenth Scottish Division 1939–1945* (The Naval & Military Press Ltd).

Chapter 7: Enter the 'Water Rats'

1. Historical Section, *Report 155, Operation Veritable: Maas and the Rhine, The Winter Offensive between the 8–25 Feb 45 (Preliminary Report)*, Canadian Military Headquarters.
2. It is often said that the Germans' digging and tunnelling in the dyke weakened it, but Dutch engineers believe that it was more likely that the dyke collapsed due to the weight of water being beyond what a winter dyke was designed to cope with.
3. The inundation of the floodplain continued with the Rhine rising from 9.7m on 2 February to a record level of 12.69m above mean level on the 17th. In a normal February, heights of 11.5m would be the norm.
4. Canadian Heritage – War Diaries, T-12018.

5. German calls for artillery fire even on registered targets took longer than those of the Allies, as the gun position officers had more parameters to calculate trading time (in excess of ten minutes) for accuracy.
6. Fowler, Robert, *Valour in the Victory Campaign: The 3rd Canadian Infantry Division Gallantry Decorations, 1945* (General Store Publishing House, 1995).
7. Rooney, Dermot, *The Psychology of Artillery effectiveness* (The Wavell Room, 2002).

Chapter 8: The Siegfried Line

1. Baggaley MC, Captain J.R.P., *The 6th (Border) Battalion, The King's Own Scottish Borderers 1939–1945* (reprint Naval & Military press Ltd).
2. Martin, Lt Gen. H.G., *The Fifteenth Scottish Division 1939–1945* (The Naval & Military Press Ltd).
3. The Mk V Churchill was designed to provide tank regiments with organic close support. Each troop had one tank with a 95mm howitzer and forty-seven HE rounds. There were 241 built in 1943.
4. Designed in the US as a radar to control anti-aircraft guns, the field mobile system as used by the Royal Signals could, as in this case, also direct aircraft to their target area when weather conditions would otherwise preclude bombing.

Chapter 9: The Advance to Kleve

1. Special Interrogation Report: General Alfred Schlemm. Quoted in Historical Section *Report 155, Operation Veritable: Maas and the Rhine, The Winter Offensive between the 8–25 Feb 45 (Preliminary Report)*, Canadian Military Headquarters.
2. XXX Corps Op Instruction No. 47 dated 3 Feb 45.
3. Lippscombe, Lt Col C.G., *History of the 4th Bn The Somerset Light Infantry in the campaign in North-West Europe* (E. Goodman & Son Ltd).
4. Parsons, Robins and Gilson, *The Maroon Square* (Franey & Co. Ltd, 1955).
5. Essame, Major General H., *The 43rd Wessex Division at War 1944–1945* (William Clowes & Sons Ltd, 1952).
6. Pinner, L.C., *A Conscript at War*, Private manuscript.
7. Jary MC, Sydney, *18 Platoon* (Sydney Jary Ltd, 1987).
8. A Sqn 4 Som LI, BSqn 4 Wilts and C Sqn 7 Som LI.
9. The *Jadpanthers* of 665 *Schwere Panzerjäger* battalion did not arrive for another twenty-four hours. They were probably misidentified.
10. Author interview, Private Jenkinson 4th Wiltshire.
11. It is estimated that 500 civilians were killed in this raid alone. The city had, however, been largely evacuated by civilians when it was bombed on the evening of 7 February 1945.
12. The British No. 24 Smoke Generator weighed about 40lb and emitted smoke for twelve to fifteen minutes,

Chapter 10: The First Attack on Materborn

1. Essame, Major General H., *The 43rd Wessex Division at War 1944–1945* (William Clowes and Son Ltd, 1952).
2. Taylor, Brigadier George, *Infantry Colonel* (Self-Publishing Associates, 1990).

Chapter 11: The Advance from Kleve

1. Pinner, L.C., *A Conscript at War*, Private manuscript.
2. Taylor, Brigadier George, *Infantry Colonel* (Self-Publishing Associates, 1990).
3. 'Tiger Corner' is one of many battlefield misnomers! The Tigers by this stage in the NWE Campaign had been sent east to stem the Soviet offensive.
4. Location of photo identified by 'Stolpi'. See Veritable on ww2talk.com.

5. Meredith, Captain J.L.J., *The Story of the Seventh Battalion, The Somerset Light Infantry* (privately published).
6. German chemical shortages led to a variety of substances being used in the manufacture of tracer ammunition, all providing different colours when fired.
7. Watson, Major D.Y., *The First Battalion, The Worcester Regiment in North West Europe* (Ebernezer Baylis & Son Ltd, Worcester).
8. Procter, Stan, *A Quiet Little Boy Goes to War* (privately published, Boron, Hampshire, June 1986).
9. The Messerschmitt Me 262 *Schwalbe* (Swallow) was the world's first operational jet fighter, entering service with the Luftwaffe in mid-1944, and was faster and more heavily armed than any Allied fighter at the time. Despite its clear advantage in the air, it came too late and in too few numbers to make a difference. Targeting the Me 262 at its air bases or when taking off and landing was a priority during VERITABLE. Flying in excess of 500mph, despite radar, conventional anti-aircraft artillery needed to be alerted at a range of 40,000 yards if it was to stand any chance of hitting the Me 262 (source: 'Red Book' Artillery, 1951).
10. Jary, Sydney, *18 Platoon* (Sydney Jary Publishing Ltd).
11. Sir John Moore (1761–1809) is considered by many to be the 'Father' of British Light Infantry.
12. Lieutenant Jary had already earned the MC back in November, coincidentally not far away on the Groesbeek Heights.
13. Forbes, Patrick, *6th Guards Tank Brigade, The Story of Guardsmen in Churchill Tanks* (N. & M. Press Ltd reprint).
14. It is now an accepted fact that where there are particularly dietary and hygiene differences between friend and foe, in some environments smelling the enemy is a factor that has to be taken into account in modern warfare.

Chapter 12: Counter-Attack

1. Zithen was a renowned Prussian military family name and regimental title. Lieutenant General Graf von Zieten commanded a corps in the Prussian Army during the Waterloo Campaign.
2. Doctrine was for fighter and fighter-bomber airfields to be established 50–70 miles from the front and those for the bombers of the Second Tactical Airforce 100–120 miles.
3. Heathfield-Robinson, Douglas, *Memoirs of a Soldier* (Bound Biographies, 2005).
4. 'Heavily pounded' is a relative term, with the Germans firing 8,000–10,000 rounds and the Allies typically having ten times that amount available.
5. Ww2talk, Guderian, Heinz, *Das Letzte Kriegsjahr im Westen, die Geschichte der 116. Pz Division, 1944–45* (SZ Offsetdruck-Verlag, 1997).

Appendix III: Confirmatory Conference Notes

1. War diary, G.O.C.-in-C. First Cdn Army, Feb 45: Appx 3.

Index